PRETENDED
SCHOOLS AND SECTION 28
Historical, cultural and personal perspectives

CATHERINE LEE

First published 2023

by John Catt Educational Ltd,
15 Riduna Park, Station Road,
Melton, Woodbridge IP12 1QT

Tel: +44 (0) 1394 389850
Email: enquiries@johncatt.com
Website: www.johncatt.com

Opinions expressed in this publication are those
of the contributors and are not necessarily those
of the publishers or the editors. We cannot accept
responsibility for any errors or omissions.

ISBN: 978 1 915261 69 4

Set and designed by John Catt Educational Limited

REVIEW

Pretended is a necessary political, social and cultural history of Section 28 and its impact on our educational spaces. In sharing her own story, Catherine Lee amplifies the experiences of all the gay and lesbian educators silenced by Section 28, and offers greater understanding to the generations of young people who were cheated out of a sound start in life because of the silence and shame the legislation planted in our schools. A brilliant book on our history, which teaches us important lessons for our future as we continue to reimagine our educational spaces as more LGBTQ+ inclusive.

Jo Brassington and Dr Adam Brett, Pride and Progress

FOREWORDS

GEORGIA OAKLEY, WRITER AND DIRECTOR OF *BLUE JEAN*

As a student, I was completely oblivious to the pain I would experience later in life due to the culture of silence propagated by Section 28. When I began researching the law in my late twenties, I felt something unlock. This hideous piece of legislation had successfully erased any positive role models I might have had. As a result, getting to know Catherine Lee has been such a cathartic experience for me. It has allowed me to unpick the messy, intergenerational trauma of my own life while empathising with the experiences of a whole generation of teachers whose lives I'd known nothing about.

When I first met Catherine, I was struck by the monumental gulf between the thoughtful, kind person she so clearly is and the decisions she'd been forced to make 30 years prior. I was profoundly moved by the way she spoke about her experiences, and it was this seed of a feeling that provided much of the emotional backbone of *Blue Jean*, the film I went on to make. Trauma locks people in a terminal state of fight or flight, and I wanted to make a film that meditated on this idea. To interrogate one woman's life and choices, while simultaneously exploring the cumulative effect of a lack of positive queer role models on a generation of kids, of which I was one.

ROSY MCEWEN, LEAD ACTOR IN *BLUE JEAN*

I met Catherine just before filming *Blue Jean*. We sat down over FaceTime and talked for a few hours – I asked her every question under the sun about her life experiences as a teacher in the 1980s and 90s. I was about to play a teacher named Jean, working in Newcastle in 1988, in a film for the BBC, so the parallels were uncanny. *Blue Jean* is partly a character study of one woman's life as a lesbian, struggling under the pressures of the social expectation of a heteronormative lifestyle, and partly a nod to the political backdrop of the time: Thatcher's Britain and the passing into law of Section 28.

The film is written and directed by the incredibly talented Georgia Oakley. I felt spoiled having Catherine to talk to, and having Catherine be so open, honest and vulnerable. The feeling that came from our conversation was, however, not what I thought it would be, but so much more. Through meeting Catherine and through my own research of the lesbian experience under Section 28, I realised how little I knew about this crushing period of history. I was shocked – and selfishly excited to develop a character who was so rich in texture, with all her struggles.

But then, after chatting to Catherine, my ego walked out of the room. I felt a responsibility to treat this story with such perfect care; to tell it right, exactly as it needed to be told and heard, and to represent it properly, as all those who were teachers during Section 28 deserved. This was more than just a film: it was a release of a time period and a story that were wholly brushed over by our cultural history.

The filming process spanned two tiring, beautiful months in the depths of an excruciatingly cold, bleak Newcastle winter. But that only added to the authenticity. As I began to step into Jean's headspace, it was like nothing I could have imagined. The constant fear and anxiety. The looking over my shoulder, conscious of every single person's looks and whispers. The overpowering fear of judgement from other people and – the saddest part – subsequently myself. Jean was forced to be so contained, to keep everything in. This was so unnatural that throughout the filming process I would wake up sobbing in the middle of the night, my body desperately trying to release all this pent-up emotion.

A few weeks into filming, we were shooting in the school that Jean taught in. Eighties-style shell suits and leg warmers were draped over each cast member. Catherine joined us on set as an adviser for all the scenes that contained students playing netball and, truly, we would have been lost without her. Despite reaching the heights of the C team in netball at school, and my extensive research into the rules of the game, I certainly didn't feel equipped to play the role of a netball coach. After two weeks of early mornings and late nights, together with all the normal dramas that come with filming (cameras breaking, running out of time, overly ambitious filming schedules), Catherine's knowledge and experience were everything we needed.

Catherine explained to us how bizarre and triggering it was to feel like she was stepping back in time to the 1980s, re-entering a sports hall where she worried about the words and whispers of her colleagues and students, just like Jean does in the film. This reminded us of how important and real this story was. Even now, 20 years after Section 28 was abolished, its effects are ingrained in the memories of every teacher who worked under it. I also thought about the students who were at school during this period – the young people with questions about their own sexuality and nobody to turn to, being told to quieten the voice in their head, desperately seeking answers to who they were, only to be met with shame and silence. How had it gone on for so long? Why was no one speaking about it now? We wanted to remove the blanket of silence that had covered a whole community of people.

Blue Jean premiered at the Venice Film Festival in 2022. We all travelled out together to watch the film we cared so much about. I had seen it once before the premiere; Catherine, however, had not. Looking back, getting to experience it alongside her was one of the most special experiences of my life. I hoped we had done justice to the stories told to us with authenticity and truth by Catherine and others. Most of all, I hoped the rest of the world would have their eyes opened to this period of history.

It was a true privilege to play Jean and to meet Catherine along the way. I spent approximately six months trying to only emulate a sliver of what life was like for her, and that just shook me to my core. That there were women experiencing the full weight of that every day for years is something I will never get my head around. But now, I hope there is space for this story – and there is no excuse to pull the blanket over it again. So, read on and educate yourself.

DEDICATION

This book is for all the lesbian and gay teachers who spent their careers under Section 28. I hope I have captured something of the struggles that affected so many of us for so many years. I also hope that by sharing my story, I might inspire you to share your story too.

This book is also for all the LGBTQ+ students in my schools between 1988 and 2003. I am sorry that I let you down. I hope this book will help you to understand why I was not there for you when you needed me most.

CONTENTS

Part III. Progress since the repeal of Section 28: current perspectives

INTRODUCTION

In June 2022, my niece and nephew entered the gates of their secondary school in rural East Anglia under a huge rainbow archway of balloons. This was just part of their school's Pride celebrations and, along with their peers, my niece and nephew spent Pride Month hearing from inspirational LGBTQ+ speakers, studying LGBTQ+ figures in history and even attending a Pride disco. I doubt many current secondary school teachers or students are surprised to read this and I imagine similar school Pride celebrations took place across the UK.

Schools were not always like this. For years, they were challenging environments for lesbian and gay teachers and lesbian and gay students, and this book aims to examine how and why this was the case.

The book has been written to coincide with the 20th anniversary of the repeal of Section 28, a law that from 1988 to 2003 prevented the 'promotion of homosexuality' in UK schools. It is a historical, political and cultural book, but it is also deeply personal. I identify as a lesbian and taught in schools for every year of Section 28. I started my career as a PE teacher in inner-city Liverpool before moving into special educational needs and pastoral leadership in rural Suffolk.

I have called this book *Pretended* because Section 28 prohibited schools from promoting 'the acceptability of homosexuality as a pretended family relationship'. These nine words were perhaps the most destructive and damaging of Section 28. Their lack of clarity caused confusion for teachers who had no idea how not to promote homosexuality as pretended. Those of us who were lesbian and gay learned in these nine words that the loving and often lifelong relationships we had with our same-sex partners were not real in the eyes of the law. A right-click for synonyms for 'pretended' in Microsoft Word offers up 'feigned', 'fake', 'counterfeit', 'imitation' and 'untrue'. Under Section 28, the partnerships of lesbian and gay teachers were then deemed feigned, fake, counterfeit, imitation and untrue, and the government mandated that we keep our relationships secret from others in schools, especially young people.

I have also called this book *Pretended* because Section 28 required that I, as a lesbian teacher, pretended to be someone I wasn't throughout my teaching career. For the 15 years of Section 28, I pretended to live alone, I pretended to have boyfriends and I pretended to be a private person so none of my colleagues asked me about my life outside school. I pretended not to be interested in promotion to school leadership, because to be a leader came with a level of visibility in the school community that was incompatible with keeping my personal life hidden.

Pretended has three distinct parts. Part I begins with a history of same-sex relationships in the UK and examines the absence of any laws for lesbians. It then explores the history of lesbian and gay teachers, considering how women who wished not to marry often used teaching as a way to live independently or with a fellow female teacher in schoolhouse accommodation. Part I goes on to examine the way in which, as teaching became synonymous with women's work and caring, male teachers historically were accused of being effeminate and wholly unsuitable as role models for male pupils. Next, consideration is given to the political and cultural narrative surrounding teachers and schools in the UK, and how this led to the introduction of Section 28 by Margaret Thatcher's Conservative government. The repeal of Section 28 is explored and the regret shown in time by the politicians who voted for it. Drawing on my research with teachers, part I then examines the legacy of Section 28 for those who taught during the era, before examining why the law called same-sex relationships 'pretended'.

Part II is a cultural and personal memoir. It draws on a number of diary entries, some of which I shared for the screenplay of the film *Blue Jean*. Covering in turn each of the years that Section 28 was law, I describe the cultural or political landscape for LGBTQ+ people, before sharing one of my own diary entries from that year that relates directly or indirectly to Section 28. I aim through the diaries to convey the challenges I faced, major and minor, and to share some more lighthearted incidents related to Section 28. Through part II, I intend to help the reader understand the extent to which Section 28 permeated my day-to-day life as a lesbian teacher, requiring me, along with lesbian and gay teachers across the UK, to careful manage the nexus of my personal and professional identities.

Part III returns the reader to contemporary issues and considers the way in which the last decade has seen significant positive shifts in schools towards LGBTQ+ inclusion. For example, it explores the leadership development work I undertake with LGBTQ+ teachers who are seeking school leadership roles as their authentic selves. It also examines significant legislative changes, such as the Equality Act 2010, and describes the way in which schools are consequently more inclusive places for LGBTQ+ stakeholders. Part III concludes by reflecting on my involvement in *Blue Jean*. I discuss why the project affected me so profoundly and how it has helped me to make peace with my time as a teacher during Section 28.

There is a good deal of material already in the public domain that celebrates the activists who protested against Section 28. *Outrageous!* by Paul Baker (2022) is excellent and powerfully shares the stories of the protests, from the lesbians who abseiled into the House of Commons to those who disrupted the BBC's *Six O'Clock News*. *Pretended* mentions some of the protests against Section 28, but they are not my main focus. As lesbian and gay teachers, we could not protest because doing so would have jeopardised our careers. Section 28 silenced us and created in schools a hostile and intimidating work environment; we lived in fear of being outed and losing our jobs. Section 28 also left a generation of young people without lesbian or gay teacher role models and denied access to pastoral support to those students who were or thought they were gay. *Pretended* is for all the teachers and students so badly let down by Section 28.

It is important that I explain my use of key terms throughout this book. I am conscious that when reflecting on the Section 28 era, I refer not to the contemporary and inclusive acronym of LGBTQ+ (lesbian, gay, bisexual, transgender, queer or questioning) but only to lesbian and gay teachers. I want to make clear from the outset that my decision to refer historically only to lesbian and gay teachers is not because my stance is gender critical. Far from it. I have chosen to focus on the experiences of lesbian and gay teachers because Section 28 referred to homosexuality, not gender. When I refer to contemporary issues of equality in schools, I apply the inclusive acronym LGBTQ+.

So why not LGB throughout instead? I have not specifically explored or referred to the experiences of bisexual teachers for two reasons. First, I am conscious that those who are gender critical use the acronym LGB and I did not want to be mistakenly regarded as trans-exclusionary. Second, the LGB acronym was not commonly used in the Section 28 era or earlier in history. I recognise that bisexual, transgender, queer and questioning people were also teachers during Section 28 and faced some of the same difficulties and many greater challenges than their lesbian and gay teacher peers. However, what little historical information exists about Section 28 tends not to overtly include bisexual, transgender, queer and questioning teachers as distinct groups. Although it is beyond the parameters of this book to share the stories of these teachers, as an urgent priority their stories must also be told.

Pretended does not constitute a complete history of lesbian and gay teachers or a complete history of Section 28. I inevitably view Section 28 and teaching from my own positionality and context. I identify as a lesbian and taught in inner-city and rural communities, and so the book is written through the lens of my own interest and experience. I left teaching more than a decade ago and my knowledge of schools today is via my work as an education academic and teacher educator. There are considerable milestones in lesbian and gay history that coincided with the Section 28 era and receive little or no attention in the book. For example, the AIDS crisis is drawn on only where politicians weaponised it, and legislative changes to the age of consent are mentioned only briefly. There are numerous books, films, TV series and other media that tell these stories far better than I ever could.

I hope to convey the everyday impact of Section 28 on the lives of lesbian and gay teachers. While the House of Lords debated semantics, including the inclusion of the word 'pretended', the impact of their omissions and inclusions affected thousands of teachers who, long after Section 28, carry scars from years of shame, exclusion and state-sanctioned homophobia. I also hope to convey the way in which Section 28 created for students educated between 1988 and 2003 a regime of compulsory heterosexuality in schools, leaving those who were LGBTQ+ entirely without support.

What happened to me as a lesbian teacher was not particularly unusual; my lesbian and gay teacher friends all encountered similar challenges. There are, however, fewer and fewer lesbian and gay teachers left in schools who experienced Section 28 first-hand and I do not want our stories to be lost. The US state of Florida recently passed the Parental Rights in Education Act, nicknamed the 'don't say gay' law. It contains many of the same restrictions applied by Section 28 in UK schools two decades ago; other states, including Pennsylvania, look set to follow Florida soon. Where the US leads, the UK often follows, and I hope this book might serve as a reminder of the adverse impact of Section 28 on teachers and students alike, so we never again introduce a law like this in the UK.

PART I

SEXUALITY AND SCHOOLS: HISTORICAL AND POLITICAL PERSPECTIVES

CHAPTER 1
A HISTORY OF SAME-SEX RELATIONSHIPS IN THE UK

This chapter describes the historical and political landscape for same-sex relationships in the UK. Unless otherwise stated, quotations are drawn from Hansard parliamentary transcripts to explore the climate for people in same-sex relationships, beginning with the reign of Henry VIII and concluding with the repeal of Section 28 in the early part of the 21st century.

Laws about intimate same-sex relationships first appeared during the reign of Henry VIII in 1533, when an Act of Parliament in England first made unlawful what was described as 'the abominable vice of buggery'. Further legislation followed in the 19th century, when the Criminal Law Amendment Act of 1885 identified homosexual acts as 'gross indecency' between men. There was absolutely no reference to sexual activity between women in these initial laws and this would continue to be the case until the late 20th century. There is a famous and widespread myth that the Criminal Law Amendment Act of 1885 originally pertained to sexual acts between women as well as men, until Queen Victoria intervened to exclude female homosexuality, not believing sex between women existed. However, closer examination of the act shows that Henry Labouchère, who proposed the legislation, did not comment on sexual activity between women in the initial proposal. Therefore, it is unlikely that Queen Victoria ever made such an intervention (Jennings, 2007).

Sexual relationships between women remained invisible and unacknowledged in UK law throughout the 1920s and 30s, although there were occasional failed attempts in Parliament to criminalise sexual activity between women as well as men. In 1921, the Conservative MP Frederick Macquisten motioned to broaden Labouchère's Criminal Law Amendment Act to incorporate 'gross indecency between female persons'. Clause 3 moved that 'any act of gross indecency between female persons shall be a misdemeanour, and punishable in the same manner as any such act committed by male persons under section eleven of the Criminal Law Amendment Act, 1885'. In the ensuing parliamentary debate, Macquisten bemoaned the demise of morality in women, which he blamed on the obliteration of Grecian civilisation and the downfall of the Roman Empire (Waites, 2002). Hansard shows that the Earl of Malmesbury disagreed with Macquisten and was appalled that the issue of sexual activity between women had been raised at all. He prefaced his contribution to the debate by apologising for raising 'a discussion upon what must be, to all of us, a most disgusting and polluting subject'.

Malmesbury went on to warn that if relationships between women were included in the clause, they, like their male counterparts, would become prone to blackmail 'without in the slightest degree decreasing the amount of this vice'. Malmesbury qualified his protestations by positing that the domestic behaviours of the sexes were entirely different. He said:

> For instance, if twenty women were going to live in a house with twenty bedrooms, I do not believe that all the twenty bedrooms would be occupied, either for reasons of fear or nervousness, and the desire for mutual protection. On the other hand, I know that when men take shooting boxes, the first inquiry is that each shall have a room to himself if possible; and a comfortable room, too.

Malmesbury concluded by stating: 'The more you advertise vice by prohibiting it, the more you will increase it.' In the same debate, the Earl of Desart argued that friendships between women could be misconstrued as lesbian if the clause was passed. He feared women may engage in lesbian acts unwittingly and said:

> We all know of the sort of romantic, almost hysterical, friendships that are made between young women at certain periods of their lives and of

its occasional manifestations. Suppose that some circumstance gave to some person who knew of it the idea, 'How easy it now is for me to make a charge.' Perhaps they do not know what the law is. Do you suppose any woman with anything in the world to lose would ever face such a charge as that? It would not be a question of defending themselves against it; it would be a question of facing it, of being brought into a public court to meet a charge of that kind. They would pay anything sooner than that. I believe that blackmail would not only be certain, but that it would inevitably be successful.

In addition to the protestations of Malmesbury and Desart, opposition to the inclusion of relationships between women was widespread. Therefore, somewhat inevitably, Macquisten's clause was defeated, leaving romantic relationships between women invisible in UK law.

Some seven years later, a lesbian did find herself involved in litigation relating to romantic love between women. Radclyffe Hall's novel *The Well of Loneliness* was published in 1928. Hall's affluence and family status enabled her to live independently from men; she resided with several different women throughout her lifetime and would dress in men's clothes. Hall was a renowned author but *The Well of Loneliness* was her first novel about a relationship between two women. The book describes the life of a fictional character, Stephen Gordon, who, like Hall, is a masculine woman from an upper-class family. Stephen becomes romantically involved with Mary Llewellyn, an ambulance driver in the First World War, but their relationship leaves the women ridiculed and ostracised. The word 'lesbian' is not used in the book at all. Instead, Stephen is described as a 'congenital invert', a phrase Hall was known to use to describe herself from time to time. Hall makes a passionate plea in the novel to 'give us also the right to our existence'. Consequently, *The Well of Loneliness* was regarded as a significant contributor to the call for recognition and acceptance of intimate relationships between women (Parkes, 1994).

Initially, reviews for *The Well of Loneliness* were positive. The *Times Literary Supplement* described it as 'sincere, courageous, high-minded and beautifully expressed' (Parkes, 1994). However, just a few weeks after the novel's publication, the editor of the *Sunday Express*, James Douglas, began undermining its success by claiming that it was obscene and immoral propaganda (Parkes, 1994). When *The Well of Loneliness* was brought to the attention of the home secretary, the Conservative and strict authoritarian William Joynson-Hicks, he sought the advice of the director of public prosecutions on what should be done. The novel was characterised by Joynson-Hicks as a 'plea not only for the toleration but for the recognition of sexual perversion amongst women' (Gilmore, 1994). The director of public prosecutions agreed with the home secretary that the book would corrupt the minds of young people and concluded that its sale in the UK was undesirable. The chief magistrate, Chartres Biron, read the book and immediately commenced the process of prosecuting Hall. Legal proceedings began but ultimately it was not Hall who was charged. Instead the publisher, Jonathan Cape, and his colleagues were summoned to Bow Street Magistrates Court, where Biron presided over the trial personally (Marshik, 2003).

Hall did not take part in any aspect of the trial; she was not called as a witness and was not invited to make a defence. She did, however, watch proceedings throughout the trial from the public gallery. More than 100 fellow authors and literary critics were called to give expert evidence on the issue of whether *The Well of Loneliness* was obscene. More than a third of the witnesses supported the book, including Vita Sackville-West and Virginia Woolf, who would later become known for their own same-sex affairs (Parkes, 1994). However, it seemed that Biron had already made up his mind and he deemed the supportive contributions by Sackville-West, Woolf and others immaterial. He decided that censorship was not pertinent to the case, positing that instead it was a matter of whether the book was obscene. The only hint at a physical relationship between Stephen and Mary in *The Well of Loneliness* was the words 'that night they were not divided'. However, Biron rejected Cape's defence that because the book did not include obscene words, and contained no reference to intimacy between Stephen and Mary, it could not be described as obscene. He applied the Hicklin test of obscenity, which stated that a work was obscene if it could 'deprave and corrupt those whose minds are open to such immoral influences', adding that Hall's call for the acceptance of 'inverts' was in itself obscene (Mullin, 2018). Biron found against Cape, who was ordered to pay court costs. In making his judgment, Biron said:

The very fact the book is well written can be no answer to these proceedings because otherwise we should be in the preposterous position where the most obscene books would be free from stricture. The more palatable the poison the more insidious. The substantial question before me is the contention that this book as a whole, does not define unnatural practices between women and does not glorify them. The unnatural acts which are the subject of this book involve acts which between men would be criminal and would involve acts of the horrible, unnatural and disgusting obscenity. The whole note of the book is a passionate and almost hysterical plea for toleration and recognition of these people. (Parkes, 1994)

Hall protested from the public gallery before the judge threatened to remove her. Biron then ordered that all copies of *The Well of Loneliness* be destroyed. Cape accepted that he must withdraw the book, but surreptitiously made arrangements for it to be published by Pegasus Press in Paris.

In 2003, when some of Woolf's unpublished notes and drafts of her writing were uncovered, they revealed the efforts she had made to obscure her own sexuality after the trial of *The Well of Loneliness* in 1928 (Sigel, 2011).

Nine years after the trial, in 1937, a debate took place in Parliament about homosexuality as grounds for divorce. Hansard shows that Viscount Dawson of Penn argued that the word 'sodomy' – which by the 1930s had been replaced by 'buggery' in common parlance – was not accurate as it related only to the 'rather vulgar crime which is only open to the male'. Viscount Dawson demanded that sexual acts between women as well as between men be included as grounds for divorce, stating:

Equality of the sexes ought to cut both ways, and it is as much a misfortune with the woman as it is with the man. You ought to protect the man against the lesbian just as you protect a woman against a male homo-sexualist.

Like Macquisten 16 years earlier, Dawson failed in his quest to have sexual activity between women recognised in law. The Conservative lord chancellor, Frederick Smith, warned that lesbian relationships should not be acknowledged in law as he doubted women had ever heard of such a thing and was concerned it may give them ideas. Smith stated: 'Of every thousand women, taken as a whole, 999 have never even heard a whisper of these practices.'

In the 1950s, as same-sex relationships between women remained invisible, homosexuality (pertaining only to sex between men) burst into the mainstream cultural consciousness. Taking a lead from the US, where high-profile gay men were arrested as part of a campaign called the Lavender Scare, the home secretary, David Maxwell Fyfe, promised to rid England of a similar 'gay plague'. The police, acting as agents provocateurs, enticed high-profile figures into sex in public places. The media reported each salacious detail, ruining the reputations of public figures including the actor and director John Gielgud and the mathematician and Second World War codebreaker Alan Turing (Bengry, 2014).

More than 1000 gay men were jailed each year and eventually the Conservative government established the Wolfenden Committee in 1954 to review the laws on homosexuality and prostitution. The committee had male and female members, but the men were worried that the female members would be shocked by the use of explicit language (Grimley, 2009). Consequently, during debate, the Wolfenden Committee agreed to refer to homosexuals and prostitutes as 'Huntleys' and 'Palmers' after a well-known biscuit brand at the time, so as not to affront the sensibilities of the female committee members (Lewis, 2016).

The Wolfenden Report of 1957 recommended that homosexual acts between men should be partially decriminalised, stating that the criminalisation of homosexuality impinged on civil liberty. The report stressed that while the law must protect young and vulnerable people from abuse, it should not encroach into private matters. Although the report pertained only to male sexual activity, it did accept that adulterous lesbian relationships were just as likely to cause marital breakdown. Furious discussions surrounded male sexual activity, but relationships between women were not discussed and remained largely taboo (Grimley, 2009).

Those seeking the complete decriminalisation of male homosexuality frequently argued on the grounds that lesbianism was legal by default as it was absent from the law. In fact, female homosexuality had no status at all, but reformers commonly drew on this to emphasise the injustice in the inequality between the sexes, sometimes positing that sexual acts between women were far worse than those between men.

In 1953, a year before the Wolfenden Committee was established, the Moral Welfare Council of the Church of England called for the decriminalisation of male homosexuality (Anderson, 2016). It also opposed the legislative disparity between gay men and lesbians. In 1956, the Moral Welfare Council published a booklet called *Sexual Offenders and Social Punishment*, which denounced the inequality in law between male and female homosexuality. The booklet stated:

> *While the male homosexual is heavily penalised for his offences ... the female homosexual is ignored and can do what she wishes with impunity. Yet socially she is often dangerous. An older woman can dominate a younger, and she can compel her to acquiesce in a lesbian liaison which may ruin her life. Even more serious, a persistent lesbian can break up a marriage by seducing the wife, or by insinuating herself into the home.* (Bailey, 1956, p.162)

The absence of lesbianism from the law while male homosexuals faced custodial sentences made the continued criminalisation of sexual activity between men challenging to support. However, opponents of the decriminalisation of male homosexuality persisted in positioning sexual relationships between women as harmless, rather than pushing to criminalise this behaviour too (Waites, 2002).

In the wake of the publication of the Wolfenden Report, the government's War Office rushed to exclude the findings from applying to the armed forces (Grimley, 2009). While male sexual relationships were prohibited in the armed forces, the War Office stated:

> *[We] do not consider that there is any major homosexual problem in relation to the women's services and they would be opposed to any suggestion that lesbianism should be an offence in the Army. In the case of women, ignorant but perfectly harmless behaviour may well be misconstrued; to have such cases subject to discipline rather than to guidance and common sense treatment would, it is felt, be far more harmful than the present administrative arrangements under which only serious cases are dealt with and which, if anything, err on the side of leniency.* (National Archives: ADM 1/25754)

The quest for a clear-cut acknowledgement of female homosexuality ensued and once again lesbianism, when and where mentioned at all, was positioned as innocuous and benign. In 1958, the judge Lord Denning captured the views of the era during a debate in the Lords about homosexuality and prostitution. Denning said: 'Dangerous driving of a motor car is a crime, but furious driving with a horse and cart is not.' A prominent opponent of the decriminalisation of homosexuality, William Shepherd MP, argued that lesbian relationships 'in many cases supply a social purpose, because they tend to be much more lasting or permanent than homosexual associations'.

In the same debate, Viscount Hailsham, who, like Shepherd, supported the continued criminalisation of male homosexuality, contended that male homosexuality resulted in the entirely deplorable feminisation of men. He said: 'A lesbian is never, or at least seldom, other than a woman, and a very feminine woman at that.' Hailsham added that lesbian relationships did not constitute sexual activity and so lesbianism was 'not, in truth, wholly analogous' to homosexuality in men.

Hailsham's unchallenged allegation that lesbianism did not compromise femininity demonstrates how little was known at the time about sexual relationships between women. At the Gateways lesbian club in London in the 1950s, a strict butch-femme binary defined the relationships that played out there (Jennings, 2006). The butch half of the partnership would often dress in a three-piece suit while the femme partners would wear dresses. The femmes were treated with chivalry by their butch partners and were not permitted to order drinks from the bar themselves. These relationships were literally driven underground to subterranean clubs such as Gateways and remained invisible in the consciousness of wider society, which was instead preoccupied with the perceived growing femininity in men (Jennings, 2006).

In the 1953 book *Society and the Homosexual*, Michael Schofield, writing as Gordon Westwood, contemplated homosexuality via a sociological framework rather than through a medical or legal lens – one of just a handful of researchers to do so. In a series of three books, Schofield investigated the lived experience of gay men in the UK; in his third title, *Sociological Aspects of Homosexuality* (1965), he compared the experiences of heterosexuals and gay and straight men in three spheres: in prison, in treatment and in the community. He concluded:

> *Homosexuality is a condition which in itself has only minor effects upon the development of the personality. But the attitudes not of the homosexual but of other people towards this condition, create a stress situation which can have a profound effect upon personality development ... A proportion of homosexuals are unable to withstand this pressure from outside and become social casualties. These are the homosexuals found most often in prisons and clinics ... On the other hand the homosexuals who have learnt to contend with social pressures can become adjusted to their condition and integrated with the community. These men are hardly ever found in prison and clinics.* (p.203)

The Sexual Offences Act finally decriminalised sex between men in 1967 and was largely acknowledged as the first judicial step towards equality for gay men. The legal age of consent was set at 21 (it was lowered to 18 in 1994, and to 16 until 2001). However, the law covered England and Wales only. Homosexuality in men remained against the law in Scotland and Northern Ireland until the 1980s.

Lesbianism continued to sit outside the law into the 1970s, when the rise of feminism led heterosexual and lesbian women to combine their efforts in a quest to achieve equality with men. The Sex Discrimination Act of 1975 established a commission tasked with eliminating discrimination between men and women and promoting equality of opportunity for women.

One of the first cases to test the Sex Discrimination Act was that of 12-year-old Theresa Bennett, who brought a case against the Football Association's ban on girls and women playing football (Griggs & Biscomb, 2010). The FA successfully defended the case but the media largely supported Theresa and other girls who came forward wanting to play football. It would take until 1991 for the ban on females playing football to be rescinded. Thirty-one years later, in 2022, England's women footballers would win the European Championship, the first major trophy since England's men won the World Cup in 1966.

The fight for gay rights emerged in the 1970s when the Gay Liberation Front (GLF) was founded in the UK. Inspired by a movement of the same name in the US, the UK GLF assembled in an old school classroom to organise protests, sit-ins, street theatre and festivals (Robinson, 2006). GLF members included lesbians and gay men, with their collective power achieving immediate impact. In 1972, the GLF organised London's first gay pride march; 50 years on, it is one of the largest LGBTQ+ Pride celebrations in the world.

In 1981, a group of largely lesbian women became visible in the mainstream consciousness by protesting against the UK government's decision to locate nuclear weapons in Berkshire. As part of the Campaign for Nuclear Disarmament (CND), the Greenham Common Women's Peace Camp at RAF Greenham Common was initially established by a Welsh group, the Women for Life on Earth (McKay, 2004). After realising that one-off events of protest were not going to get the missiles removed, the women began to camp at Greenham Common to continue their protest. The women's peace camp movement, which was largely comprised of lesbians, had emerged.

While these lesbians sought to affect cultural and political change in the UK, they remained wholly absent from the law. As other countries unambiguously included same-sex intimacy between women in their homosexuality laws, the UK would not criminalise lesbian identities or relationships until the introduction of Section 28 in 1988.

Having set out the historical and political landscape for same-sex relationships in the UK, I look closely in the next chapter at the history of the lesbian teacher in Western society. Beginning with an exploration of the spinster as teacher, I focus in particular on the way in which lesbianism became synonymous with women in the teaching profession, and how teaching became a career in which women who wished not to marry men could live independently, or sometimes with other female teachers in lesbian relationships.

CHAPTER 2

SPINSTER OF THE PARISH: A HISTORY OF THE LESBIAN FEMALE TEACHER

As chapter 1 revealed, at the start of the 20th century, women were positioned culturally and politically as sensitive and easily shocked by references to sex. It would take until the sexual liberation of heterosexual women in the 1970s for society to tolerate discourses in which women engaged in sexual activity for any reason other than childbearing. Madiha Didi Khayatt (1992) states that, for centuries, society viewed women as 'passionless, incapable of sexual feelings, submitting to male aggressive desire only for the purpose of procreation' (p.15). The enduring absence of lesbian women from the homosexual narrative also served to erase lesbian relationships from public consciousness.

As documented by Judith Butler in her seminal text *Gender Trouble* (1990), sexuality becomes bound up with male and female gender categories because it is recognised in relation to whom a person desires. Butler describes sexuality and gender as multiple and fragmented, constructed in relation to others and within society's systems of power and knowledge identities.

The prevailing polarisation of gender roles in UK society determined social behaviour and provided the model for gender-based sexual expectations and behaviours for years to come. According to Khayatt (1992), 'a woman who actively desired another woman ceased to be a woman, [she] became masculinized' (p.15). Khayatt asserts that the 'masculinization' of lesbians prompted men to become concerned about female attempts to gain power.

The binary identifiers of masculinity in men and femininity in women served to preserve male dominance and subdue female assertiveness. When women presented as masculine, mainstream society rejected them for transgressing what were inconceivably narrow expectations of femininity.

Until the beginning of the 19th century, teaching was the sole territory of the educated male. Members of the teaching profession were highly respected pillars of society who were beyond reproach. However, as the 20th century loomed, perceptions of the teaching profession slowly began to shift (Blount, 2000). Teaching began to be considered a caring profession, with the education of children akin to the maternal duties of raising children and thus aligned with domestic or women's work (Apple, 1985).

The earliest female teachers were nuns who, because of their vow of poverty, did not draw and keep a wage for their roles (Hufton, 1984). As teaching became synonymous with care, men left the profession in numbers, leaving women to fill vacant positions. Until the 1970s, there was a ban in most Western countries on married women working in teaching and other clerical jobs (Borjas, 2007). Upon marriage, women were obliged to leave their posts to become housewives. According to Khayatt (1992), teaching was one of few routes that allowed unmarried women to achieve economic liberation. Female teachers earned their own wage and usually gratis accommodation at the school, meaning they did not rely on a man for financial support.

Over time, somewhat inevitably, the terms 'spinster' and 'teacher' became inextricably linked with one another (Munro, 1998). The term 'spinster' first entered common parlance in the late 15th century and referred to girls and women who spun wool (Young, 2019). Women did not work once they were married, so 'spinster' became the name for any woman who was old enough to marry but remained single. Spinster continued to be the denotation for unmarried women until 2005 in the UK, where the bride-to-be was described as a 'spinster of this parish' in the Church of England marriage banns (Young, 2019).

Female teachers came to be seen as failures by society at large, as their presence in the classroom symbolised that they had been unable to attract a man, become a wife and have a family – in those days an achievement much more lauded by society than having a career. Those women who entered teaching were labelled as masculine, regardless of their appearance. Being educated or intelligent were, at the time, attractive traits in a man but not in a woman (Blount, 2000).

Soon, the spinster teacher – an intelligent and accomplished woman, but not desirable enough to attract a man – became vilified by Western capitalist society (Jeffreys, 1997). Cultural references began to characterise female teachers as evil, or at best callous, and they were usually portrayed as humourless and masculine in appearance (Allen, 1982; Lugg, 2003). The reputation of female teachers as necessarily masculine ensured the spinster and lesbian labels became intertwined; the status and respectability of the spinster teacher was challenged as they shared with lesbians a space that sat outside the dominant heteronormative patriarchal discourse of the early 20th century (Blount, 1996).

By the 1920s, the status of both male and female schoolteachers was problematic. Teaching was seen as too feminine for men and too masculine for women. According to Jackie Blount (1996), teaching became conflated with gender transgression and so was inextricably associated 'in the popular mind with homosexuality and all of its attendant taboos'. When compared with their male peers, however, female teachers were inexpensive to employ. As schools were largely independent and often run for the monetary gain of benefactors, there were financial benefits to employing women rather than men.

In the US, Catharine Beecher founded the American Woman's Educational Association (AWEA) in 1852, an organisation committed to extending educational opportunities for women (Eisenmann, 2001). Beecher posited that women were naturally maternal and had inherent caring qualities that made them ideal teachers. According to Beecher, teaching was an extension of childcare and so a natural extension of motherhood. Blount (1996) observes that Beecher and her peers at AWEA were troubled by the spinster teacher trope and, via their organisation, encouraged female teachers to display overtly feminine characteristics, hone their domestic skills and, alongside their teaching posts, prioritise preparation for marriage and motherhood.

In the US and the UK, teaching was slowly being reframed and became a stopgap for young women before marriage. Many schools found that female teachers left the profession soon after their careers commenced, which was disruptive and inconvenient. Over time, schools began to prefer to appoint 'old maid' or committed spinster teachers, as they were likely to stay in the role for longer (Blount, 1996).

By the late 19th and early 20th centuries, the spinster teacher had become established in the cultural landscape in British and American society. Spinster teachers emerged in novels and films – stereotypically prim and stern, with their hair scraped off their faces into severe buns (Blount, 2000). As the number of spinster teachers grew and they committed to their employment for the long term, schools began providing housing to accommodate them. Many spinster teachers boarded in houses together in small groups. It also became commonplace for pairs of spinster teachers to set up home together.

Research by Blount (2000) uncovered a declaration by a spinster teacher in 1934. She said of her life:

> *The very conveniences of living at present make the single life more agreeable than it once was ... [and] makes the assistance of a strong masculine hand or the protection of masculine presence unnecessary. The domestic-minded spinster is no longer driven to the deprivations of the boarding house or the small hotel.*

The commitment of the spinster teacher to her career meant that society valued her contribution. The communal living arrangements of spinster teachers were accepted as the norm and by the 1930s female teachers were afforded genuine independence. Living with other spinster teachers liberated them from the demands of becoming a wife and a mother, and allowed these women to prosper on their own terms.

Theodore Roosevelt, US president from 1901 to 1909, observed a tendency in educated young white women to pursue the teaching profession as a way of actively avoiding marriage and motherhood. Roosevelt said this behaviour constituted 'race suicide' and expressed concern that the spinster teacher was responsible for the downfall of the white middle classes in America (Blount, 2000).

Over time, the tendency of women to remain unmarried was perceived as a threat to traditional gender roles. As spinster teachers attained leadership positions in education, sometimes over men, a backlash emerged (Blount, 2000). The once harmless and useful spinster teacher was no longer seen as a benevolent presence and her contentment outside the institution of marriage came under criticism. By the late 1930s, spinster teachers had begun to be described as deviant and those living together in pairs were scrutinised for what became known as homosexual traits (Cavanagh, 2005).

Avid viewers of the BBC television series *Gentleman Jack*, about the life of the lesbian Anne Lister of Shibden Hall in West Yorkshire, may have heard characters reference a lesbian teacher scandal. In series two, episode six, Captain Sutherland, the brother-in-law of Anne Lister's lover, Ann Walker, attempts to prevent the women from combining their considerable estates – he wants Walker's money for himself. Sutherland sets out on a mission to destroy Lister's reputation, insisting to Walker's solicitor that it would be irresponsible of him to sign the division, given Lister's 'unnatural' hold over his sister-in-law. Sutherland alleges to their accountant that the women are in a scandalous romantic relationship that should be stopped. To further labour his point, he references a similar lesbian scandal in an Edinburgh school between two spinster teachers.

In 1809, Marianne Woods, aged 27, and Jane Pirie, aged 26, opened a highly selective girls' school in Drumsheugh Gardens in Edinburgh (Faderman, 2013). The school soon attracted some of the city's most prominent and wealthy families, earning a reputation as one of the best and most highly regarded schools for girls in Scotland. The school was described as a compact facility, with the two teachers and 10 students sharing just two bedrooms. While this is unthinkable today, it was commonplace at that time for teachers and children to sleep in a single room in schoolhouses (Faderman, 2013). The practice was largely regarded as beneficial in the supervision and support of boarding school children.

Among the students at Drumsheugh Gardens was Jane Cumming, the grandchild of Lady Helen Cumming Gordon, a Scottish aristocrat. Lady Cumming Gordon's son had conceived Jane with an Indian servant, causing shame and embarrassment for his family. Lady Cumming Gordon did, however, care for the child and secured her education at this top-class Edinburgh school (Faderman, 2013).

In November 1810, Jane visited her grandmother and during their conversation mentioned that her teachers, Woods and Pirie, displayed 'inordinate affection' for each other (Faderman, 2013). After questioning Jane about the relationship, Lady Cumming Gordon was appalled and wrote to all parents with children at the school to let them know of the immoral behaviour of the two teachers. She encouraged every parent to remove their child from the school and withdrew Jane with immediate effect. Within two days, every girl at Drumsheugh Gardens had been dramatically whisked away from the school. The schoolhouse stood empty, except for the two distraught teachers. Woods told a concerned parent, 'I am utterly ignorant of what was laid to my charge, and I am not conscious of anything' (Faderman, 2013).

When Woods and Pirie learned of the allegations by Lady Cumming Gordon, they each sued her for libel (Singh, 2020). This set in train a protracted court case that attracted significant media attention and caused intimate details of their lives together to be shared across the world. Several of the schoolgirls were called as witnesses; some alleged that the teachers called each other 'darling' and had been seen by a number of girls lying on top of one another. Jane Cumming testified in the case, claiming she was often woken at night when Woods visited Pirie's bed. Jane also alleged that she 'was more often than once disturbed early in the morning . . . they were speaking and kissing and shaking in her bed'. Jane added, 'I heard Miss Woods one night ask Miss Pirie if she was hurting her ... Miss Pirie said "No". Then another night I heard Miss Pirie say: "Oh, do it, darling". And Miss Woods said: "Oh, not tonight, for it may waken Miss Cumming and perhaps Miss Stirling" ... So then at last she came in and she lay above Miss Pirie. And then Miss Woods began to move and she shook the bed' (Faderman, 2013).

Another witness, Janet Munro, supported the claims of Jane, describing to the court her recollections of seeing the teachers in bed together. 'I believe her clothes were off and one lay above the other,' she said. 'Miss Pirie was uppermost. The bedclothes tossed about and they seemed to be breathing high. I said: "Miss Pirie, I wish you would go away, for I can't get sleep".

Then Miss Woods said to Miss Pirie: "You had better go away, Jane, for I'm afraid you'll catch cold standing there". But I knew she wasn't standing. She was in bed' (Faderman, 2013).

Despite the vivid accounts by the girls, the majority of the judges presiding over the case were not convinced. Lord Justice Meadowbank, doubting the existence of sexual relationships between women, stated that a sexual relationship between the two teachers was 'equally imaginary with witchcraft, sorcery or carnal copulation with the devil'. Another of the judges, Lord Justice Hope, said it was as likely as 'thunder playing the tune of *God Save The King*' (Faderman, 2013).

The judges questioned Jane's background and, in particular, her early years with her mother in India. Meadowbank mused on the likelihood that Hindu servants had discussed sexual exploits within the hearing range of Jane, exposing her to knowledge of such sordid acts between women as those she had described in court (Faderman, 2013).

During the court case, lawyers made much of Jane's dark complexion and revealed that Lady Cumming Gordon had kept Jane at arm's length since she was brought from India. Before telling her grandmother about the alleged lesbian relationship between the two teachers, Jane had confided her feelings in a notebook. The notebook showed that Jane had developed a crush on Woods and that Woods had rejected her advances. Scorned, Jane had gone on to proposition a classmate who also rejected her, causing Jane to run away from the school (Faderman, 2013).

The lawyer for Woods and Pirie produced a number of good character references for the teachers and stressed that both Jane Cumming and Janet Munro had been admonished by the strict Pirie. Their lawyer went on to argue that both teachers were afflicted with rheumatics and would often massage each other, accounting for their physical contact in bed and providing an explanation, perhaps, for the shaking bed the girls had witnessed (Roughead, 1931).

The court initially found Lady Cumming Gordon not guilty of defamation of the two teachers by a 4-3 majority. Woods and Pirie appealed against the decision and their appeal was upheld 12 months later, also by a 4-3 majority. However, even then, Lady Cumming Gordon continued to pursue the teachers. She took the case to the House of Lords, where it continued in the public domain for nine further years after the original claims. The House of Lords rejected her appeal, triggering a further protracted dispute over the financial damages the teachers were owed (Faderman, 2013).

Having claimed £10,000 each from Lady Cumming Gordon, the now destitute Woods and Pirie collected approximately £1000 each after legal costs. Their victory came at the cost of their reputation and finances, both of which were left in tatters. The women also parted company. Woods gained employment teaching part-time in London and Pirie was left in hardship and ill health in Edinburgh.

Over time, the lesbian teacher scandal of the Drumsheugh Gardens school was largely forgotten. However, in 1930 papers pertinent to the case were found at the Signet legal library in Edinburgh by the prominent lawyer and crime writer William Roughead. He went on to feature the case in a book of infamous legal cases called *Bad Companions* (1931) and so the scandal gained publicity all over again.

Lillian Hellman was an American playwright and screenwriter renowned for her achievements on Broadway, as well as her communist views. She read Roughead's book and turned the story of Woods and Pirie into a controversial play called *The Children's Hour*. Hellman relocated the story from Edinburgh to New England in the US and changed the names of the protagonists. Woods and Pirie become Karen Wright and Martha Dobie, and Jane Cumming became Mary Tilford. *The Children's Hour* otherwise remained true to the original story. Tilford absconds from the school and, to escape being returned, informs her grandmother that the two teachers are having a lesbian affair. As in real life, the play shows how the child's allegations destroy the lives and careers of the two teachers (Faderman, 2013).

The Children's Hour was first performed at the Maxine Elliott Theatre on Broadway in 1934, before moving in 1936 to Paris and to London's Gate Theatre Studio. A Hollywood film followed in 1961 starring Audrey Hepburn and Shirley MacLaine; the film was released under an alternative title, *The Loudest Whisper*, in New Zealand, Australia and the UK.

The play was produced for the radio in 1971 as part of the BBC's Saturday Night Theatre series and starred Prunella Scales (*Fawlty Towers*) and Jill Bennett (*For Your Eyes Only*). In 1994, the play was revived for radio by the BBC's Monday Play series, this time starring Buffy Davis, Clare Holman, Miriam Margolyes and Margaret Robertson. In 2011, *The Children's Hour* returned to London and was introduced to a new generation, with Elisabeth Moss (*The Handmaid's Tale*) and Keira Knightley (*Atonement, Bend it Like Beckham*) playing the two teachers.

The Children's Hour was not the only depiction of lesbian relationships within the school setting. In 1917, *Regiment of Women* was published as the debut novel of Winifred Ashton writing as Clemence Dane. *Regiment of Women* is set in Edwardian England and, like *The Children's Hour*, it describes the relationship between two female teachers at an elite boarding school for girls. Clare Hartill, the older of the two women, is in her mid-thirties but is in poor health. She lives alone in a small flat without gas or electricity but full of books. The girls at the school are devoted to Hartill, despite her high standards and academic demands. They see that Hartill is ambitious for them and this makes her a popular teacher.

Alwynne Durand, the second teacher, is just 19 years old and has no formal teacher training. Hartill and Durand soon become friends: Durand spends all her spare time in Hartill's home, staying overnight on occasions, and the teachers holiday together during the school summer break. Durand's aunt, Elsbeth Loveday, with whom she lives, becomes jealous of Hartill; the novel describes acute antagonism between the two older women as they vie for Durand's companionship.

The relationship between Hartill and Durand is severely tested when one of their pupils, Louise, takes her own life by jumping from a schoolhouse window. The suicide is declared a case of accidental death. However, Louise's suicide appears to have resulted from Hartill's severe criticism of her performance in the school play. Over time, Hartill manipulates the facts and shifts the burden of guilt on to Durand's shoulders. Hartill displays increasingly bizarre behaviour and is consistently cruel to Durand. Loveday spots the breakdown of their relationship and attempts to remove her niece from the teaching post, arranging for her convalescence when she catches the flu.

But Loveday's scheme to keep the women apart includes more than her niece's recuperation. She introduces Durand to a potential suitor, Roger Lumsden, a kind, educated and attractive man who runs his own gardening business. However, Durand is not attracted to Lumsden and longs to return to Hartill and her teaching post. On her return to the school, Durand continues to be treated badly by Hartill; eventually, the younger teacher recognises that the relationship is abusive. Durand leaves the school, sending Hartill a telegram informing her that she is to be married.

This unhappy ending for the two teachers is symptomatic of the criticism Clemence Dane has for spinster teachers. In a 1926 collection of essays, *The Women's Side*, Dane highlights the tensions that can exist between teachers and students in girls' schools. Dane is particularly vociferous in her essay 'A problem in education'.

Exploring the subject of power in relationships between female students and female teachers, 'A problem in education' describes the issue of emotional attachments between members of the same sex and is critical of the hothouse atmosphere of single-sex schools. Dane observes that when spinster teachers have no life beyond their career, they devote their time and energy to the intrigues within the school. She notes a peculiarity arising from the social isolation of women and girls in single-sex schools and blames the effect of the marriage ban in creating spinster teachers. According to Dane, the need for spinster teachers to maintain respectability means they spend their lives completely immersed in the closed world of schools. In the essay, Dane asks:

> But what opportunity has a woman to mix freely with men and women alike, so as to understand her own outlook on these matters, to test her feelings, to differentiate between her need of friendship and her need of love? Her sole emotional outlook is her fellow-mistresses and her students. (1926, p.53)

A teacher herself, Dane was a friend of Violet Trefusis and Vita Sackville-West, who famously had a lesbian affair. According to Emily Hamer (2016), Dane was almost certainly a lesbian herself but deployed elaborate strategies to keep her private life from others. Drawing on documentary evidence including Dane's will, Hamer suggests that Dane had been in a long-term romantic relationship with Elsie Arnold, who lived with her. When that association ended, Dane began an intimate relationship with another woman, Olwen Bowen-Davies. Supposedly, Dane's forthright views on the claustrophobic nature of schools for the spinster teacher were based on her own experiences, although one cannot avoid the conclusion that her critical stance was a ploy to evade scrutiny of her own circumstances and relationships (Hamer, 2016).

Though rare, there is further evidence of lesbian teachers in history and literature. Hamer (2016) notes that Edward Carpenter was an English gay rights activist, socialist and philosopher. He was best known for his book *Civilisation: its cause and cure* (1889), in which he describes civilisation as an illness of sorts, through which human societies pass. As an early campaigner for sexual liberation and equality, Carpenter was well connected. He was known to have had an influence on the writings of DH Lawrence and was thought to have inspired EM Forster's homoerotic novel *Maurice*.

According to Hamer (2016), Carpenter received many letters of thanks from lesbians who appreciated his activism in support of gay rights. Bob Rogers was a young woman living in Derby; in a letter to Carpenter in 1925, she wrote:

> *I feel I am acting as the spokesman of thousands who think and feel as I do in writing to express my great deep gratitude ... Although I am known as Bob, physically I am a girl, still in my twenty-first year. I have been teaching slum boys since I left college nearly two years ago. It was at college that I met and learned to love a girl, who, in almost every respect, is quite different from me ... I had no idea but love between two of the same sex could possibly exist.* (In Hamer, 2016, p.66)

Lillian Barker was a schoolteacher and lesbian living in London in the early 1900s (Hamer, 2016). She specialised in educating students referred to at the time as delinquent, but whom we would recognise today as having special educational needs. According to Hamer, Barker met her partner, Florence Francis, when both women worked as Sunday school teachers. In 1914, Barker moved in with Francis and the women cohabited for 40 years, until Barker died in 1955.

Barker served in the Second World War at the Royal Arsenal, Woolwich, where as superintendent she was responsible for 30,000 female workers. After the war, in 1923, Barker became governor of the Borstal Institution for Girls in Aylesbury. In this role, she led significant reforms that centred on the education and rehabilitation of the girls. She was appointed Dame Commander of the Order of the British Empire (DBE) in 1944 for her services in connection with the welfare of women and girls (Hamer, 2016).

In the 1997 book *The Spinster and her Enemies*, Sheila Jeffreys suggests that as far back as the 19th century, spinster teachers were considered a threat to the children they taught. By way of example, Jeffreys cites Alec Craig, the socialist and 'sexual modernist' who wrote that spinster schoolteachers were dangerous to the young because they were not having sexual intercourse, and so had a dangerous energy that he referred to as 'dammed up sexual urge'. Without describing what the effects of this might be, Craig said that seeking another channel or outlet was rarely satisfactory in its results. According to Jeffreys, there was a good deal of suspicion around the potential evils resulting from the almost exclusive employment of women in the teaching profession. She cites the example of Walter Gallichan, editor of the *Free Review*, a magazine that carried progressive ideas on sexual reform. Gallichan warned his readers and society in general of the danger of the 'frigide' as a teacher. He believed such a teacher would educate girls to become women who were critical of men. Jeffreys argues that at the heart of the harsh depiction of the spinster teacher by Craig, Gallichan and their peers was the possibility that these women might not need men and might be having sex with each other.

By the early 1900s, medical research in the field of human sexuality was thriving. Any transgressions from heterosexual relationships came under intense scrutiny and homosexuality was considered pathological (Bullough, 1976). Lawrence Averill (1939) suggests that in cohabiting, spinster teachers were largely thought to have suppressed 'fundamental instincts to the point of extinction, instead of sublimating them and finding peace and satisfaction in other compensating and stimulating ways' (p.10). Spinster teachers remained a cause for apprehension, however. The psychologist G. Stanley Hall, in his 1905 article 'Certain degenerative tendencies among teachers', asserted that psychological processes were at play that caused spinster teachers to become sour, frustrated and negative.

Society more generally also denounced spinster teachers for deviating from expected gender roles. Many were seen as aberrant or pathological, and all were soon deemed unsuitable for working with children.

In the 1920s, Katharine Bement Davis, a social activist and sex researcher, conducted research that concluded spinster teachers might in fact be lesbians (Bullough, 1988). Davis surveyed 2200 college-educated women and sought to compare patterns of sexual behaviour between the married and single women. Davis established that half the spinsters had experienced intense emotional relationships or sexual relationships with other women (Davis, 1929). Her study made a significant contribution to the association of spinsters with lesbianism in the US.

Determined to suppress lesbianism in spinster teachers, American school administrators campaigned for women to retain their teaching positions after they married. In *The Status of the Married Woman Teacher* (1934), David Peters describes the prejudices directed against married women teachers and concludes that single and married women teachers were comparable in their effectiveness in the classroom. However, Peters also identifies that 'the measured mental growth of the students taught by the married women teachers exceeded the measured mental growth of the students taught by the single teachers' (p.87).

The findings of Peters were welcomed by the US's National Education Association, which decided that abolishing the celibacy rule would help to rid female teachers of the 'old-maid schoolteacher' cliché. The association justified this by positing that the old maid trope was distasteful and was adversely affecting the recruitment and subsequent morale of younger members of the profession.

The Civil Rights Act of 1964 ended discrimination against married women teachers. By outlawing discrimination based on sex, the act forced local school districts to treat married female teachers as they treated their married male counterparts. As a consequence, the number of married female teachers doubled after 1964, surpassing the increase in the percentage of married women in the entire US workforce.

Now that the teaching workforce was replenished with heterosexual teachers, society in the US resumed its vilification of spinster teachers.

In shades of McCarthyism, right-wing politicians and the press began alleging that homosexual teachers were a danger to children (Bérubé & D'Emilio, 1984). Blount recalls that in the popular *Coronet* magazine, a 1950 article with the headline 'A moral menace to our children' claimed that 'each year, literally thousands of youngsters of high school and college age are introduced to unnatural practices by inveterate seducers'. The article encouraged parents and education leaders to be vigilant for teachers who might corrupt their students. Around the same time, in the UK, Frank Caprio's book *Female Homosexuality: a psychodynamic study of lesbianism* (1954) alleged that a young girl, aged 15, had committed suicide because a female teacher had conducted an 'immoral' relationship with her. Caprio concluded that the homosexual problem with teachers was pressing.

The notion of the lesbian teacher as predator continues to prevail in modern consciousness. Sheila Cavanagh (2008), researching child welfare in a lesbian teacher sex scandal in Canada, posits that protecting students from a lesbian teacher is actually a pretext for a more 'deeply entrenched worry about the proliferation of queer identifications in school' (p.388). Cavanagh argues that the reason for challenging 'child protectionist discourses' is not to make students sexually available to teachers, but to 'wrest youthful (often queer) sexualities from the clutches of adult projections' (p.388). Cavanagh is also clear that such discourses perpetuate heterosexuality as compulsory in schools.

Having explored the history of the lesbian teacher, in chapter 3 I turn to the history of men in teaching. I explore the feminisation of the profession once women were permitted to enter and consider why men in teaching were considered effeminate. Finally, I examine the impossibility of teaching as a profession for gay men. Just as the female teacher became synonymous with lesbianism, the male teacher soon became the effeminate homosexual in public consciousness and, like lesbians, became regarded as a danger to children.

CHAPTER 3

BEWARE THE EFFEMINATE MAN: A HISTORY OF THE GAY MALE TEACHER

While the previous chapter revealed the uncomfortable relationship with teaching endured by spinsters and lesbians, this chapter explores how men – and in particular gay men – have similarly encountered vilification, prejudice, contempt and hostility within the teaching profession. It should be noted that lazy historical tropes related to sexuality and teaching equate heterosexuality with masculinity and homosexuality with femininity in men. I want to stress that, in describing the historical and cultural climate for men in teaching, I do not personally accept that effeminate men are necessarily gay and masculine men are always straight, just as I don't accept that lesbians are necessarily always masculine and feminine women are always heterosexual.

Teaching was initially a male-only occupation that garnered the same level of respect as careers in medicine or law, but by the middle of the 19th century, in the UK and the US, spinster teachers had entered the profession and so began teaching's reputation as women's work. Once women entered teaching, the profession became less desirable for men. Geraldine Joncich Clifford (1989) refers to concerns conveyed by Chicago's Board of Education in 1884 about the increasing number of female teachers in the city's schools. These female teachers were deemed 'irritable' and lacking in 'self-control' (p.296) and the board worried that the result of this behaviour would be to influence boys in their classes towards 'effeminacy'. Between 1885 and the First World War, much of the education media in the US lamented the growing feminisation of teaching, which, according to Clifford, was '[driving] the last man from the field' (1989, p.298). John Abbott (1991) too indicates that school trustees and leaders across Western society expressed anxiety about the number of men leaving teaching, fearful that it could 'tend towards effeminacy and eventually breed a generation more fit to be apparelled in petticoats than pants' (p.52).

As the First World War arrived, most men remaining in teaching were forced to leave the profession to participate in the conflict and women, of course, filled these vacancies. According to Clifford (1989), the war had 'direct effects upon both sexes' roles in education' (p.307). Fifty-thousand men exited teaching to fight in the war and never returned to their careers in schools because, Clifford posits, post-war they obtained better-paid posts in other professions. The men who remained in teaching during the war were, then, those seen as not fit enough to fight and therefore emasculated at the very time when strength and masculinity were most lauded. As Jackie Blount (2000) states, 'Properly masculine men would leave the toils of the classroom for the rough and tumble world of work with other men' (p.85). Those men who remained in teaching were seen as unusual and effeminate for undertaking women's work.

According to Blount (2000), men who remained in teaching once it became the domain of the spinster were accused of displaying 'cross-gender behaviours and characteristics' (p.84). She adds that men who taught children were broadly considered as weak and submissive. In the US in 1920, men accounted for just 14% of all teachers in schools. Blount notes that 'clearly, by the turn of the century the gender definition of schoolwork had shifted so dramatically that men could transgress their gender-appropriate boundaries simply by wielding chalk' (p.87).

Blount (2000) observes that it was problematic for men who remained in teaching to be intelligible to others as masculine, although there were attempts, particularly in the US, to redefine male teachers and boost their 'flagging sense of manliness' (p.86). The US responded by developing male teacher societies and associations in the early part of the 20th century. These organisations were set up to attract more male teachers into schools to counter the growing concern that female teachers were having an adverse impact on male pupils. In 1911, male teachers and school principals in New York launched a campaign to attract men into elementary teaching because it was widely considered that the paucity of men in elementary schools was responsible for a growing effeminacy in boys (Blount, 2000). Although men in headteacher or other leadership positions were considered a little more masculine and 'less subject to defects', men in classroom teacher roles were deemed to be 'doing women's work' and increasingly became stigmatised as sissies and figures of fun (p.86).

Martin Ashley (2003) notes the movement in the US to reverse the softening of boys in school at the hands of women and feminine men. By the early 20th century, a wave of patriotism and a nostalgia for the American frontier and wilderness led to the advent of the male scoutmaster. The Boy Scouts of America was seen as an important institution to compensate for the feminisation of boys in school. Jeffrey Hantover (1998) recalls the ideal attributes of a scoutmaster. He states that in the early 20th century, the ideal scoutmaster would not be 'sissy' but would be a patriot 'with common sense and moral character ... no Miss Nancy need apply' (p.102).

Rebecca Coulter and Christopher Greig (2008), writing about the history of the male teacher in the Canadian education system from the late 1800s, note that Alberta's education department accused male teachers of lacking 'one or all of the three G's: Go, Grit and Gumption'. The Ontario school board was similarly overtly critical of the men attracted to teaching, stating:

> Years ago, the men who became teachers were really men. But the last few years have brought us nothing but effeminate types. The students are better off with a sensible woman than with a man like that. The ones this Board hired last year should have joined the FWTAO [Federation of Women Teachers' Associations of Ontario]. (In Ellis, 1971, p.37)

Wayne Martino (2009) observes that this fear of men in teaching was compounded by a growing belief that the men attracted to teaching were deviant and lacked interest in finding a wife. He states that by the middle of the 20th century, public fears about gender nonconformity had become a tool of social control and surveillance that sought to ensure only heterosexual people became teachers. Ashley (2003) points to the common belief in mid-1900s America that too much contact with women made boys gay.

According to Martino, by the 1950s, male teachers were explicitly expected to model appropriate masculinity for the children in their classrooms. In the US, Blount describes numerous national campaigns advocating the employment of masculine male teachers in schools. In 1969, the academic Patricia Cayo Sexton declared in her book *The Feminized Male: classrooms, white collars and the decline of manliness*, 'Putting a man, any man, in place of women in school will not do. A man who is less than a man can be more damaging to boys than domineering mothers' (pp.29-30).

Sexton's quote captures perfectly the obsession with the feminisation of schooling and its impact on the masculinity of boys during the 1960s and 70s. Sexton purports that schools fostered in children passive conformity, which bred in male pupils harmful levels of femininity that were counter to the natural presentation of healthy masculinity. She adds that male teachers who lacked overt masculinity encouraged rebellious streaks in boys, causing them to become 'outsiders and misfits' who were 'stunted in normal masculine growth' (1969, pp.10-11).

In *The Feminized Male*, Sexton mounts a pernicious attack on male teachers, making sweeping and unsubstantiated claims about men who are attracted to teaching. She claims that men thinking of entering the teaching profession are 'neuter in gender', adding that they have a 'rather feline quality commonly ascribed to women' (p.38). Sexton adds that male teachers are the embodiment of a 'mama's boy gone bad' (p.38). Although she concedes that not all male teachers are feminised, she insists that at the very least they are disturbed and unstable, as a consequence of having repressed their masculinity. Sexton's references to male teachers having a 'feline quality' of course hints at the cattiness or bitchiness associated with the worst of women. She accuses male teachers of resorting to figuratively 'biting and scratching their rivals' (p.39).

Despite her scurrilous attack on the male teacher, Sexton is not content that the solution is teaching as a women-only profession. She criticises female teachers for driving norms of appropriate and acceptable behaviour that force male pupils to engage in feminine standards of presentation if they are to succeed in school. This, according to Sexton, involves boys presenting themselves as 'polite, clean, obedient, neat and nice' (1969, p.55). She adds that real boys – that is, those she describes as the 'masculine types' (p.55) – have 'a tougher time in school than those who look and act more like girls', adding 'I have felt that school makes sissies out of many boys and feminizes many more by insisting that they act like girls' (p.55).

Blount (2000) asserts that homophobia was the motivation behind the regulation of strict gender roles for teachers in the 19th and 20th centuries. She observes that the male teacher was overwhelmingly portrayed as effeminate; a transgressor who displayed deviant sexualities. By the mid 20th century, effeminate behaviour in men had become perceived as completely intertwined with homosexuality. Ashley (2003) suggests that the conflation of paedophilia with male sexuality is a further reckless impediment in an ill-informed discourse that was driven by the media.

Research by the psychologist G. Stanley Hall purported that teaching reduced masculine men to effeminate homosexuals. Hall professed that the men who worked in schools alongside female teachers risked 'some deterioration in the moral tone of [male teachers'] virility and [loss of] power to cope successfully with men' (in Blount, 2000, p.91). Willard Waller, an eminent sociologist, also cautioned that teaching caused effeminate behaviour in men. In his book *The Sociology of Teaching* (1932), Waller caused significant moral panic when he claimed that homosexual male teachers were 'transmit[ting] abnormal attitudes to their students' (in Blount, 2000, p.91).

Some 50 years before the AIDS epidemic, the use of language such as 'transmit' by Waller hints at the extent to which homosexuality was at the time medicalised and remained stubbornly synonymous with contagion of an infectious disease.

Although Sexton is keen to see men return to school classrooms in the US as role models for male pupils, she is at pains to stress that only 'real men' with untainted masculinity are required. According to Martino (2009), the effect of views such as Sexton's was to perpetuate binary gender categories in education, with masculinity and femininity distinctly defined in oppositional terms. I suggest that Sexton causes much more harm than that. Her depiction of schools as the preserve of feminised male teachers and masculine female teachers is a deliberate attempt to cause moral panic by describing all those in the teaching profession as harmful to children. Of course, some 20 years later in the UK, it would be the perception that children needed to be protected from such harmful teachers that would drive Section 28 on to the government's statute books.

Emma Renold, writing in the UK in the year before Section 28 was finally repealed, observes the malevolent stereotypes that continue to make teaching a treacherous profession for men (and particularly gay men) to enter. Renold (2002) contends that men fear they will be branded as paedophiles for working with children and this deters them from entering the profession. James King, who identifies as gay and was for years a teacher, describes the impossibility of primary teaching for gay men. He asserts that male teachers must adopt a culturally validated, hegemonic form of masculinity to survive as a teacher. The insistence on masculinity, according to King, is an attempt to deter any association of deviancy surrounding the 'unnamed, silent accusation of paedophilia' (2004, p.27). King goes on to contend that this homophobic tactic positions men who are not overtly masculine as, at best, a poor influence on male children and, at worst, perverts with a sexual interest in boys.

Paul Sargent (2005), in common with King, suggests that the male teacher is caught in a bind. Sargent states that male teachers 'find themselves caught between doing a subordinated form of masculinity that would make them successful teachers and structural demands for them to do a form of complicit masculinity that is more supportive of the patriarchal gender regime' (p.253). I would add that male teachers who are gay are caught in a double bind. Being both a teacher and a gay man serves to prove the point that teaching is not an occupation for 'real' men. Even where hypermasculinity is enacted in the school workplace, the reprehensible conflation of the gay man with the potential paedophile hints that they may have a disingenuous reason for entering the profession and immediately makes them the target of suspicion.

Tor Foster and Elizabeth Newman (2005) researched the lived experience of men training to be primary school teachers in the UK. The men reported receiving disapproving remarks from family and friends about their career choice, with the common refrain that teaching was not a 'masculine thing to do' (p.351). Foster and Newman concluded that, over time, pejorative comments and questions by family and friends led to a form of 'identity bruising' for the trainee teachers, with some deciding to use their teaching degree in another career instead.

Debbie Epstein and Richard Johnson (1998) argue that in UK schools, homophobia drives the insistence that male teachers must embody overt masculinity in order to be suitable role models for children. Although writing in the Section 28 era when homophobia was sanctioned by the UK state, Epstein and Johnson observe that men routinely use expressions of homophobic abuse against male peers whenever they are perceived as doing something to diverge from hegemonic masculinities. They add that homophobia serves to naturalise gender performance and creates in children fears of being different. Epstein and Johnson observe that boys or men who fail to embody hegemonic forms of masculine behaviours are often seen as being traitors to masculinity and this makes them an obvious target for bullying.

The school curriculum is highly gendered and nowhere more so than in secondary schools, where teachers specialise in a subject. What a male teacher specialises in can determine whether he is seen as sufficiently masculine and heterosexual. STEM subjects (science, technology, engineering and maths) are seen as the most challenging and so occupy the position of being most prestigious. These subjects are seen as suiting boys better than girls, and because boys are pushed towards STEM subjects, they are more likely to study these subjects at university and may ultimately become STEM teachers. Male teachers who work in the traditionally feminine areas of the curriculum – such as dance, drama, English, music or food technology – are more likely to be subordinated within a school's social organisation and seen as effeminate. The reverse is not necessarily true for girls and female teachers, however. Girls and women who study STEM subjects are seen as high-achievers, somehow able to succeed and compete with the boys and men in these most taxing of subjects. Rather than teasing their female peers, girls and women tend to admire those who can compete with boys and men in the STEM arena.

Of course, history and culture show us that it was not strong women, effeminate men or the feminisation of schooling that created climates in which male pupils were encouraged to become gay; quite the contrary. The hypermasculine, prestigious boys' schools in the UK, where the teachers were historically all male, have overwhelmingly been the school environments in which boys were exposed to and experienced intimacy and sexual activity with other boys. Schools such as Eton, Marlborough, Harrow and Charterhouse, where boys are sent in preparation to occupy the upper echelons of power, are often revealed through the memoirs of former pupils as schools in which boys have sexual experiences with someone of the same sex.

The idea of the British fee-paying or public school system was to prepare boys for a spartan life, devoid of female company. Boys were taught to become loyal and dutiful administrators of the British empire. The leading colonial administrator Lord Lugard (1858-1945) lauded the 'public school spirit' as essential for British imperialism (Kushnier, 2002). However, in reality, history shows that the British public schools for boys had a distinct culture entrenched in homosexuality. For example, new boys to the schools were commonly 'fags' to the prefects (older boys), who gave them women's names to denote their submissive sexual role. Jennifer Kushnier (2002) observes that public schools were responsible for the homosocial bonds at the heart of British patriarchal power and that Eton in particular was a homosocial environment. Kushnier cites one former Etonian from the 1850s who referred to extensive homosexuality at the school. He recalled a roll call of childhood 'perpetrators' who would later achieve prominent roles in the leadership of the country.

Tim Card (1994) observes that, at Eton, a homosexual phase among boys was tolerated in the school as long as they snapped out of their homosexuality when they matured and entered the 'intolerant' social life beyond school. Paul Hammond (1996) too maintains that 'intense bonds between men … were first fashioned at school' (p.126). Alan Sinfield (1994) writes that 'public schools were crucial in the development of homosexual identity because, despite the official taboo, they contributed, in many instances, an unofficial but powerful cultural framework within which same-sex passion might be positively valued' (p.66).

In chapter 4, I introduce Section 28 – the axis on which this book pivots and the law that would deeply affect lesbian and gay teachers for years. After a brief introduction to the medical and criminal status of homosexuality, I trace the history of Section 28, from Lord Halsbury's initial bill in 1987 right through to its repeal in 2003. I reveal how Section 28 rendered lesbian and gay teachers fearful that they would lose their jobs should their sexuality be revealed in the school workplace, and left an entire generation of LGBTQ+ young people without pastoral support throughout their adolescence.

CHAPTER 4
SECTION 28: AN INTRODUCTION

Section 28 of the Local Government Act became law on 24 May 1988. It changed the working practices of all teachers for the next 15 years. The lesbian and gay teachers who taught under Section 28 were changed forever.

Section 28 aimed to prevent staff in local authorities from talking about same-sex relationships (Baker, 2022). All state-maintained schools at the time came under local authority control and so Section 28 affected every teacher and every student. The wording of Section 28 was, however, protracted and dense, so it was unclear what was and was not permitted (Baker, 2022). Teachers, governors and other school staff widely assumed that Section 28 prevented adults in schools from mentioning same-sex relationships and that out lesbian or gay teachers were incompatible with the prevailing culture and environment of UK schools, which at the time were entirely heteronormative. Section 28 stated:

1. *A local authority shall not –*

    (a) *intentionally promote homosexuality or publish material with the intention of promoting homosexuality;*

    (b) *promote the teaching in any maintained school of the acceptability of homosexuality as a pretended family relationship.*

2. *Nothing in subsection (1) above shall be taken to prohibit the doing of anything for the purpose of treating or preventing the spread of disease.*

Kathryn Rhodes (2020) observes that Section 28 was the first time in UK parliamentary history that lesbian and gay identities and lifestyles were denounced, rather than the homosexual acts. It was also the first act of Parliament to include lesbians, who until this time had remained absent from the law. According to Rhodes (2020), Section 28 constituted institutional homophobia and, throughout the 15 years that it was law, it prevented the possibility of lesbian and gay teachers 'achieving liveable professional lives' in the school workplace. Lesbian and gay teachers were forced to hide in plain sight in the school workplace in order to protect themselves from scrutiny and homophobic discrimination.

Back in the 1980s, 'homosexuality' was a term used much more frequently than it is today. In common parlance, it referred to any same-sex relationship (Baker, 2022). As chapter 1 demonstrated, the label 'homosexual' was initially used to denote either a medical condition or a crime.

THE MEDICAL ORIGINS OF HOMOSEXUALITY

The *Diagnostic and Statistical Manual of Mental Disorders*, maintained by the World Health Organization (WHO), and the *International Classification of Diseases*, published by American Psychiatric Association, both cited homosexuality as a mental disorder. Jack Drescher (2015) observes that the pathologising of homosexuality ensured it was regarded as an illness that needed a cure, not a difference that should be accepted by society. The WHO did not remove homosexuality from its list of mental disorders until 1990. Therefore, as Section 28 was introduced in 1988, questions about homosexuality continued to focus on the causes, treatment and cure of homosexuality.

Homosexuality was, then, a problematic term for inclusion in Section 28. According to Paul Baker (2022), it was contextually inappropriate in terms of being something schools might 'promote'. As Baker states, it would not be appropriate for schools to be prevented from 'promoting' the flu, yet, in 1988, homosexuality had the same status as the flu and any other illness or mental disorder.

Once homosexuality was removed from the WHO's list of mental disorders in 1990, one ordinarily might have expected the mainstream consciousness to pivot to consider questions such as 'How do we support the needs of homosexual people?' However, in the UK, the wording of Section 28 served to maintain the pathological and medical connotations of homosexuality, positioning it as something that must be avoided at all costs and, in particular, kept away from impressionable young people to whom it could be transmitted (Baker, 2022).

THE CRIMINAL ORIGINS OF HOMOSEXUALITY

As chapter 1 explained, the Criminal Law Amendment Act 1885 prohibited *any* male homosexual act in Britain, so even acts that took place in private could be prosecuted. Often, a letter expressing terms of affection between two men was all that was required to bring a prosecution. Like Section 28, the Criminal Law Amendment Act 1885 was ambiguously worded and as a result became known as the 'blackmailer's charter'. Most famously, the poet and playwright Oscar Wilde was prosecuted for homosexuality and sent to Reading Gaol. Female sexual activity was not explicitly criminalised by legislation. Sexual activity between two women was never punishable in the UK because historically it was assumed to never take place. As outlined in chapter 1, female homosexuality was discussed for the first time in Parliament in 1921 with a view to introducing discriminatory legislation, later to become the Criminal Law (Amendment) Bill of 1921. The House of Commons and House of Lords initially rejected it, anticipating that the creation of such a law might draw the attention of women to homosexuality and encourage them to explore something of which they were previously unaware.

In the case of Section 28, 'homosexuality' appears to be used (inaccurately) as a catch-all term for same-sex relationships or same-sex couples. But, of course, homosexuality was not a relationship in 1988, it was a disease (Baker, 2022). UK politicians were, however, keen to repurpose the term so that it could be applied to schools and local authorities. The reason for this is unclear, but Baker suggests that preventing homosexuality in schools and local authorities might have been a response to the AIDS virus, which had first been diagnosed in the UK in 1981 and was referred to in the media at the time as the 'gay plague'.

Section 28 referred to homosexuality but in fact described same-sex relationships and couples, both male and female (Baker, 2022). Further confusion was caused when the phrase 'pretended family relationship' was inserted into the bill as it moved first through Parliament and then the House of Lords. When the bill that would later become Section 28 was discussed in the House of Lords on 16 February 1988, the inclusion of the word 'pretended' was debated furiously with Baroness Cox, one of the main supporters of the bill, who worried that without the word 'pretended', some homosexual relationships might be promoted in schools by way of a loophole (Baker, 2022).

It is worth considering again the language of Section 28. It stated:

1. *A local authority shall not –*

    (a) *intentionally promote homosexuality or publish material with the intention of promoting homosexuality;*
    (b) *promote the teaching in any maintained school of the acceptability of homosexuality as a pretended family relationship.*

The *Collins English Dictionary* defines the word 'pretended' as 'insincerely or falsely professed; feigned, fictitious, or counterfeit'. Section 28, then, prohibited teachers in schools and staff in local authorities from promoting a mental disorder (homosexuality) as an insincerely or falsely professed, feigned, fictitious, or counterfeit family relationship (Baker, 2022). There is little wonder that Section 28 caused fear and confusion in schools.

EDUCATION IN THE SECTION 28 ERA

The Conservative MP Margaret Thatcher became the UK's first female prime minister in 1979. She went on to clash with the Greater London Council (GLC), led by the left-winger Ken Livingstone. In the GLC elections of 1981, Labour won nine more seats than the Conservatives and developed a reputation under Livingstone's leadership of being the champion of the disadvantaged, the racially diverse and those who were sexual minorities (Toulouse, 1991).

Until the Conservatives came to power in 1979, teachers had largely been left alone to determine what to teach. This allowed them to shape the curriculum in ways that ensured relevance to the communities they served. Teachers were pillars of integrity in their communities, respected and largely trusted to teach whatever they thought it was important for children to know.

Under the Conservatives, the incidence of poverty among children increased dramatically. For example, the number of families receiving benefits rose from 4.4 million in 1979 to 7.7 million in 1983 (Gillard, 2018). According to Max Morris and Clive Griggs (1988), 'By any reasonable criterion, some nine million, or one-sixth of the population, were living in poverty ... and the numbers were to increase' (p.11).

Teachers, of course, saw for themselves the adverse impact of the Conservative government on the lives of the children they taught and so the left-wing leanings of many teachers were not without foundation. Two years into Thatcher's government, in 1981, the education and science secretary, Mark Carlisle, and the Welsh secretary, Nicholas Edwards, published a document entitled *The School Curriculum*. This was the first time that central government had provided guidance for schools in England and Wales on what should be taught. The foreword by Carlisle and Edwards stated that the document offered guidance to the local education authorities that presided over schools on how the curriculum could be further improved. Carlisle and Edwards stated:

> *Parents, employers and many others also care about our schools. The paper explains to them where the government stands on a matter which lastingly affects our national prosperity and the whole nature of our society. Technological and other changes require an urgent response from our schools.*

The School Curriculum covered the entirety of compulsory education for ages 5-16. What was taught at school had to be adapted to the needs of every student, including the gifted and those with special educational needs, so that each child was appropriately prepared for the practical demands of adult and working life.

The Education Reform Act of 1988 followed and led to a dramatic shift for schools. The act was designed to put schools in competition with one another. It also introduced General Certificates of Secondary Education (GCSEs), which replaced Ordinary or O-levels and CSEs (Certificates of Secondary Education). The main changes for schools through the Education Reform Act were league tables, open enrolment, formula funding, a new inspection regime (Ofsted) and a new national curriculum.

LEAGUE TABLES

The introduction of school league tables meant that, for the first time, schools were ranked from best to worst according to the performance of their students in examinations. League tables are published online and in national newspapers, and are used by parents to inform decisions about where they will send their children to school. Thatcher's government claimed that league tables would drive up standards in schools, because no parent would send their child to a failing school. In reality, of course, league tables triggered the creation of property hotspots in the catchment areas of highly ranked schools. Those parents in well-paid jobs can buy the more expensive properties but, conversely, poorer families are left in cheaper school catchment areas where the school's unfavourable league table ranking drives down property prices. Inevitably, then, school league tables have created an environment in which a child's access to a good state school is determined in large part by their parent's income.

OPEN ENROLMENT AND SELECTION

The Education Reform Act 1988 introduced open enrolment for schools: children apply to multiple schools ranked by their parents in order of preference. As a result, highly rated schools are oversubscribed, allowing them to introduce selection criteria, although schools were not initially permitted to select children based on their academic ability. In time, some highly ranked schools were allowed to become 'specialist schools' that could select 10% of their intake based on aptitude in a particular subject, such as mathematics, science or music. Faith schools are permitted to select children on the basis of religious affiliation, driving some parents to adopt or change religions to ensure their child gains a place at a highly ranked school.

FORMULA FUNDING

The Education Reform Act also introduced formula funding. For the first time, schools were funded according to the number of students enrolled. Accordingly, oversubscribed schools are rewarded financially, while less popular schools – those ranked lower in the league tables – receive less funding as fewer families want to send their children there. Without adequate funding, those schools cannot afford to spend on the education of their students in the way that more successful schools can, meaning class sizes are large and the support of teaching assistants is not always available. Over time, a vicious cycle has emerged, with schools not performing well precisely because they lack the resources to give the children the support needed to achieve good grades, and so improve the ranking of the school (Gillard, 2018).

OFSTED

The Office for Standards in Education (Ofsted) was also established as part of the Education Reform Act. Since 1992, schools have been inspected by government-appointed officials who grade them according to the quality of the teaching observed, student behaviour and parental feedback. Like examination results and league table rankings, Ofsted inspection reports are made available publicly and schools may be taken over or closed down completely if they do not recover quickly from a poor Ofsted rating.

THE NATIONAL CURRICULUM

The Education Reform Act introduced the national curriculum. This requires all state schools to teach the same topics throughout a child's compulsory education, from Reception to Year 11. From 1988, the year that Section 28 was introduced, the core subjects of English, mathematics and science became compulsory, and SATs (statutory assessment tests) were gradually introduced in Years 2, 6 and 9. The national curriculum ensures that all students are taught and assessed in the same way, enabling comparison between schools for the purposes of the school league tables (Gillard, 2018).

Within the body of the initial national curriculum documentation, sex education was described as requiring the 'fullest consultation and cooperation with parents' and local authorities would be obliged to inform parents of the way in which sex education were taught in schools. The main purpose of sex education was to teach abstinence from sexual activity (Epstein & Johnson, 1998; Ringrose, 2016) and to prepare young people for parenthood and family life. The move by the Conservative government to insist on a sex education curriculum promoting only heterosexual family values was to lay the foundations for a bitter battle with Labour-controlled London boroughs (Baker, 2022). In particular, the support by the GLC and Haringey local authority for gay and lesbian groups and organisations was seized upon by the Conservatives and manipulated to create moral panic by the Tory tabloid press (Baker, 2022). The Conservatives defended their national curriculum, and in particular their state-regulated sex education, by accusing Labour-controlled local authorities of wasting taxpayers' money on lesbian and gay groups.

Those opposing the government's sex education curriculum and in favour of local authority support for lesbian and gay groups were labelled the 'loony left' by the Conservatives and shown to conflict with the Conservatives' alleged return to family values. The Conservatives painted any move towards lesbian and gay equality as militant, radical and completely at odds with their quest to champion the heterosexual family. At the same time, AIDS had begun taking hold across the UK, leading the most right-wing to claim that AIDS was a fitting retribution for those who were gay. The largely Conservative-supporting media soon took every opportunity to claim that all homosexuals were promiscuous disease-spreaders (Baker, 2022), sentiments that would be echoed in the House of Lords when Section 28 was eventually debated.

THE LITTLE YELLOW BOOK

The children's book *Jenny Lives with Eric and Martin* was first published in Danish as *Mette bor hos Morten og Erik* in 1981. The author, Susanne Bösche, wrote the book in response to her perception that an increasing number of children in Denmark had same-sex parents (Baker, 2022). *Jenny Lives with Eric and Martin* was translated into English in 1983 by Louis Mackay and bought by a small independent publisher in the UK. The book had a bright yellow cover and, rather than illustrations, included black and white photographs of 'Jenny' with her two dads.

In 1986, the *Daily Mail* newspaper in the UK reported that the book had been purchased by school libraries in the Inner London Education

Authority and other left-wing authorities. A few days later, *The Times* quoted the arts minister Richard Luce, who described the book as 'totally unacceptable for stocking on open library shelves' (Baker, 2022).

Buoyed by the media support and detecting moral panic among parents, the Conservatives intensified their efforts to expose Labour's funding of lesbian and gay groups as reckless, radical and, of course, 'loony' (Baker, 2022). During a debate in the House of Lords, Baroness Cox made reference to *Jenny Lives with Eric and Martin*. According to the Hansard parliamentary transcripts, Cox alleged that there was an urgent need to investigate the teaching of the occult, witchcraft and homosexuality. It is symptomatic of the era that aligning homosexuality with witchcraft and the occult was not challenged by anyone. In the same debate, Viscount Buckmaster, a member of the newly formed Conservative Family Campaign, also referred to *Jenny Lives with Eric and Martin*, noting that books such as this advocated incest and homosexuality (Baker, 2022).

Determined that more must be done to challenge the left, the Conservative government and the Tory press did everything within their gift to make ordinary people believe the Labour party was filled with radical extremists. Central to their approach was the insidious assertion that lesbians and gay men were a danger to children. *Jenny Lives with Eric and Martin* became a symbol of this assertion and the right-wing press capitalised on it. For example, *The Daily Mail* ran headlines in 1986 that included 'Save the children from sad, sordid sex lessons' (4 June 1986), 'Bizarre truth about happy family in the gay schoolbook' (22 September 1986) and 'Courses on homosexuality and lesbianism for all students from nursery schools to further education'. *The Sun* featured articles entitled 'Kids get lessons in gay love' and 'Vile book in school: students see pictures of gay lovers', while *The Daily Telegraph* complained of 'An official sex industry that is at work in the classroom and is poisoning the minds of children' (Baker, 2022).

Inevitably, teachers became collateral in this vicious fight between the right and left of politics. Once trusted to teach whatever they felt was in the best interest of their students, teachers were now under suspicion from parents, with their integrity questioned at every turn.

As the moral panic gathered momentum, a 1986 booklet by Rachel Tingle entitled *Gay Lessons: how public funds are used to promote homosexuality among children and young people* listed monies awarded to various gay and lesbian groups. On the website for the Forum of Christian Leaders, the following biography accompanies a picture of Tingle:

> *Rachel Tingle is an economist and journalist with a wide range of experience working in economic research and consultancy; in print and television journalism ... Her booklet,* Gay Lessons: How Public Funds are Used to Promote Homosexuality Among Children and Young People *led directly to the Section 28 legislation in Britain which, for 15 years ... banned the promotion of homosexuality using public money.*

With the public alarmed, the Conservatives drew up an amendment to the bill that would become the Education (No. 2) Act 1986. Viscount Buckmaster brought a 'moral considerations' amendment to the House of Lords, which was approved before being debated in the House of Commons. It said that sex education 'shall have due regard to moral considerations and the promotion of stable family life.' The then education secretary, Kenneth Baker, supported Buckmaster's amendment, stressing that it was important 'to give a clear signal reinforcing the institution of marriage as the foundation of a healthy family life and the very bedrock of our civilization.' Section 46 of the Education (No. 2) Act 1986 required that:

> *The local education authority by whom any county, voluntary or special school is maintained, and the governing body and head teacher of the school, shall take such steps as are reasonably practicable to secure that where sex education is given to any registered pupils at the school it is given in such a manner as to encourage those pupils to have due regard to moral considerations and the value of family life.*

Guidance circulated to local authorities in September 1987 stated:

> *19. The Secretary of State considers that the aims of a programme of sex education should be to present facts in an objective and balanced manner so as to enable pupils to comprehend the range of sexual attitudes and behaviour in present day society; to know what is and is not legal; to consider their own attitudes, and to make informed, reasoned and responsible decisions about the attitudes they will adopt both while they are at school and in adulthood. Teaching about the*

physical aspects of sexual behaviour should be set within a clear moral framework in which pupils are encouraged to consider the importance of self-restraint, dignity and respect for themselves and others, and helped to recognise the physical, emotional and moral risks of casual and promiscuous sexual behaviour. Schools should foster a recognition that both sexes should behave responsibly in sexual matters. Pupils should be helped to appreciate the benefits of stable married and family life and the responsibilities of parenthood. ro thanks

20. Schools have a responsibility to ensure that pupils understand those aspects of the law which relate to sexual activity. Pupils should understand three things in particular, which are that:

i. except in certain very restricted circumstances, it is a criminal offence for a man or boy to have sexual intercourse with a girl under 16, irrespective of whether she consents;

ii. homosexual acts (defined as buggery or gross indecency) between males constitute a criminal offence unless both parties have attained the age of 21 and the acts are committed with the consent of both in private (ie, where only the two parties are present); and

iii. it is an offence to make an indecent assault on a person; and a girl or boy under 16 cannot in law give any consent which would prevent an act being an assault for the purpose of this offence.

21. Schools cannot, in general, avoid tackling controversial sexual matters, such as contraception and abortion, by reason of their sensitivity. Pupils may well ask questions about them and schools should be prepared to offer balanced and factual information and to acknowledge the major ethical issues involved. Where schools are founded on specific religious principles this will have a direct bearing on the manner in which such subjects are presented.

*22. **There is no place in any school in any circumstances for teaching which advocates homosexual behaviour, which presents it as the 'norm', or which encourages homosexual experimentation by pupils. Indeed, encouraging or procuring homosexual acts by pupils who are under the age of consent is a criminal offence** [my emphasis]. It* *must also be recognised that for many people, including members of various religious faiths, homosexual practice is not morally acceptable, and deep offence may be caused to them if the subject is not handled with sensitivity by teachers if discussed in the classroom.*

As the general election of 1987 drew ever closer, the Tory press became increasingly aggressive in their characterisation of Labour as the champion of lesbians and gay teachers, who in turn were positioned as a danger to children. Headlines from *The Sun* included 'Labour picks rent boy as school boss' and 'Lesbian plots to pervert nursery tots' (Sanderson, 2021).

THE EMERGENCE OF SECTION 28

In 1986 in the House of Lords, Lord Halsbury, a crossbench peer, brought the Local Government Act 1986 (Amendment) Bill, subtitled 'An act to refrain local authorities from promoting homosexuality'. Hansard shows that Halsbury said the following:

I should like your Lordships' leave to read the terms of what I moved nearly 10 years ago, on 14 June 1977, against the late Lord Arran's bill reducing the age of homosexual consent from 21 to 18 ... What I then said of homosexuality, at col. 14, was this: 'Given any disability whatever, one has the alternatives of either making the best or making the worst of the situation in which one finds oneself. Homosexuals have this choice. It is as open to them as to anyone else. Those who make the best of their situation are the responsible ones who would no more molest little boys than a responsible heterosexual would molest little girls, or go down the streets soliciting strangers, or reject stabilised relationships for promiscuity.

The law does not concern itself with them and nor do I. Those who make the worst of their situation are the sick ones who suffer from a psychological syndrome whose symptoms are as follows: first of all, exhibitionism; they want the world to know all about them; secondly, promiscuity; thirdly, proselytising; they want to persuade other people that their way of life is the good one; fourthly, boasting of homosexual achievements as if they were due to and not in spite of sexual inversion; lastly, they act as reservoirs of venereal diseases of all kinds. Ask any venerealogist: syphilis, gonorrhoea, genital herpes and now AIDS are characteristically infections of homosexuals.

I was referring to male homosexuals. I did not think then that lesbians were a problem. They do not molest little girls. They do not indulge in disgusting and unnatural practices like buggery. They are not wildly promiscuous and do not spread venereal disease. It is part of the softening up propaganda that lesbians and gays are nearly always referred to in that order. The relatively harmless lesbian leads on to the vicious gay. That was what I thought then and what I still in part continue to think, but I have been warned that the loony left is hardening up the lesbian camp and that they are becoming increasingly aggressive.

One of the characteristics of our time is that we have for several decades past been emancipating minorities who claimed that they were disadvantaged. Are they grateful? Not a bit. We emancipated races and got inverted racism. We emancipate homosexuals and they condemn heterosexism as chauvinist sexism, male oppression and so on. They will push us off the pavement if we give them a chance. I am, in their jargon, a homophone, a heterosexist exploitationist. The whole vocabulary of the loony left is let loose in a wild confusion of Marxism, Trotskyism, anarchism and homosexual terminology.

funny how the rhetoric hasn't changed at all

According to Sue Sanders and Gill Spraggs (1989), underlying Halsbury's speech was the panicked dismissal of any move towards a more inclusive and equal society. In essence, the members of the ruling class had successfully colluded to keep blacks, lesbians and gays (among so many others) 'off the pavement'. But, say Sanders and Spraggs, just beneath the surface of Halsbury's speech was the fear that having kept minorities off the pavement, so to speak, the minorities would, given half a chance, retaliate and overthrow the ruling elite.

In common with the rest of the Lords, Halsbury was not an elected representative and so, unlike his colleagues in the Commons, he could afford to make explicit his prejudice and disdain for the marginalised without fear of reproach. In fact, Hansard transcripts of speeches in the run-up to Section 28 demonstrate that Halsbury was in the company of many like-minded peers. For example, Lord Longford, speaking in support of Halsbury's bill, said:

Homosexuals, in my submission, are handicapped people. Of course, some of them do not confine themselves to relations with their own sex. I suppose Oscar Wilde is one of the most famous examples. I am not referring to people who attempt to have it both ways, but I am talking of people whose tendency is so strong that they can have relationships only with their own sex. I think particularly of male homosexuals because, as I think the noble Earl, Lord Halsbury, brought out, lesbians are no danger.

The tragedy of such people is that they cannot enjoy family life and they cannot have children. If only for that reason I suppose that not many of us – perhaps none of us – would wish our children or grandchildren to grow up homosexuals. But, as I think I indicated earlier, in so far as these people are handicapped they deserve our fullest compassion and understanding.

In so far as an attempt is being made to expand homosexualism throughout this community, the outcome can only be fatally disruptive for the family. It is bound to be of profound concern to Christians and to everyone else who wishes to maintain a healthy community. I am not saying that the promotion of acts of homosexuality should necessarily be made illegal. That might or might not be discussed on some other occasion. I say only that it should not be financed by public bodies in a country that still claims to be Christian. I support the noble Earl, Lord Halsbury.

Lady Saltoun of Abernethy, like Longford, spoke in enthusiastic support of Halsbury's bill. In a now-famous quote, she states:

This is a small bill – a David of a bill that sets out to kill a Goliath of an evil. I wish it well. Decent people, parents all over the country, will wish it well. As my noble friend has said, he has had a great many letters from people wishing it well. Let us not disappoint them.

Halsbury's bill had in fact been drafted by Lord Campbell of Alloway, a British judge, barrister, author and life peer. According to Sanders and Spraggs (1989), during the debate, Campbell attempted to make explicit that the proposals in Halsbury's bill would not rule out the appointment of a homosexual teacher. Instead, Campbell stressed that the bill aimed only to inhibit the promotion of lesbian and gay rights in schools, and the provision of explicit books such as *Jenny Lives with Eric and Martin*. Campbell positioned his bill therefore as a motion to curb an abuse of rates (rates were a charge made by local authorities to householders, much like the council tax we are charged today). Sanders and Spraggs (1989) stated that, given the concern expressed on behalf of the ratepayer, one would be forgiven for thinking that lesbians and gay men were classes exempt from local taxation themselves, and that the sums spent on projects for lesbian and gay community groups were extortionate. In reality, as Sanders and Spraggs observed, the money being spent on the lesbian and gay community was paltry in comparison to other budgets and to local authority budgets as a whole.

Halsbury's bill passed easily through the House of Lords. The Conservative MP Jill Knight then led the bill through the House of Commons. Hansard shows that Knight claimed children as young as two years old had been given gay and lesbian books in Lambeth, South London. She also described same-sex relationships as 'perverted' and 'desperately dangerous'. Knight is widely known as a key force behind Section 28 and a 'dedicated – not to say fanatical – anti-gay MP' (McGhee, n.d.). According to Sanders and Spraggs (1989), as one of the most vociferous and persistent supporters of homophobic legislation, Knight's approach was distinct. She was prone to sensationalist and unsubstantiated outpourings, many of which strayed noticeably from the issue under debate. Knight stated: 'This bill came into being for a very good reason … it is before the committee because there is evidence in shocking abundance that children in our schools, some as young as five years, are frequently being encouraged into homosexuality and lesbianism.'

During the parliamentary presentation of Halsbury's bill, Knight's speech deviated on to concern for the drummer boys of the Indian army under the Raj. Eventually returning to the threat of homosexuals, she alleged: 'Millions outside Parliament object to little children being perverted, diverted or converted from normal family life to a lifestyle which is desperately dangerous for society and extremely dangerous for them' (Sanders & Spraggs, 1989). Finally, Knight warned of the danger that AIDS presented to society, alleging that teaching about homosexuality in schools would lead in due course to the spread of AIDS.

Knight's impassioned if not meandering oratory saw the bill pass through stage 1 in the Commons. Its further passage was interrupted by the 1987 general election. On 11 June, Thatcher's Conservative party returned to government with a landslide victory. However, Halsbury and Knight's bill was not initially reintroduced by the Conservative government upon its re-election, despite their resounding mandate.

In December 1987, a new Conservative MP, David Wilshire, proposed an amendment to the new Local Government Bill that was intended to be equivalent to Halsbury's bill. The amendment was debated, firstly as Clause 27 and later as Clause 28. The government decided to support the tabling of the amendment in exchange for the unpredictable and unorthodox Knight standing down from the Health and Medicines Bill standing committee, where she was hindering the progress of legislation. Wilshire's amendment was supported by Michael Howard, local government minister, and Michael Portillo, parliamentary secretary.

The amended bill was read initially in the Lords and there were a number of calls for exclusions. A Social Democratic Party peer, Viscount Falkland, proposed a compromise amendment to the clause to exempt the arts from a ban on the promotion of homosexuality. The Conservative Lord Somers did not support this and countered:

> One has only to look through the entire animal world to realise that it is abnormal. In any case, the clause as it stands does not prohibit homosexuality in any form; it merely discourages the teaching of it. When one is young at school one is very impressionable and may just as easily pick up bad habits as good habits.

The narrowing amendment was unsuccessful, but the Lords voted in favour of the clause the next day. The Local Government Bill went to the House of Commons. Here, the Conservative MP Michael Colvin raised concerns about a sudden removal of funding for lesbian and gay groups by local authorities. Colvin was considered by Thatcher to be a 'wet', a label she assigned to Conservatives she regarded as feeble and willing to compromise with the trade unions. On 8 March 1988, Colvin asked the environment minister, Christopher Chope, who would in time preside over the introduction of the council tax, whether the government would discuss with the Association of London Authorities the degree of funding to be permitted by local authorities in London to distribute to gay and lesbian groups. Chope replied: 'No. Clause 28 of the Local Government Bill will ensure that expenditure by local authorities for the purpose of promoting homosexuality will no longer be permitted.' The following day, the Labour MP Tony Benn, in a debate in the House of Commons, said:

> If the sense of the word 'promote' can be read across from 'describe', every murder play promotes murder, every war play promotes war, every drama involving the eternal triangle promotes adultery; and Mr Richard Branson's condom campaign promotes fornication. The House had better be very careful before it gives to judges, who come from a narrow section of society, the power to interpret 'promote'.

In defence of his clause, Wilshire countered Benn's assertion by stating that 'there is an awful lot more promotion of homosexuality going on by local government outside classrooms'.

None of the amendments designed to temper the clause were passed and Clause 28, which later became Section 28 of the Local Government Act 1988, remained largely intact, affecting schools, local authorities and the arts. The Conservatives' defence of Section 28 was that it protected the family and in particular normal family life. Thatcher herself, in many of her speeches, summoned 'the family' as moral justification for Conservative policies in general and positioned lesbian and gay people as the enemy of normal family life. Neither she nor her party seemed able to define what was meant by a 'normal family'.

Sanders and Spraggs (1989) point out that, in reality, the traditional heterosexual family with a stay-at-home mother and a working father was disappearing fast in the UK. By 1985, only 37% of women remained at home as housewives and 14% of children lived in households with only one parent. Divorce rates had risen steadily throughout the 1980s, with 150,000 couples divorcing in 1985 and the median duration of marriages less than nine years. There was an increase in the popularity of co-habitating as opposed to marriage, with children and young people increasingly raised by an adult who was not their biological parent in what we know today as blended families.

At the Conservative conference in Blackpool on 9 October 1987, children were the focus of Thatcher's conference speech. In it, she warned against 'extremist teachers'. Thatcher alleged that children were being taught 'anti-racist mathematics' and 'political slogans', and in a now infamous part of the speech, she purported that 'children who need to be taught to respect traditional moral values are being taught that they have the inalienable right to be gay'.

Thatcher's 'inalienable right to be gay' soundbite made the television and radio news, bringing her reckless assertion to the attention of millions. Of course, Thatcher did not explicitly accuse lesbian and gay teachers of corrupting children in her speech; she accused the teaching profession in general. This stain on schools by the government inevitably led heterosexual staff to distance themselves from their lesbian and gay colleagues in an attempt to recover the integrity of the profession (Lee, 2019). Unsurprisingly, heterosexual teachers grew resentful of their lesbian and gay counterparts and no doubt began to wonder whether there could be any smoke without fire (Thompson-Lee, 2017). Fractions and factions started to emerge and school staffrooms began to feel like hostile places for the few lesbian and gay teachers who dared to be out (Lee, 2019).

Section 28 of the Local Government Act 1988 was enacted as an amendment to the UK's Local Government Act 1986 on 24 May 1988. It was a historic day that would be forever associated with the struggle for lesbian and gay equality.

OPPOSITION TO SECTION 28

Despite the chilly climate for lesbians and gay men in the 1980s, there were some critics of Section 28. During the parliamentary debate in February 1988, Baroness Stedman opposed the word 'promote' and expressed concern that Section 28 would make countering prejudice illegal. Baroness Blackstone contended that the inclusion of the phrase 'pretended family relationship' was offensive to same-sex couples. Lord Peston agreed, describing Section 28 as 'nasty and vindictive', adding, 'Are we asked to believe that homosexuals are less useful to society than the rest of us?' (Baker, 2022). This modest opposition in Parliament was, however, dwarfed by the vehement protests against Section 28 by lesbians and gay men and their allies.

PROTESTS AGAINST SECTION 28

On 2 February 1988, 10 lesbians entered the House of Lords to protest against Section 28. After peers voted in favour of the bill, the lesbians abseiled into the chamber of the House of Lords to bring national attention to the proposed new law. Sally Francis, one of the 10 and the person who coordinated the plot, recalled the events 30 years later in the *Guardian* newspaper (Godfrey, 2018):

> *We had done lots of actions, lots of blockades and breaking into places. But this was different. The day before, one of my friends was in the chamber of the House of Lords wondering what we could do there. She had the idea of swinging from the microphones hanging from the ceiling. We thought they were probably not strong enough.*
>
> *In the end, we bought a washing line in Clapham market and knotted it up on the bus on the way up – it was pretty low-tech stuff. I smuggled the rope in under my donkey jacket and didn't set off any alarms.*
>
> *Ten of us set off for the action, but only six of us got into the Lords, four as guests of one of the peers. Those of us in the public seats would try to block the security from getting to the other women on the balcony.*
>
> *We waited till the vote went for the clause. If they had voted against it, we weren't going to do it. But they voted for it. When the vote finished, we were all looking at each other; the other group was going: 'Oh, God, we can't do it,' and we were going: 'Don't fucking do it.' Then, all of a sudden, two of them went over.*
>
> *The security panicked. The women who had gone over the balcony with the washing line were thrown out of the House of Lords. The rest of us were arrested and put in a cell up by Big Ben. They didn't know what to do with us.*
>
> *After about six hours, we were released and met up with the women who had been thrown out. They had spoken to the press, but the press didn't believe they had done it because they didn't understand why they hadn't been arrested.*
>
> *When we were all reunited, we went to the pub by the bridge on Whitehall – a real press haunt. There were a lot of journalists there*

and I remember us telling them: 'If you all buy us a drink, we'll tell you what happened and what we did.' I remember it feeling really special.

The Ideal Home Exhibition in London was also the target of a series of protests against Section 28. According to Baker (2022), in March 1988 a large group of lesbians took over one of the show homes inside the exhibition centre to demonstrate against the inclusion of the phrase 'pretended family relationships' in Section 28. Banners displayed from the windows of the show home stated: 'One of these days these dykes are gonna walk all over you', 'The ideal home is one without any men in it' and 'Stop Clause 28'. The protesters were part of a group called DykeStrike and remained in the show home for almost 30 minutes, until they were removed by police and ejected from the exhibition (Baker, 2022).

Lesbian political activists also demonstrated against Section 28 outside Buckingham Palace. The demonstration was held on 8 March 1988 to coincide with the 70th anniversary of women gaining the right to vote. In common with the suffragettes, some of the lesbians chained themselves to the palace railings. Booan Temple describes in *The Guardian* (Godfrey, 2018) how the women 'chained themselves to the railings at Buckingham Palace like the suffragettes did'. They unfurled a number of banners including 'Dykes against the clause', 'Lesbians against Clause 28', 'International Womyn's Day' and '70th anniversary of Suffragettes'.

The most high-profile of the protests against Section 28 took place on 23 May 1988, the evening before Section 28 became law. Lesbian activists entered the BBC News studio, where presenters Sue Lawley and Nicholas Witchell were introducing *The Six O'Clock News*. Booan Temple was one of the protesters and recalled the incident in an interview with *The Guardian* (Godfrey, 2018).

The LGBT community had been getting more vociferous in the 80s. We were starting to demand more rights, not least of which was the right to live in safety.

I, and many of my loved ones, had been attacked in the street. There was an atmosphere that 'the other' needed to be eradicated and I think the LGBT community was seen as a threat to the institution of the family. Section 28 was part of that.

I was engaged with a lesbian feminist network, but the campaign against section 28 was not an organised campaign in the traditional sense. Many women and mothers felt duty-bound to protect themselves, their families and their friends ... there were massive marches in Manchester and in London. Lots of women came up with loads of very innovative protests, but none of it got reported. We couldn't get our arguments out there. So a small group of us decided to go into the Six O'Clock News studio. By getting on the news, we would be the news.

Once in the BBC building, we waited until the 'live' light came on and ran into the studio wearing T-shirts saying 'Stop the Clause'. One woman handcuffed herself to a camera, and one to the news desk, where Nicholas Witchell held her down very aggressively. He has since apologised for his heavy-handed behaviour. I was rugby-tackled to the ground and dragged away.

We were held in an office until we were arrested and taken to Shepherd's Bush police station. I believe the BBC and others had a meeting and decided not to press charges, so we were released without charge and made our way to the Houses of Parliament to join the protesters there, as section 28 passed in to law at midnight.

Despite this series of passionate and courageous protests against Section 28, lesbian and gay teachers overwhelmingly did not demonstrate against Section 28. The protests had gathered significant media attention and so those of us teaching at the time were, for the most part, too frightened of being seen by pupils, their parents or school colleagues to participate. To be spotted protesting against Section 28 could be construed as supporting or 'promoting' homosexuality, and this could have been career-ending (or at least we believed this was the case). Many lesbian and gay teachers have written retrospectively about the fear they felt working under Section 28; in part II of this book, I write at length about my own experiences as a teacher between 1988 and 2003.

Next, in chapter 5, I consider the academic literature of the Section 28 era, to get a sense of the impact of the law on gay and lesbian teachers.

CHAPTER 5

THE IMPACT OF SECTION 28 ON LESBIAN AND GAY TEACHERS

This chapter uses academic research and literature to examine the lived experience of lesbian and gay teachers during the Section 28 era. Drawing on publications from the 1980s and 1990s, when Section 28 was law, the chapter reveals a number of common themes, including institutionalised heterosexuality in schools, the management of personal and professional identities, the psychological impact on teachers of being marginalised, and covert and overt workplace harassment.

Research by and about teachers during Section 28 was scant, not least because the law drove lesbian and gay teachers underground. They were frequently not prepared to participate in interviews or questionnaires for fear of identification. A year into Section 28, Gillian Squirrell lamented the 'dearth of sensible writing and discussion to counterbalance the sensationalism of press and parliament' (1989, p.17).

The work of Gill Clarke, Debbie Epstein, Epstein and Richard Johnson, Andrew Sparkes, and Clare Sullivan in the UK was an exception to what Helen Lenskyj (1997) described as a conspiracy of silence about the lived experience of lesbian and gay teachers. Under Section 28, the disclosure of a lesbian or gay teacher's sexuality would jeopardise their employment prospects. However, the alternative of remaining closeted and silent perpetuated the myth that all teachers were heterosexual, leaving discrimination in schools unchecked and unchallenged.

The state-sanctioned silencing of lesbian and gay teachers by Section 28 led them into feelings of enforced dishonesty and deceit. Over time, this duplicity adversely impacted their integrity, sense of self, wellbeing and ultimately mental health (Lee, 2019). Clarke (1997) observed dissonance and a sense of deceit in lesbian teacher relationships with both colleagues and students, and revealed the extent to which invisibility for all her teacher participants became 'a measure of survival and avoidance of harassment and discrimination in the classroom' (p.37). Many of Clarke's lesbian teacher participants claimed they lived double lives under Section 28, and were isolated and lonely in the school workplace.

Under Section 28, lesbian and gay teachers were enveloped by the oppressive nature of homophobia and heterosexism. Rigidly managing the intersection of their personal and professional identities and assimilating to heteronormative school cultures during Section 28 placed a significant additional burden on top of an already highly demanding and tiring job. Clarke (1996) noted that 'the holding of dual identities i.e. pseudo-heterosexual and lesbian' created 'great dissonance and personal turmoil' (p.196) for the lesbian teachers she interviewed. According to Clarke, during Section 28, the lesbian (and gay) teacher was under constant surveillance by others, who looked for inconsistencies in their 'stories' and monitored them closely for transgressions from the heterosexual norm. This covert harassment served to remind lesbian and gay teachers of their 'outsider status' (Kitzinger, 1994, p.501) and affected the way in which they experienced the school workplace.

The Section 28 era preceded our current internet and social media age, so graffiti left anonymously around the school was a major way in which a lesbian or gay teacher could find their personal life thrust into the public domain (Mason & Tomsen, 1997). Although easier to contain than online comments that can be reposted worldwide, homophobic graffiti about lesbian and gay teachers was nonetheless devastating. When homophobic graffiti was found in schools, teachers and other adult members of the heteronormative school community had, under Section 28, the option of either challenging or ignoring it. Those challenging the homophobia risked accusations under Section 28 that they were promoting homosexuality and could be accused of being lesbian or gay themselves. The presence of graffiti inevitably ignited rumours and served to encourage students to engage in acts of further harassment under the cloak of anonymity, compounding the distress of the lesbian and gay teacher and keeping their sexuality in the public domain.

Jacqueline Underwood (1995) found that the lesbian teachers in her study tried to remain as invisible as possible so as to avoid drawing attention to themselves, acknowledging that this strategy was not conducive to job promotion nor to a positive sense of self. It is little wonder that during the Section 28 era, many lesbian and gay teachers left the profession altogether. And of course, when lesbian and gay teachers were invisible, the young people who experienced their own education under Section 28 endured a complete absence of lesbian and gay role models and no doubt saw teaching as a profession solely for heterosexual people.

Much of the literature on lesbian and gay teachers during the Section 28 era portrays them as marginalised by the heterosexual hegemony of the school community (Clarke, 1996; Epstein & Johnson, 1998; Sparkes, 1994). While this literature gives a voice to lesbian and gay teachers, their stories of oppression collude with the negative dominant social understandings of this most challenging of eras. Research about lesbian and gay teachers undertaken during and after Section 28 attributes the reproduction of normative gender and sexual identifications in schools to institutionalised heteronormativity (Epstein & Johnson, 1998; Waites, 2005; Gray, 2010; Rudoe, 2010).

Some of the research shows the way in which lesbian and gay teachers attempted to compensate for their covert personal identities by developing a professional identity that was beyond reproach and respected by their colleagues (Griffin, 1992; Kissen, 1993; Singer, 1997; Litton, 1999; King, 2004). Lesbian and gay teachers were shown to put inordinate amounts of time and energy into their teaching, overperforming in order to develop a highly positive professional reputation. Pat Griffin (1992) describes this overperformance as something of an insurance policy, designed to counteract the loss of credibility that lesbian and gay teachers would experience at work if their sexuality became public knowledge. Griffin identified a number of interrelated behaviours that lesbian teachers used to manage their sexuality. Some sought to acquire the reputation of being someone 'not to mess with' (1992, p.173), while others would withdraw entirely from the staff community, sitting in their classrooms at break and lunch times to avoid personal questions about their private lives. Griffin's participants admitted to endlessly rehearsing how they would respond to confrontation in relation to homophobic remarks or behaviours.

The Section 28 era literature demonstrates overwhelmingly that lesbian and gay teachers took great care to conceal their sexuality at work (Clarke, 1997; Sparkes, 1994; Sullivan, 1993). There is some evidence, however, that a decade or so into Section 28 it was just about possible for lesbian and gay teachers to be out discreetly among some of their trusted colleagues in progressive schools. Clarke observed that their sexuality was more likely to be tolerated or accepted when the individual did not flaunt it or make it visible. Clarke (1996) referred to this teacher as the 'good homosexual' – someone who did not challenge the heterosexual status quo. Ten years into Section 28, Clarke cautioned against lesbian teachers coming out in the school workplace:

> *Whilst on the surface it may appear that there is some degree of tolerance for sexual minorities it is clear that what 'we' do in the private sphere is 'acceptable' and tolerated only so long as we do not step over the boundaries into the public domain.* (1998a, p.88)

Epstein and Johnson (1998) identified further requirements for negotiating an openly lesbian or gay identity in the Section 28 era:

> *It is possible – just – to be gay, 'out' and publicly approved of in Britain. This approval, however, is conditional, if not on a certain quietude, certainly on otherwise exemplary behaviour. A homosexual life or act must leave unchallenged the dominant sexual and other categories – heterosexuality, marriage, coupledom ... Where these are challenged ... retribution is likely to follow.* (p.25)

While fear of job loss as a consequence of Section 28 troubled lesbian and gay teachers, another fear was prevalent yet not as readily articulated at the time, even by those teachers brave enough to participate in research during Section 28. Clarke (1996) observed that her lesbian teacher participants feared being 'viewed as paedophiles, child molesters and perverts' (p.201). Sheila Cavanagh (2008), Simon Borg (2017) and Catherine Thompson-Lee (2017) also found that lesbian and gay teachers worried excessively that their heterosexual colleagues, and parents of pupils in their care, would align their identity with discourses of hypersexuality and paedophilia. Heather Piper and Pat Sikes (2010) observed that the 'fear of the paedophile taints adult-child relationships in general' (p.567). And although, according to Preston (2018), all teachers are potentially under suspicion, Piper and Sikes assert that 'when the focus is on sex that is regarded as being outside of the norm, the difficulties are magnified' (2010, p.567).

Emily Gray (2010) reflects that 'the perceived link between homosexuality and paedophilia ... contributes to the (re)production of the heteronormative discursive practices that dominate schools as educational institutions' (p.40). When schools allow such attitudes to prevail, they are complicit in the rejection of all other depictions of sexuality.

LESBIAN AND GAY TEACHERS: THE INTERNATIONAL PICTURE

Although Section 28 was a piece of UK legislation, it is worth considering the climate for lesbian and gay teachers across other Western countries during the Section 28 era. At first glance, in the US, Canada and Australia, lesbian and gay teachers were protected by anti-discrimination legislation in the school workplace. A number of pieces of equalities legislation aimed to improve the rights of lesbians and gay men. For example, Title VII of the Civil Rights Act 1964 prohibits employment discrimination on the basis of sexual orientation or gender identity. The Equal Employment Opportunity Commission interpreted Title VII to cover LGBT employees. In 1982 in Canada, Section 15 of the Charter of Rights and Freedoms offered protection from discrimination. In Australia, the Human Rights and Equal Opportunity Commission was established in 1986 to investigate employment discrimination on the grounds of sexual orientation.

However, the literature shows that legislation at the macro level in these countries did not contribute to individual lesbian or gay teachers necessarily feeling able to come out in their school communities. After changes to Canada's equalities legislation to include sexual orientation, Madiha Didi Khayatt (1992) assessed the amendments and evaluated the views of the Canadian lesbian teachers she interviewed:

It would not guarantee the attitude of people who are made privy to that knowledge. It would not shelter one from their prejudices, from their antagonism, from their unwillingness to cooperate with a teacher who would declare herself publicly as lesbian. (p.207)

Myrna Olson (1987), studying lesbian and gay teachers in the US, found that they feared rejection by other adults and feared alignment with mythologies that linked homosexuality with child molestation, promiscuity, effeminacy, mental instability and disease. Researching the experiences of lesbian teachers in Australia, Tania Ferfolja too observed that they were marginalised by colleagues who assumed they were heterosexual. Ferfolja (2010) argued that lesbian teachers were victims of oppression and were forced to deploy, at times, elaborate strategies to conceal their lesbian identity in the school workplace. Strategies included the careful monitoring of their personal presentation, behaviour and conversations with others, which often included the creation of fictitious opposite-sex partners or the changing of pronouns to suggest a female partner was instead male (Ferfolja, 2009).

James King (2004) described the concerns and pressures that preoccupied gay teachers in the US. He reflected on his own worries about how parents and colleagues perceived him when he was around children. King self-consciously monitored his behaviour, describing a multifaceted regime in which his own paranoia eventually caused him to question whether he was in fact a negative influence on the children he taught. On reflection, King realised that by going through the paralysing ordeal of monitoring his own behaviour in the classroom, he unintentionally propagated the heteronormative and homophobic underpinnings responsible for his self-monitoring. King was perpetually anxious that colleagues and parents would see his interactions with children as predatory and, over time, began to internalise their concerns and become obsessively preoccupied with his own behaviour.

Regretting his own self-censorship, King (2004) claimed gay teachers had to strike a 'bad bargain' (p.123) with their schools that was distracting and damaging for those who felt bound to subscribe to it. King asserted that gay male teachers were permitted to remain in post only in exchange for a complete denial of their sexual identities. Self-consciously monitoring their own behaviour as seen through the eyes of others was necessary, as was policing themselves for evidence of their sexual identity, in case a colleague, parent or school leader jumped to conclusions that jeopardised their teaching career, saw them moved on elsewhere, or even led to their dismissal.

Griffin (1992) developed a descriptive framework for lesbian and gay teachers in the US. This identity-management typology, consisting of four stages, was developed via analysis of interviews with lesbian or gay teachers. Their behaviours were grouped into four categories: passing; covering; implicitly coming out; and explicitly coming out. Griffin described the four identity management strategies as follows.

'Passing' is where 'an individual actively says or does something to suggest they are heterosexual so that their sexual identity is invisible. Or, more passively, they may simply not challenge the assumption that they are heterosexual' (in Sparkes, 1994, p.99).

'Covering' relates to circumstances where a lesbian or gay teacher is made intelligible to others as heterosexual by concealing their non-heterosexual identity. An example might be using gender neutral language when speaking about a romantic partner. Griffin (1998, p.138) denotes covering as 'a middle ground between passing as heterosexual and actually coming out'.

'Implicitly coming out' is similar to covering but relates to speaking about personal circumstances without unambiguously verifying that one is lesbian or gay.

Finally, 'explicitly coming out', according to Griffin (1998), entails a lesbian or gay teacher making a declarative statement in which they describe themselves to others as lesbian or gay.

In her seminal text *Epistemology of the Closet* (1990), Eve Sedgwick posits that the coming out narrative for lesbians is complex and, for better or worse, often serves merely to confirm the suspicions of others. Sedgwick states:

> *Coming out is a matter of crystallizing intuitions or convictions that had been in the air for a while already and had already established their own power-circuits of silent contempt, silent blackmail, silent glamorization, silent complicity.* (1990, pp.79-80)

it might change

Literature referring specifically to lesbian teacher discourses of coming out suggests additional layers of complexity are present, which are intertwined with the discourses of knowledge and power that surround institutions such as schools and society more widely. Khayatt (1997) challenges the assumptions that (Canadian) lesbian or gay teachers have a duty to come out and act as advocates for lesbian or gay students, and suggests that coming out may not necessarily be that helpful for the students or the teacher. Khayatt interrogates the benefit of coming out in the classroom, particularly through a 'declarative statement' (p.130). She argues that coming out through a declarative statement is unsound because personal identities are continually in a state of flux. Khayatt contends that the act of making a declarative statement is to freeze identity, which does not, in Khayatt's view, do justice to the identity of the teacher presenting herself in class.

Mary Lou Rasmussen (2004) explores the political and pedagogical matters that inevitably influence educational discourses of the closet and coming out. Rasmussen is critical of coming out discourses in schools in the US, as she claims they tend to forge a relationship between inclusivity and coming out – a relationship that, she claims, situates the closet 'as a zone of shame and exclusion' (p.144). Rasmussen asserts that encouraging gay and lesbian teachers to come out leaves those who are unable to do so feeling that they have somehow abdicated their moral responsibility as a role model to young people. Rasmussen is particularly critical of steps taken in the US by the Human Rights Campaign to introduce a National Coming Out Day – something the UK has now also adopted. This calls upon people, including teachers and students in schools, to come out and be honest and open about their sexuality. According to Rasmussen, this implies that those who feel unable to do so, for whatever reason, are somehow failing young people who may need their support.

In her book *The Last Closet* (1996), Rita Kissen tells the stories of American lesbian and gay educators as they battle for respectability in the face of homophobia. She describes the predicament and tension facing lesbian and gay teachers, noting paradoxical circumstances in their status. Kissen observes how lesbian and gay teachers desired to come out to end the silence and myths surrounding them, yet ironically were compelled to remain hidden because of the power of the same silence and myths. In Kissen's research, many teachers who felt unable to come out in their professional context experienced significant guilt about remaining closeted (see also Woods & Harbeck, 1992; Sullivan, 1993). As Ferfolja (2009) notes, this sense of guilt places an inordinate burden on individuals who are potentially already marginalised (p.386).

There are, however, some academic discourses from across Western societies that position lesbian and gay teachers as agents of resistance who contested and still do contest heteronormative discursive practices. According to Ferfolja (2009), some lesbian and gay teachers challenge and resist heterosexist presumptions and subvert non-heterosexual identities in schools. By drawing on Judith Butler's theories of performativity (1990), Ferfolja argues that even teachers who remain closeted and silenced, or who pass as heterosexual, have power and agency. She argues that maintaining a silence is an act of considerable subversive power because it troubles the presumption of heterosexuality. Ferfolja states that 'lesbian and gay teachers, through their very presence, highlight the falsity of the constructed naturalness of heterosexuality, which is of itself a very powerful statement' (2009, p.391).

Despite teacher coming out discourses being most often associated with courage and bravery, not coming out or simply remaining silent about one's sexuality is not synonymous with failure, nor a dereliction of responsibilities to young people in schools. Remaining in the closet, censoring oneself and navigating the hazardous terrain of the heteronormative school can be the more courageous option for the lesbian or gay teacher. It is certainly the option that demands the most energy.

JANE BROWN: A LESBIAN HEADTEACHER'S STORY

Throughout the 15 years of Section 28, the vast majority of lesbian and gay teachers in the UK were hiding in plain sight in the school workplace, carefully managing the nexus of their sexual identities and identities as teachers. Hiding in the workplace is not, of course, conducive to being promoted and so lesbian and gay teachers tended not to be raised to headships and other positions of school leadership at the same rate as their heterosexual peers.

According to Jackie Blount (2003), heterosexual, white, masculine and able-bodied are attributes entrenched in Western conceptualisations of the school leader. Despite a teaching workforce in the West that is largely female, the traditional notion of the headteacher is one in which the traits of masculine, white and male stubbornly preside.

However, one lesbian teacher, Jane Brown, attained a headship as her authentic self during the Section 28 era, albeit in the gay-friendly, Labour-controlled London borough of Hackney. Brown was to become, though, caught in the Section 28 crossfire and eventually pilloried by the Tory tabloid press, leaving her career and personal life in tatters.

In 1994, Brown's school, Kingsmead Primary, was offered subsidised tickets to a performance of the ballet *Romeo and Juliet*. The children at Kingsmead were seen as underprivileged and so not likely to access such a cultural experience with their families. However, Brown declined the tickets, allegedly dismissing *Romeo and Juliet* as a story depicting only heterosexual love. Davina Cooper (1997), writing about the incident, states that 'price, logistics, and educational planning were all factors' (p.501) in Brown's decision, yet the only factor that attracted public attention was Brown's reference to *Romeo and Juliet* being about heterosexual love. The tabloid press reported that Brown had lacked good professional judgement in declining the tickets on behalf of the students at her school. However, rather than simply criticising Brown's decision, they seized on her sexual identity. The press then created a scandal, portraying Brown as a 'loony left' lesbian teacher who would not let her students access a cultural experience because it portrayed only heterosexual love.

The right-wing tabloids universally drew on Brown's physical appearance and dress in their criticism of her. Epstein (1996) argues that 'this coding of Jane Brown as being a butch lesbian ushered in a series of attacks on her primarily for her sexuality' (p.254). Angelia Wilson (1995) notes that *The Sun* newspaper used derogatory language, describing Brown as a 'hatchet-faced dyke' who must be sacked immediately.

Brown's physical appearance became a weapon with which to destroy her reputation as a headteacher. She was branded as an inappropriate person to be leading a school because she was a lesbian. In *The Daily Mail* on 21 January 1994, Brown was described as 'wearing a blue donkey jacket, red jeans and boots – her customary school attire'.

As I assert throughout this book, Section 28 was the result of a fierce battle between the left and right of UK politics. Margaret Thatcher frequently cited the use of local authority funds for lesbian and gay issues to exemplify what she saw as the recklessness of the loony left. There could be no garment more politically charged at the time than the donkey jacket. The Labour leader Michael Foot, who lost to Thatcher in the 1983 general election, famously wore a donkey jacket, and the miners with whom Thatcher went to war in the 1980s wore donkey jackets with the initials NCB (National Coal Board) across the back.

Brown was also caught in the middle of a ferocious struggle for power between the governing body of her school and the education department of Hackney local authority. The Conservative government had recently introduced its Local Management of Schools (LMS) policy. Under LMS, schools were given more autonomy than they had previously, and the governing body of Kingsmead Primary used the Brown case to test its new responsibilities and power. While the governing body stood by Brown, New Labour was preparing to challenge for leadership of the country. Cooper (1997) claims the lack of support for Brown by Hackney local authority was down to New Labour members of the authority wishing to distance themselves from the left of the party. The lesbian headteacher and her donkey jacket served to embody all that the Conservatives alleged was wrong with the loony left and Brown came to symbolise for the Tories just why Section 28 was needed.

According to Cooper (1997), lesbian activists united to support Brown and so Kingsmead became a focal point of sorts for the lesbian community. Parents of children at the primary school were largely supportive of Brown but were critical of Gus John, Hackney's director of education, because of his failure to support the headteacher. Epstein (1996) interprets the support from parents differently, however, suggesting that certain parental support for Brown was rooted in racism against John, who was black.

Epstein and Johnson (1998) assert that Brown's case was symbolic of how teacher sexualities were politically charged and aggressively policed in schools during Section 28. They argue that the media, the church and the state all contributed to the excessive scrutiny of teachers thought to be lesbian or gay. Brown's identity as a lesbian teacher cost her dearly. She was forced to issue a public apology, which seemed to be sought more for her lesbian identity than the missed theatre trip. According to Epstein and Johnson (1998), the *Romeo and Juliet* incident led to the invasion of Brown's privacy, her partner being outed in her workplace, and her partner's children and ex-partner being harassed. Brown received hate mail and her career as a headteacher was inevitably devastated.

Rather than her being seen as courageous, Brown's case served as a cautionary tale to other lesbian and gay teachers during Section 28. With her sexuality at the heart of the media narrative, her poor professional judgement was seen to be entirely attributable to her lesbianism. Epstein and Johnson (1998) note, a decade into Section 28, that the media's portrayal of Brown was an 'attempt to define lesbian teachers ... as inappropriate people to head a school and ... to teach there at all' (p.90).

The case of Brown – and in particular the way in which her physical appearance was attacked in the press – shows the importance of personal appearance for the lesbian teacher. While dress codes for males in school seem overtly prescribed and so relatively straightforward for gay men, for lesbian teachers, dress and appearance are crucial to the appropriate performance of gender and sexuality in the school workplace. Amy Wallis and Jo VanEvery (2000) cite the example of a lesbian teacher who said:

> When I go to work, I put on my 'uniform', neat cardigans and smart blouses and trousers with a crease ironed down the front, clothes that I would never wear outside work. Although I realize there are many things I choose to edit in the school environment, most of the information that I censor about myself is related in some way to my sexuality. (p.413)

Catherine Lugg and Autumn Tooms (2010) similarly observe that 'every organization has a professional uniform that is the mandated presentation of self. The dress code of the lesbian is a significant factor in the telling of identity and is a crucial point at which the personal and professional identities intersect' (p.84). Lisa Edwards et al. (2016) too posit that in balancing a lesbian identity with teacher identity, some lesbian teachers that they interviewed compensated for their sexual identity by deploying an overly feminine dress code to distance themselves from a masculine lesbian stereotype.

To conclude, Section 28 had a profound effect on the way in which lesbian and gay teachers experienced their school workplaces for the 15 years that it was law. Teachers were forced to carefully manage the intersection of their personal and professional identities, leaving them isolated and caught in a web of deceit among their colleagues and students. Lesbian and gay teachers taught in a climate of fear, worrying constantly that their sexuality could be exposed, resulting in the loss of their job and, worse, the potential label of paedophile.

In the next chapter, I explore how Section 28 was repealed some 15 years after its introduction in 1988. I examine the election to government of New Labour and its initial failed attempt to repeal Section 28 in 2000. I consider the efforts of Conservative peers to resurrect the homophobic rhetoric that had led to Section 28 and describe how, even after its repeal in 2003 in England, many heterosexual teachers were unaware that the law on sexual identities in schools had changed. Finally, I consider the introduction of the equalities legislation that provided some occupational security for lesbian and gay teachers, and reflect on the apologies made by Conservative MPs for Section 28.

CHAPTER 6
THE REPEAL OF SECTION 28

The Labour party remained conspicuously quiet on Section 28 as it grew ever more centrist in its quest to win the 1997 general election. Strategically, it continued to distance itself from traditional Labour values, rebranding itself New Labour in an attempt to appeal to more people and shake off the labels of 'radical left' and 'loony left' that Margaret Thatcher and the Conservatives had deployed so effectively. *still are*

When New Labour did come to power in 1997, under Tony Blair's leadership, many lesbian and gay people were optimistic that the party would end Section 28 immediately. However, New Labour was aware that among significant elements of the electorate, Section 28 was popular. Once in government, it made no immediate move to quash the legislation and, instead, carefully monitored public perceptions of same-sex relationships using social attitudes data as a barometer.

Meanwhile, members of the House of Lords, sensing that New Labour may seek to repeal Section 28, ramped up their homophobia, returning to the vicious rhetoric that had helped to pass the law back in 1988. According to Paul Baker (2022), Lady Saltoun of Abernethy, who had previously described Section 28 as 'a David of a bill that sets out to kill a Goliath of an evil', asked the rhetorical question in the Lords, 'Why do homosexuals proselytise?'

Hansard parliamentary transcripts show that, in response to her own insidious question, Saltoun stated:

I think it is rather in the same way that drunks try to persuade everyone round them to drink too – because they feel more comfortable if all around are the same as them. If I were purple with orange spots, I should probably want every one of your Lordships to become purple with orange spots, so that I should feel at home.

Saltoun's rhetoric was representative of the claims other peers would make to protect Section 28. However, despite their sinister efforts, Saltoun and her contemporaries failed to avert an attempt by the New Labour government to repeal Section 28 as part of the Local Government Act 2000.

In February 2000, New Labour cautiously attempted to begin to repeal Section 28. Mindful of public opinion, the party went to great lengths to stress that it did not wish the repeal to be seen as permission for schools to promote homosexuality (Thorp & Allen, 2000). Therefore, as a defence against any such accusations, New Labour simultaneously proposed an amendment to the Learning and Skills Bill (1999-2000). The amendment offered a new duty on schools to follow statutory guidance on sex and relationships education that prohibited teaching about same-sex relationships, describing it as inappropriate.

Opposition to the repeal of Section 28 was led by Baroness Young in the House of Lords. Young was made leader of the Lords under Thatcher (the only woman to feature in a Thatcher cabinet). She was a sponsor of the right-wing and Christian-aligned lobbying group Family and Youth Concern (Baker, 2022) and an enthusiastic supporter of Section 28.

Hansard shows that the following words were spoken by Baroness Young in her quest to maintain Section 28:

I must make it clear that the government amendment is not a substitute for what has come to be known in shorthand as Section 28 ... I know that I am speaking for the overwhelming majority of the population which does not want the promotion of homosexuality in schools. I have had some 4,000 letters begging me to stand firm; letters from teachers, doctors, nurses, social workers, hundreds of church-goers, parents, grandparents and even a few homosexuals. For the issue which we are debating has touched a chord in the British people. ...

Today, we are standing for the protection of children and the support of parents. In today's world, parents find it very difficult to bring up children, with all the temptations before them. When their children are in school, they do not want homosexuality to be promoted; nor do they want their children to be subjected to the literature which many of us have seen.

Saltoun also rallied the homophobic rhetoric. She alleged that when parents protested about homosexuality in schools, they were subjected to abuse and even violence. Saltoun claimed 'some councils would merrily spend large sums of council tax payers' money on gay jamborees, raves and so forth', adding:

Like other Members of the Committee, I have received a great many letters from anxious parents and grandparents imploring me to support the amendment moved by the noble Baroness, Lady Young ... the majority of people in this country look to this House to save Section 28 for them so that their children and grandchildren can grow up without being subjected at a very young age to the kind of indoctrination described in Bankrolling Gay Proselytism which Section 28 prevents.

Bankrolling Gay Proselytism was an inflammatory document published by the Christian Institute that provided examples of spending by local councils and health authorities on projects to support gay and lesbian people.

The repeal of Section 28 was not successful in 2000. The future prime minister Theresa May, at the time the shadow education and employment secretary, urged the government not to try to repeal the law for a second time, telling a student newspaper that 'most parents want the comfort of knowing Section 28 is there' (Becket, 2017).

In the newly devolved Scottish Parliament, the repeal of Section 28 was successful in 2000. As part of the Ethical Standards in Public Life (Scotland) Act 2000, Section 28 was repealed on 21 June 2000 with an overwhelming majority of 99 to 17.

Keeping an ever-watchful eye on the lesbian and gay public opinion data, in 2003, New Labour tried once again to repeal Section 28. The Conservatives remained steadfast in their opposition to the proposed repeal, having committed in their 2001 manifesto pledge 'to retain Section 28 of the Local Government Act'. Baroness Blatch, a former leader of Cambridgeshire County Council, told the House of Lords:

> *Many parents are concerned about the use of inappropriate materials in schools, which is why Parliament has regulated sex education. Those who ... seek the repeal of Section 28 have failed adequately to grasp this point. They have failed to grasp that sexuality – just like politics or religion – is a controversial area where parents have strong concerns ... the vast majority of parents do not want homosexuality promoted in schools ... Section 28 was introduced for a reason. Some local authorities were actively promoting homosexuality in schools.*

The only openly gay peer, Labour's Lord Alli, attempted to make the case for the repeal of Section 28, seeking to allay fears that homosexuality would be taught in schools if the repeal was successful. He said:

> *Sex education in schools is not governed by Section 28. No matter how many times the other side repeat it, it does not make it true. They know that maintained schools must have a written policy on school sex education ... Because of Section 352 of the Education Act 1996, they know that the governing body and head teachers must ensure that sex education encourages people to have due regard to moral considerations and the value of family life. Because of Section 403 of the Education Act 1996, they know that parents have the right to withdraw their children from all or part of sex education ... Section 28 is about one group of people trying to use the law to embody their own prejudices. Section 28 has no place in the protection of children, let alone in a modern, civilised society.*

When Parliament voted in 2003 on the repeal of Section 28, MPs of note who voted to keep the law included Iain Duncan Smith, Anne Widdicombe, David Davis and the future prime ministers Theresa May and David Cameron.

According to Kathryn Rhodes (2020), it was the UK's membership of the European Union that hastened the repeal of Section 28 and helped to expedite further equalities legislation in the UK. Sasha Roseneil and Shelley Budgeon (2004) too note that European statutes augmented the speed of the repeal by providing workplace protection for lesbian, gay and bisexual people and recognising same-sex relationships.

Eventually, on 18 September 2003 – 15 years, three months and 25 days after the introduction of Section 28 – the law was finally repealed. Section 122 stated simply: 'Repeal of prohibition on promotion of homosexuality Section 2A of the Local Government Act 1986 (c. 10) (local authorities prohibited from promoting homosexuality) ceases to have effect.'

The Section 28 legislation had left an entire generation of lesbian and gay young people without access to lesbian and gay role models and suitable pastoral support at the most challenging time in their adolescence. It caused gay and lesbian teachers to fear they would lose their jobs if they were outed in the school workplace. It starved lesbian and gay groups and projects of public funding and, through its ambiguous and unfathomable wording, presided over an enduring and intolerable culture of fear and confusion in schools.

No teacher was ever prosecuted as a consequence of Section 28 and, in retrospect, the same vague and confusing wording that caused such fear among lesbian and gay teachers probably made Section 28 unenforceable. It was far from a benign presence, however. In Scotland in May 2000, the Glasgow resident Sheena Strain, with the backing of the Christian Institute, cited Section 28 in a case that she brought to the Court of Session (the supreme civil court of Scotland). Strain objected to her council tax being used to fund a project for HIV and AIDS care and education that distributed a safe sex leaflet entitled *Gay Sex Now*.

The case was eventually settled out of court. As part of the agreement, Glasgow City Council pledged to send a covering letter to all council grant recipients stating that they must not spend council tax income on the promotion of homosexuality or on the publication of any material promoting homosexuality. Even after its repeal, Section 28 was cited in legal attempts to withdraw funding for HIV and AIDS prevention work.

One might imagine that after 15 difficult years under Section 28, the repeal would trigger considerable celebration and fanfare. Not a bit. The news went almost entirely unreported by the UK press. The left-leaning *Guardian* included a short article buried on page 6, but no other mainstream outlet carried mention of it. As this was a repeal of a local government act, and not an education act, schools were not notified that Section 28 was no longer in force. They continued much as they always had, with heterosexual school stakeholders largely oblivious that Section 28 had been repealed.

Protective legislation for lesbian and gay teachers followed. Protection initially came via the Employment Equality (Sexual Orientation) Regulations 2003, then through the Equality Act (Sexual Orientation) Regulations 2007 and then by means of the current legislation, the Equality Act 2010. The act prohibits discrimination in the workplace on the grounds of 'protected' characteristics, including gender reassignment and sexual orientation. It also introduced a single public duty necessitating that all publicly funded bodies, including schools, proactively promote equality across the board (Colgan & Wright, 2011).

APOLOGIES FOR SECTION 28

Public attitudes continued to shift in support for lesbian and gay identities, and Conservative politicians were left running to catch up. In his first conference speech as leader of the Conservative party in 2006, David Cameron demonstrated how he had moved on in his beliefs about lesbians and gay men after being on what he called a 'journey'. Acknowledging the introduction in 2005 of civil partnerships for same-sex couples by New Labour, Cameron said: 'There's something special about marriage. Pledging yourself to another means doing something brave and important … You are making a commitment. And by the way, it means something whether you're a man and a woman, a woman and a woman, or a man and another man. That's why we were right to support civil partnerships, and I'm proud of that' (Watt, 2009).

In 2009, seeking election as prime minister, Cameron made a speech apologising for Section 28 at a Conservative fundraising event for Pride. During this speech, Cameron described Section 28 as 'offensive to gay people', adding, 'Yes, we may have sometimes been slow and, yes, we may have made mistakes, including Section 28, but the change has happened' (Watt, 2009). Cameron confessed that he had a less than ideal voting record on gay rights, but stated:

In wanting to make the party representative of the country, I think we have made some real progress. If we do win the next election, instead of being a white, middle-class, middle-aged party, we will be far more diverse. The Conservatives had the first woman prime minister and we are bound to have the first black prime minister and the first gay prime minister. (Watt, 2009)

Cameron became prime minister in 2010, but despite his rhetoric about the mistakes of Section 28, he did not rush to enact laws to improve rights for gay and lesbian people. In fact, it took Cameron and the Conservatives until March 2014 to legislate in favour of same-sex marriage.

When Cameron stepped down as prime minister, after the Brexit vote of 2016, he stated that same-sex marriage was his proudest achievement. Reflecting as part of Pride celebrations in June 2022, Cameron told the *i* newspaper:

I supported gay rights and civil partnerships, but I wasn't immediately sold on the case for full-on equal marriage. It took time, lots of thinking and conversations with my wife, Sam, and other friends to become so committed to the policy that I was willing to fight for it. And it was a fight. Opposition was fierce – from constituents, voters, religious organisations, and many in my own party. There was huge pressure to drop it. But we continued the fight – and we were right. Equal marriage is absolutely necessary. People should be able to get married, whoever they are, and whoever they love ... It is easy to take these things for granted now and assume that society just becomes more equal as time passes. The truth is that gay rights were never a given. They happened because of brave and dedicated men and women from the gay community and from wider society. Pride has played a huge role in that progress. In the year I was born, homosexuality was still illegal in Britain. Today, I live in a country where people of all sexualities proudly fly the rainbow flag. My children's generation talk about their LGBTQ+ friends and sexuality as something that is completely unremarkable. (*i*, 2022)

Another Conservative leader and former prime minister, Theresa May, also apologised for her voting record on Section 28 and other anti-LGBT legislation. May voted against the repeal of Section 28 in 2000, and earlier against the equal age of consent and against same-sex adoptions. However, in 2010, May conceded that she had changed her mind and would now vote differently on the legislation (Grindley, 2016). On succeeding Cameron as prime minister in 2016, May said:

There's some things I've voted for in the past that I shouldn't have done and I've said sorry. Section 28 obviously would have been one of those things … I hope people will see the fact I recognise that I shouldn't have taken that view on Section 28. I have developed my views. I want to be seen as an ally of the LGBT community here in the UK. (Braidwood, 2018)

[handwritten margin note: not 'I am sorry'?]

[handwritten margin note: not 'I am an ally'?]

[handwritten note under text: pure virtue signalling in line with changes in public opinion]

May went on to say, in 2018, that so-called gay conversion therapy had 'no place in modern Britain', adding: 'We are determined as a government to end it. We are going to consult on the best way of doing that and we're very clear that this is something that does not have a place in our society' (Brown, 2018). However, she failed to ban conversion therapy during her tenure as prime minister.

Reflecting on the 50th anniversary of UK Pride in June 2022, May told the *i* newspaper:

Thanks to people like Peter Tatchell and the commitment of many other long-standing campaigners, we can take pride in how much, and how profoundly, attitudes have changed. I include myself in that – looking back now, there are issues I would have voted on differently, were I to vote on them today … I was proud, as Prime Minister, to launch the country's first National LGBTQ+ Survey. More than 100,000 people responded. Some of the results were encouraging. Most gay and lesbian people told us they felt comfortable living in the UK and the majority of LGBTQ+ people – almost 60 per cent – feel able to be open about their sexuality or gender identity at work. Yet at the same time, two in five LGBTQ+ people said they had experienced verbal or physical abuse because of their sexuality or gender identity. And nearly two-thirds avoid holding hands with same-sex partners for fear of a negative reaction. Few people, reading the accounts of trans people in our survey, would disagree that they still face indignities and prejudice, when they deserve understanding and respect. It is nearly five years since that survey was launched and in that time the debate about trans people has grown more, not less, divisive. We need to strive for greater understanding on both sides of the debate. Just because an issue is controversial, that doesn't mean we can avoid addressing it. To that end, the government must keep to its commitment to consider the issue of transgender conversion therapy. If it is not to be in the upcoming Bill, then the matter must not be allowed to slide. For, whatever our sexuality or gender identity, we are all equally deserving of acceptance; LGBTQ+ rights are human rights. That was the lesson of 50 years ago and while we have come a long way, it is something we still need to remind ourselves of today. (i, 2022)

Even John Major, who was prime minister for almost half of Section 28 (between 1990 and 1997) expressed regret about the way in which the Conservative party had treated lesbian and gay people. Also speaking to the *i* newspaper, Major stated:

Social progress to protect minorities is often painfully slow, but I warmly welcome the advances that have now been made – and continue to be made. I recall being shocked by the bigotry and intolerance that followed a meeting I held with Sir Ian McKellen over thirty years ago when, as Prime Minister, I was seeking to better understand the difficulties faced by the gay community. Sir Ian – whose brave advocacy I admired – was one of the reasons that Parliament voted to lower the age of consent in 1994. Slowly, but surely, tolerance and understanding have grown from that time – although, alas, there are still hurdles to overcome. (i, 2022)

Boris Johnson, the Conservative prime minister from 2019 to 2022, had a mixed record on lesbian and gay rights. He did vote to repeal Section 28 in 2003 but was largely absent for many other votes on legislation promoting LGBTQ+ equality and inclusion. Johnson was also notorious for making homophobic slurs. According to Reiss Smith (2021), before becoming prime minister, Johnson was criticised for pervasive anti-gay rhetoric in his newspaper columns for the right-wing *Daily Telegraph*. Johnson described gay men as 'tank-topped wearing bum boys' and attacked Labour for allegedly encouraging the teaching of homosexuality in schools. Despite voting in favour of civil partnerships in 2005, Johnson was critical of same-sex partnerships in his book *Friends, Voters, Countrymen*

(2002), written to woo the Conservative party faithful. Johnson wrote, 'If gay marriage was OK – and I was uncertain on the issue – then I saw no reason in principle why a union should not be consecrated between three men, as well as two men; or indeed three men and a dog' (Williams, 2008).

In contrast, while serving as mayor of London from 2008 to 2016, Johnson participated in the city's Pride parade. In 2010, he became the most senior Conservative to support marriage equality. However, Johnson's proclivity for gaffes was apparent when he addressed an audience of LGBTQ+ activists. He joked about gay men taking their husbands 'up the Arcelor', the large red observation tower in Stratford's Olympic Park. He later apologised.

Johnson's successor as prime minister, Liz Truss, did not become an MP until 2010 and so does not have a voting record on Section 28. However, Truss voted in favour of same-sex marriage in 2010, in 2013 and in 2019, when same-sex marriage was extended to Northern Ireland. She also voted to make same-sex marriage accessible to armed forces personnel outside the UK in 2014.

However, during her time as equalities minister (2019-2022), Truss oversaw the Conservative government's decision to exclude transgender people from the ban on conversion therapy. Although Truss reduced the cost of applying for a gender recognition certificate, she also abandoned plans to allow for gender self-identification, designed to help trans people to change their gender without medical approval. Her plans to reform the Gender Recognition Act 2004 were eventually scrapped, after members of the LGBTQ+ advisory board resigned under her tenure in protest against her views. Truss claimed that trans women are 'not women' and she believes in the right to restrict access to spaces on the basis of biological sex. Truss became the UK's shortest-serving prime minister, resigning on 20 October 2022 after just 45 days in office over decisions taken that were detrimental to the economy.

Rishi Sunak succeeded Truss. The MP for Richmond (Yorkshire) was elected to Parliament in 2015. After launching his bid to become prime minister, an ally of Sunak's claimed in the *Mail on Sunday* that, as PM, Sunak would urge schools to be 'more careful' on how LGBTQ+ topics are taught (Kelleher, 2022). On becoming PM on 25 October 2022,

Sunak appointed Suella Braverman as his home secretary; Braverman has claimed that gender dysphoria is spreading by social contagion in schools.

Taking part in a question-and-answer session on the Mumsnet website, Sunak was uncompromising in his views on transgender people. He asserted that, on gender, "biology is important, is fundamental" when it comes to toilets and sports. He went on to say he "absolutely" agreed with Johnson, who had been criticised for saying trans women should not compete in women's sports (Kelleher, 2022).

The initiator of Section 28, Margaret Thatcher, did not apologise, either for Section 28 or for her treatment of lesbians and gay people. As a Conservative peer, Thatcher was an infrequent attendee at the House of Lords as she was in poor health after suffering several strokes. However, one of Thatcher's last political acts was to attend the House of Lords debate in July 2003 and vote to retain Section 28 (Baker, 2022). Ten years after the repeal of Section 28, in April 2013, Thatcher died at the Ritz Hotel in London, where she was living. Might Thatcher have also apologised for Section 28 had she still been alive in 2022? Who knows, but somehow I doubt it.

In chapter 7, I explore what, if anything, changed for lesbian and gay teachers in schools once Section 28 had been repealed. I also draw on my research with lesbian and gay teachers in 2018 to argue that Section 28 continues to cast a long shadow in schools and has left a damaging legacy for all those teachers who experienced it.

CHAPTER 7
THE LEGACY OF SECTION 28 FOR LESBIAN AND GAY TEACHERS

Despite the apologies from Conservative leaders and a new era of acceptance for the LGBTQ+ community, in the years after Section 28, schools remained entrenched in a culture of caution and confusion over lesbian and gay identities. Consequently, very little progress was made towards lesbian and gay inclusion in schools.

Three years after the repeal of Section 28, a survey by the Teacher Support Network found that 80% of gay and lesbian teachers had experienced homophobia in their school workplace. Abuse ranged from offensive jokes to physical assault, with 86% of victims reporting that pupils were the worst offenders and 17% saying they were too scared to go to work.

The survey found that 43% of gay and lesbian teachers had experienced homophobia from colleagues, 40% from their managers, 14% from pupils' parents and 6% from school governors (Press Association, 2006).

Ten years after Section 28, Emily Gray too presented a picture of largely heterosexual school leaders who were disinclined to support teachers who wished to come out as lesbian or gay to their students. Gray (2013) identified many acts of resistance by heterosexual school leaders, including the refusal to hold Pride assemblies, failing to use the word 'homophobia' in a report on bullying, and even furtively removing books with LGBTQ+ themes from school libraries.

Ann Hardie (2012) found that malicious stereotypes about lesbian teachers were stubbornly persistent in schools. She argued that these malevolent tropes served to keep sexualities secret in the school workplace. Hardie, a lesbian PE teacher, describes not declaring her own lesbian identity in school because she feared being accused of child abuse:

> *I felt on edge and vulnerable because of my sexuality; thus, I made sure I never supervised showers and, in this way, I maintained a professional boundary that prevented the possibility of any allegation of sexual impropriety or paedophilia.* (p.274)

Writing for the Herts for Learning blog in 2022, Michael Gray recalls his experiences as a teacher in 2011 and the way in which the repeal of Section 28 was ignored by his headteacher. Gray states:

> *Even after Section 28 had been repealed, it left a legacy. In my second year of teaching, I remember being summoned to the Head's office. He had been informed – by anxious parents – that there were rumours in the playground that I was gay. He stated that he had no problem with this at all, but advised me, very firmly, to keep my private life and my professional life separate. This issue was then never spoken of again. This was 2011 – eight years after Section 28 had finally been repealed.*
>
> *In retrospect, I'm angry. I'm livid. Throughout my life I was made to feel as if I were an embarrassment. I was made to feel like I was abnormal and, worst of all, I felt alone. However, I was also lucky: I had and still have a very loving and supportive family. I had good friends at school – without whom life could have been far worse. In fact, I probably owe far more to my friends and family than I could ever know. But what happened to the children who were not as lucky as me? I am sure that there were thousands of children during those years who were totally alienated from society, who felt abnormal, who felt ashamed and who felt alone. All this – in large part – from one piece of legislation which, in my opinion, caused more destruction than we can possibly imagine.*

Two years earlier, in 2009, I left a 21-year career as a teacher in schools under very similar circumstances to those described by Gray. Section 28 had long since been repealed and a raft of equalities legislation was in place to protect my rights as a lesbian teacher in the school workplace.

However, a parent complained about my sexuality to my headteacher; like Gray's head, he failed to protect me and left me completely without support. Some years later, I wrote an account of this incident for the book *Heteronormativity in a Rural School Community* (Thompson-Lee, 2017). Here is an extract:

> *In June 2009, the Freemans moved in next door to the Suffolk cottage my partner Jo and I shared. Theirs was the only other property for half a mile and, after the summer break, the Freeman family enrolled three of their six children at the school at which I was assistant headteacher. The Freemans had a garden of six acres, but placed a trampoline immediately abutting our boundary, no more than 15 feet from our kitchen and bedroom windows. The Freeman children loved the trampoline, not least I'm sure because when jumping they got an intermittent view of their teacher and her female partner. After worrying about it for weeks, Jo and I decided to go and introduce ourselves and welcome the Freemans to the village, hoping in the process for an opportunity to mention the trampoline issue.*

> *Mr Freeman showed us around the grounds of his new property and Jo sensitively broached the subject of the trampoline, explaining that I was a teacher at the school his children attended and that it was important for his children and for me that professional and personal boundaries did not become blurred. Mr Freeman moved the trampoline, we thanked him for appreciating our position and rounded off the encounter in a cordial and neighbourly manner.*

> *Later that evening, banging on the front door interrupted our conversation. Mr Freeman was pacing on and off the doorstep shouting that he would not be told what to do by a pair of lesbians and was going to make our lives a living misery. We stood paralysed as Mr Freeman spat out more and more frustrated threats.*

> *The following weeks were unhappy and uncomfortable. Though no further words were exchanged with the Freemans, Mr Freeman pursued and provoked us at every opportunity. He called us 'dykes' and 'lesbians'; he urinated in our garden, appeared at our windows late at night, and tried to run us off the narrow country lanes in his enormous black four-wheel drive. We staunchly attempted to enjoy the*

summer sunshine, but we had become an obsession to Mr Freeman. He shouted, howled, or laughed loudly and inexplicably at us. He threw things over the fence to startle us; on one occasion it was a bucket and on another the Freeman family bag of clothes pegs.

Inevitably, the Freeman children began to tell their friends at school that I was a lesbian. A teaching assistant told me that I had been the topic of conversation in the class she was attached to and before long the walk from my classroom to my office or the playground was an ordeal of student whispers and comments, perceived or real.

On 1 December 2009, my headteacher asked to see me in his office. As we walked together to his room he reassured me that it was nothing to worry about. As I closed the door, my headteacher said simply, 'A parent has been in.' I immediately suspected it would be Mr Freeman but fell silent as my head recalled the meeting. Mr Freeman had come into school to tell my headteacher that I was a lesbian and express concern that I was teaching. He had qualified his concern by alleging that I had been staring lustfully at his daughters on their trampoline.

I remained in the head's office unsure of how to proceed and began to tell him about the harassment from Mr Freeman at home. I let him know that Jo and I had put our house on the market and were trying to find a new home well away from Mr Freeman. I explained that I was too scared of retributions to contact the police about Mr Freeman but when we were eventually in a safe place, I intended to report his behaviour.

The headteacher looked worried, though I was to learn that he was not worried about me. His concern was for Mr Freeman. The headteacher said initially that I was overreacting and that it was 'no big deal'. I could not agree and firmly replied to the head that I hoped that when I reported Mr Freeman to the police, he would support me by telling the police about this visit to school. Annoyed at my challenge, the head snapped that his priority was to get along with Mr Freeman, particularly as he had so many children passing through the school. He added that, if and when I found myself in court, he had no intention of testifying on my behalf and my private life should be just that in school, private! As I made my way out of the headteacher's office, he added: your personal life is nothing to do with school, so keep us out of it.

This extract shows that heterosexual school leaders like mine and the one Michael Gray worked for appeared to be largely unaware of the repeal of Section 28. Or perhaps they were aware, but chose not to move on from a culture of pervasive homophobia created during Section 28 and still stubbornly entrenched in schools. Whatever the reason, despite equalities legislation protecting gay and lesbian teachers, I learned that parent power was far more compelling to my headteacher than his duty to me, his colleague.

The spirit of Section 28 continued in government guidance for schools on sex and relationships education (SRE). New Labour's concession in the Education and Skills Act 2000, which helped to get Section 28 repealed, left schools with a policy stating that teaching about same-sex relationships was inappropriate.

After a coalition of Conservatives and Liberal Democrats ousted the New Labour government in the 2010 general election, financial incentives were offered to schools to become academies and sit outside local authority control. A policy on free schools soon followed, encouraging parents and local community groups to set up schools that, like academies, were not required to adhere to the policies and practices of the local authority. In August 2013, a decade after the repeal of Section 28, LGBTQ+ activists working with the British Humanist Society identified 46 schools in England with SRE policies that either replicated Section 28 or stated that the law was still in force (Baker, 2022).

Despite these pockets of poor practice, schools have generally made progress towards LGBTQ+ inclusion since the repeal of Section 28. In guidance to schools in England entitled 'Inspecting teaching of the protected characteristics in schools' (2021), Ofsted states:

The Public Sector Equality Duty in section 149 of the Equality Act 2010 requires Ofsted, when exercising all our functions, to have due regard to the need to:

- *eliminate discrimination, harassment, victimisation and any other conduct that is prohibited by or under the Equality Act 2010*

- *advance equality of opportunity between persons who share a relevant protected characteristic and persons who do not share it*
- *foster good relations between persons who share a relevant protected characteristic and persons who do not share it*

The guidance goes on to cite examples of how primary and secondary schools might include teaching about LGBT identities in the curriculum. Kathryn Rhodes (2020) observes, however, that despite the introduction of laws and policies to protect LGBTQ+ teachers in the school workplace, limited legal recognition and protection is offered to lesbian and gay teachers who work in faith schools. Rhodes cites the example of a Conservative government guidance document entitled *Staffing and Employment Advice for Schools*, which makes special dispensation for the employment status of teachers on the grounds of religious belief in voluntary-aided schools. The guidance states:

> *6.1 The governing body in a voluntary-aided school may give preference with regard to the appointment, remuneration and promotion of teachers at the school, to persons:*
>
> - *whose religious opinions are in accordance with the tenets of the school's religion; ...*
>
> *6.2 The governing body may also have regard, in connection with the termination of the employment of a teacher at the school, to any conduct by the teacher which is incompatible with the precepts of, or with the upholding of the tenets of the school's religion.* (Department for Education, 2021)

Rhodes points out that governing bodies in schools with a religious foundation must 'ensure that the application of these powers does not contravene employment law' (6.8). Nevertheless, under the government's caveat for faith schools, it is difficult to conceive of a faith school environment in which lesbian and gay identities are condemned in religious doctrine yet lesbian and gay teachers feel sufficiently comfortable to be out in such a school workplace.

The 2021 Ofsted guidance on teaching the protected characteristics sheds a little more light on the position of LGBTQ+ identities and teaching in faith schools. It states:

[Faith] schools are at liberty to teach the tenets of any faith on the protected characteristics. For example, they may explain that same-sex relationships and gender reassignment are not permitted by a particular religion. However, if they do so, they must also explain the legal rights LGBT people have under UK law, and that this and LGBT people must be respected. (Ofsted, 2021)

THE LASTING IMPACT OF SECTION 28

My own research in 2018 with LGBTQ+ teachers across the UK identified that Section 28 had left a damaging legacy for those who experienced it. To coincide with the 15th anniversary of the repeal of Section 28, I sought to investigate how LGBTQ+ teachers experienced their workplaces, via a survey of 105 teachers who self-identified as LGBTQ+. Implicit within the research was an appreciation that a complex network of factors has a bearing on the way in which LGBTQ+ teachers experience their school workplaces. Experiences varied according to geographical and demographic factors, as well as type of school, age range taught, and the age, status and level of confidence of the LGBTQ+ teacher.

The study aimed to reach a wide range of LGBTQ+ teachers across England, providing a forum in which they could anonymously reveal, should they wish, quite personal details about their sexual and gender identities without fear of being identified. The questionnaire consisted of multiple-choice, closed, structured and unstructured questions. The UK's leading lesbian lifestyle magazine, *Diva*, promoted the survey online and in print but no equivalent magazine or online outlet for gay men did this. The result was that the majority of participants were lesbian, bisexual or queer women, comprising 85 of the 105 taking part.

The data showed that the participants had spent between one and 36 years in teaching, with the average career spanning 13.5 years; 39% of respondents taught in the primary phase and 58% in secondary schools. The other 3% taught in all-through schools (schools for students aged 4-18) or in early years or preschool education.

I expected and hoped to find a workplace culture in schools that had largely recovered from the constraints of Section 28. As I analysed the results, I noticed a stark difference in responses between LGBTQ+ teachers (young and mature) who had entered teaching after Section 28 and those who were still in teaching after experiencing Section 28 first-hand. For the purpose of comparison, these teachers are referred to as either 'Section 28 teachers', meaning they taught between 1988 and 2003, or 'post-2003 teachers', meaning Section 28 had been repealed before they entered the teaching profession.

Participants were initially asked which school stakeholders were aware of their sexual or gender identity. Only 20% of Section 28 teachers indicated being out to all school colleagues; this contrasted with 88% of post-2003 teachers. Meanwhile, 45% of post-2003 teachers were out to their students, compared with only 20% of Section 28 teachers.

Some of the Section 28 teachers who were not out to students described their frustration at not being able to be a role model to young people. One respondent stated:

> I know that I have a responsibility to LGBTQ+ kids in school and it upsets me when I see them struggling like I did … but I worry what parents will think of me if I try to help. Sometimes I feel like I'd be viewed as a predator or something. (Section 28 lesbian teacher)

A small number of post-2003 teachers, but no Section 28 teachers, described running Pride clubs and other extracurricular activities for LGBTQ+ students and allies at school. Post-2003 teachers also seemed less concerned about parental perceptions of their sexual and gender identity than their Section 28 peers, for whom parental complaints were a recurring fear. This post-2003 teacher was confident that the law would protect her:

> Stuff them – we've a duty to look after all kids at the end of [the] day – the law is on our side! (Post-2003 bisexual secondary school teacher)

Many of the LGBTQ+ teachers described grappling with an internal paradox in which they wished to come out to students to dispel the myths, speculation and gossip they knew surrounded them, while simultaneously feeling compelled to keep their sexual or gender identity private because of the hetero- and cis-normative power perpetuating the silence. Section 28 teachers, especially those in secondary schools, wrote of feeling guilty about not being able to come out in the workplace, perceiving largely that they had failed in their duties as role models for LGBTQ+ students.

The survey asked whether participants lived inside the school catchment area – the geographical location from which the school takes its students. The differences between the Section 28 teachers and post-2003 teachers were notable. Just 18% of the Section 28 teachers lived within their school's catchment area, compared with 43% of the post-2003 teachers. Section 28 teachers described guarding their privacy fiercely and creating elaborate ways of being that separated their personal and professional identities and ensured they never collided. One Section 28 teacher said:

> *I keep my home life and school life apart. I don't want to bump into kids and their parents when I'm out with my girlfriend. I want to be as far away from school as possible when I'm being my gay self.* (Section 28 lesbian secondary school teacher)

Section 28 lesbian and gay teachers guarded their privacy outside school in order to create a safe space and actively protect themselves against public scrutiny or interest in their personal lives (Thompson-Lee, 2017). Living outside the school catchment area is one way in which the participants in this study achieved the privacy they needed. There were fundamental differences in the way in which the Section 28 and post-2003 teachers engaged socially within their school communities – for example, at end-of-year events or celebrations. When asked whether they took their same-sex partner to school social functions, 60% of Section 28 teachers reported never taking their partner to school social events and no Section 28 teacher always took their partner. This contrasted sharply with the responses of post-2003 teachers: almost three-quarters usually took their partner to a school event. One Section 28 teacher described how he struggled with school social and celebration events, adding that this had curtailed any plans he had to become a school leader:

> *I don't ever want to be a headteacher, it's all the social events that put me off. Can you imagine, the head turning up to the Christmas play with his boyfriend? But then not having a partner there would look equally weird.* (Section 28 gay male primary school teacher)

Section 28 teachers described additional challenges at the intersection of their personal and private selves. Only one-fifth of Section 28 teachers said they were able to be completely themselves in the classroom, while half of their post-2003 counterparts said they were able to be their authentic selves. Lisa Edwards et al. (2016) state that when self-censorship occurs for LGBTQ+ teachers, heterosexuality is the only sexual identity represented to young people and this denies them LGBTQ+ role models.

A similar picture emerged when participants described their relationship with the school staffroom. While 88% of post-2003 teachers said they were completely themselves in the staffroom, only 60% of Section 28 teachers said the same. David Nixon and Nick Givens (2007) argue that Section 28 imposed a narrow view of sexuality on schools that, in calling lesbian and gay relationships 'pretended', privileged the heterosexual family and the institute of marriage (which at that time was only permitted between a man and woman).

The teachers taking part in the study were asked whether they thought their sexual and teacher identities were compatible. Just 12% of post-2003 teachers thought the two identities were very incompatible, compared with 40% of Section 28 teachers. Fifteen years after the repeal of Section 28, it was apparent that those teachers who had worked under the legislation continued to spend inordinate amounts of time and energy managing the point at which their personal and private identities met. Section 28 teachers continued to be cautious and actively self-censored in their conversations with colleagues. As a consequence, they reported often feeling isolated and lacking a sense of belonging in their school community. Two Section 28 teachers described some of the behaviours they continued daily in school:

> *Sometimes when I'm teaching, I find myself stopping mid-sentence to check that what I'm planning to say isn't going to out me to the kids. I must appear very strange to them sometimes.* (Section 28 gay male primary school teacher)

> *Some parents think gay teachers shouldn't be in the classroom and I'm worried about what might get back to them all the time. It's easier to keep myself to myself in the classroom and the staffroom.* (Section 28 lesbian primary school teacher)

LGBTQ+ teachers often find that in separating out the personal from the professional, they enter into an implicit 'don't ask, don't tell' contract with their school community. Originating in the US military in 1993, during the Clinton administration, and lasting until 2011, the 'don't ask, don't tell' policy was perceived initially as an act of tolerance by the left-wing Democrats. The policy stated that lesbian and gay military personnel could serve in the military provided they did not make a declarative statement about their sexuality. According to Eric Anderson (2002), 'don't ask, don't tell' proved that 'what cannot be discussed is just as powerful a weapon of heterosexual hegemony as what can be discussed' (p.874). Renee DePalma and Elizabeth Atkinson (2009) applied 'don't ask, don't tell' to schools and argued that its pseudo-tolerance serves as a powerful heteronormative discursive practice in schools. When a teacher is not given the opportunity to speak their authentic self into existence in the school workplace, they are literally silenced, falsely perpetuating the 'heterosexist assumption that all teachers and parents are heterosexual, and all girls and boys will grow up and eventually (want to) marry a person of the opposite sex' (DePalma & Atkinson, 2009, p.839).

All the LGBTQ+ teacher participants in my research described being cautious when applying for positions in new schools. One post-2003 teacher commented:

> *I haven't faced explicit homophobia in my workplace, but I find that my applications for new jobs go further when I do not include [reference to] my school LGBTQ+ inclusion work.* (Post-2003 gay male secondary school teacher)

In common with this teacher's experience, Adele Bates (2018) found that when teachers showed links to the LGBTQ+ community on their CV – by mentioning past voluntary work with an LGBTQ+ organisation, for example – they were less likely to be invited to a job interview.

My research investigated the perceptions of the LGBTQ+ teachers of homophobia and the use of homophobic language in their schools. The results were quite unexpected: 38% of post-2003 teachers reported experiencing homophobia within the past five years of their careers, compared with only 20% of Section 28 teachers. There are a number of possible explanations for this. One may be that post-2003 teachers perceive homophobia more acutely than their Section 28 counterparts, who endured teaching in more challenging and overtly homophobic times. Alternatively, perhaps those post-2003 teachers who are out at work do not hear homophobia, as colleagues and students curb their language when in their presence. This was borne out in a comment from a post-2003 lesbian teacher who was out to her students and suggested that her students regulate their language because they know she is gay:

> *I do hear comments now and again, usually it's teasing and banter between kids. Since I've come out at school, a few of them do stop themselves or apologise if they say something inappropriate in front of me.* (Post-2003 lesbian secondary school teacher)

The comment demonstrates the power and importance of exposure to diversity and diverse role models when it comes to promoting inclusion in schools.

The Section 28 teachers appeared to experience the school workplace more negatively than their post-2003 peers, but seemed to have accepted homophobia as an endemic part of working in a school. This was reflected in responses to the question 'Have you ever left a teaching role because of homophobia or heteronormativity?' While 15% of post-2003 teachers reported leaving a role due to homophobia or heteronormativity, none of the Section 28 respondents had done so. Although Section 28 teachers reported more significant challenges in the school workplace, they also appeared more resigned to the status quo. The two quotations below, one from a post-2003 teacher and another from a Section 28 teacher, reflect quite separate expectations of their school workplace.

> *I should be able to bring my whole self to work. I couldn't stay at a school if I had to keep details of my private life a secret. If anyone had a problem with me I'd expect my Head to back me 100%.* (Post-2003 bisexual secondary school teacher)

> *I keep myself to myself at school. In the early days, I used to make up girlfriends but now I can't be bothered to lie, so I don't tell anybody anything about my life outside school.* (Section 28 gay male secondary school teacher)

Some LGBTQ+ teachers still make inordinate amounts of effort to assimilate into the heteronormative school environment, adding a layer of additional stress on top of an already demanding job. All teachers can feel under surveillance by colleagues and students from time to time, but for LGBTQ+ teachers this surveillance can feel constant and over time may become overwhelming. LGBTQ+ teachers who keep their sexual or gender identities private live in a constant state of anxiety, fearing that their personal life may be thrust into the public domain (Thompson-Lee, 2017; Neary, 2013). Homophobic harassment, posts on social media or, in the Section 28 era, graffiti on desks or classroom walls show how some LGBTQ+ teachers may become 'visible in circumstances not of [their] choosing' (Mason & Tomsen, 1997, p.28).

When a homophobic comment about an LGBTQ+ teacher is made or written, their sexuality becomes explicit in space and time whether online or in the physical school environment. For example, websites like Rate My Teachers have presided over the outing of staff in a way that is indelible and damaging for those teachers named.

In my study, the LGBTQ+ teachers were asked whether they had ever accessed help for anxiety or depression linked to their sexual or gender identities and role as a teacher. They were also asked to disclose whether their anxiety or depression had led them to take time off work. Almost half (48%) of Section 28 teachers reported having suffered from anxiety or depression linked to their sexuality and role as a teacher, but none had been absent from work as a consequence of this. Half as many post-2003 teachers (24%) reported suffering from anxiety or depression but, in contrast to Section 28 teachers, one in five said they had taken time off work as a consequence. One post-2003 teacher described the challenges she had faced:

> *I seem to burn out much quicker than everyone else but it feels like because I'm gay, I'm trying to manage lots of things on top of my job. I feel guilty half the time for not being a role model for the students that are struggling with their sexuality, but at the same time feel terrified when I think about the parent power at my school.* (Post-2003 lesbian all-through teacher)

Among the general teaching population, an average of 18% access help for anxiety or depression (Education Support Partnership, 2018), meaning that both the post-2003 (24%) and Section 28 (48%) teachers are over-represented here. Ilan Meyer (2003) identified that minority stress was a significant and often recurring feature of the lives of LGBTQ+ people. Paula Mayock et al. (2009) concurred, noting that the concealment of sexual or gender identity becomes routine or normalised over time, and it is then challenging for a person to revise their position. Meyer (2003) observes that a sense of harmony with one's environment is the basis for good mental health, adding that 'when the individual is a member of a stigmatised minority group, the disharmony between the individual and the dominant culture can be onerous and the resultant stress significant' (2003, p.676).

This research into the legacy of Section 28 has shown that LGBTQ+ teachers are prone to poor mental health, such as anxiety and depression, as a result of their compulsory participation in heteronormative social processes, social institutions and social structures, leading to repeated messages of exclusion (Meyer, 2003). Crucially, the self-reported rates of anxiety and depression by my participants show that those LGBTQ+ teachers who endured Section 28 suffer with poor mental health more acutely and chronically than those who entered teaching after Section 28 had been repealed.

The research also shows that the LGBTQ+ teachers who experienced teaching during Section 28 were still, some 15 years later, deeply affected by it. The Section 28 era created a legacy of caution, self-censorship and complex identity management that lingers for LGBTQ+ teachers today. Those who taught in schools during Section 28 are significantly less likely than their post-2003 peers to be out to school stakeholders such as colleagues, students and parents, and less likely to participate in school social activities, particularly with their partner. They remain less able to be themselves in the classroom and staffroom school environments than LGBTQ+ teachers who entered the profession after Section 28 had been repealed.

Section 28 teachers do appear to be more resilient or perhaps just more resigned to cope with school environments that are not inclusive. They are more practised at managing the intersection of their personal and professional identities, and achieve this in large part by separating the two aspects of their lives completely and carefully censoring the information they share with students and colleagues.

For 15 years, Section 28 served as the jewel in the crown of the Conservative party's return to family values. It created a toxic moral panic in schools that positioned every young person and their lesbian or gay teacher in a preposterous binary of potential victim of abuse and potential groomer/abuser. The legacy of Section 28 has endured and the teachers most affected by it continue to withstand professional and personal dissonance, adversely impacting their mental health.

In the concluding chapter of part I of this book, I consider the phrase 'pretended family relationship' from Section 28. I explore how the description of same-sex relationships as 'pretended' invalidated lesbian and gay couples and their families for a generation.

CHAPTER 8
PRETENDED FAMILY RELATIONSHIPS

Section 28 prohibited schools and local authorities from promoting homosexuality as a 'pretended family relationship'. Lord Halsbury was the original architect of Section 28 and it is worth reminding ourselves of its wording:

(1) A local authority shall not –

(a) intentionally promote homosexuality or publish material with the intention of promoting homosexuality;

(b) promote the teaching in any maintained school of the acceptability of homosexuality as a pretended family relationship.

The inclusion of the word 'pretended' in the Halsbury bill, first as Clause 28 and eventually Section 28 of the Local Government Act 1988, was debated long and hard in the House of Lords on 16 February 1988. To illuminate the meaning of the phrase 'pretended family relationship', the Hansard parliamentary transcripts show that Halsbury offered a few words of clarification. He said:

We all learnt at school – did we not? – of the Old Pretender and the Young Pretender? What does 'pretender' mean in that context? Somebody who makes the pretence of claiming to the throne or whatever it may be? This is a claimed family relationship and that is the reason for the choice of the word 'pretended', which seems to me to be fully justified by its dictionary meaning.

Halsbury's comment appears to contend that those in same-sex relationships had wrongfully claimed the term 'family' and as such were pretenders, with no right to use the word to describe their partnerships, even when they had children. However, like Section 28 itself, Halsbury's assertions about the term 'pretended' were far from clear.

Lord Monson, a cross-bench hereditary peer and a close ally of Halsbury, rushed to his aid during the debate, but in trying to offer clarity he rather contradicted his friend. Monson stated:

> I largely agree with my noble friend Lord Halsbury. I contend that Amendment No. 72 would give us the worst of all worlds. It would confine the restrictions which are to be imposed by Clause 28 solely to the question of homosexuality as a pretended family relationship, whatever that curious phrase may mean. Thereby it implies that promiscuous homosexual relationships – such as those which, until recently, were said to be found in the bathhouses of San Francisco and New York in which men were said to have sexual relations with 200 or 300 different men every year – are in some way preferable to stable, quasi-family homosexual relationships. Given the AIDS epidemic, that must appear to most people to be quite insane.

The Labour peer Lord Gifford was not comfortable with the inclusion of 'pretended family relationship' in the bill and presented a scenario in which the phrase could cause problems in the classroom. Gifford said:

> Where the child of a homosexual relationship was being bullied at school, any teacher who was trying to introduce tolerance, to help the child and to give it support, would be in terrible difficulty. Once the teacher sought to say, 'Don't worry. Your parents' relationship is one of many kinds of relationships in the world. There is nothing wrong with it. It is just different from other people's and you should not be bullied because of it', then that teacher would be raising in the classroom the 'acceptability of homosexuality as a pretended family relationship'.

Gifford went on to say that unless the local authority took action against that teacher for their attempts to introduce tolerance for diversity in the classroom, 'the authority will be in danger of being said to promote the teaching of homosexuality as a pretended family relationship'. In describing this scenario, Gifford exposed the way in which Section 28 would become almost impossible to navigate for all teachers. Lord Rea, a committed socialist and a GP in North London, used this debate about the word 'pretended' to talk about his own childhood in a so-called pretended family relationship with lesbian parents. Rea said:

> I was brought up by two women, one of them my mother, in an actual family relationship. There was no pretence there ... It was a good family, and I maintain that there is nothing intrinsically wrong with a homosexual couple bringing up a child. I consider that I had as rich and as happy a childhood as most children who are reared by heterosexual couples, and far better than many I see in my daily practice as a doctor. I do not think any of the defects in my character, of which I have an average number, have arisen from my being brought up by two women. My sexual orientation is, I am told, also pretty average and so is that of my children.

Here Rea rejects the inclusion of the word 'pretended' in the bill, asserting that his childhood with two mothers was authentic and positive. Rea also challenges the bedrock of the Conservatives' attack on Labour's support for lesbian and gay people. At its root, Section 28 supposed that children could become homosexual through exposure to same-sex relationships. Rea is keen to point out that despite growing up in a lesbian family, he is heterosexual.

Baroness Seear, leader of the Liberal party in the House of Lords, also called for the removal of the word 'pretended', stressing her objection to the entire bill. She stated:

> My Lords, I do not wish to carp about the wording of paragraph (b). But even taking account of the changes that have been made and the fact that the wording now stops at the word 'relationship', it is most confusing. The term 'pretended family relationship' is still most unsatisfactory. I do not like the clause. However, if the Minister insists on saying what he intends to say, would he not agree that some such words as 'promote the teaching of homosexuality in any maintained school as an acceptable basis for a family relationship', leaving out the word 'pretended', is much clearer and more acceptable? I do not like what the Government are trying to say, but if they are going

to say it, it should be said in a way that is clear and makes sense. I suggest that my wording is better than the term 'pretended family relationship'.

The Conservative peer Malcolm Sinclair, Earl of Caithness, wished to see 'pretended' remain in the bill so that teachers could not imply same-sex relationships were in any way comparable to heterosexual ones. Caithness said:

There is no attempt to deny that there exist relationships which have all the appearance of a normal family relationship but where two adults are of the same sex. The purpose of the phrase 'teaching … the acceptability of homosexuality as a pretended family relationship' is to indicate that the local authorities should not be using their powers … to encourage the teaching that relationships between two people of the same sex can and should play the same role in society as the traditional family.

Later, Caithness pointed his colleagues towards the importance of the word 'family' when compared with 'pretended'. He added:

The word 'family' is an essential element of the phrase we are discussing. We are not concerned with pretended relationships. There is no doubt that two people of the same sex living as part of the same household have a relationship. There is nothing pretended about it. The word 'pretended' in the phrase relates more to the concept that such a relationship is a conventional family relationship or the portrayal of it is as equally valid as the traditional family relationship.

Lord Willis, a Labour peer and a critic of Section 28, called 'pretended' a 'dirty word' when partnered with the word 'relationship'. He added that the clause was 'a bit of a dog's breakfast'. It is difficult to disagree with him.

The inclusion of the phrase 'pretended family relationship' in Section 28 is worthy of exploration beyond the House of Lords. Sasha Roseneil and Shelley Budgeon (2004), writing soon after the repeal of Section 28, state that 'the idea of family retains an almost unparalleled ability to move people, both emotionally and politically' (p.135). Lauren Berlant and Michael Warner (1998) argue that heteronormative societal belonging is constructed through the restriction of 'a historical relation to futurity' (p.554) and a discourse that privileges a generational narrative that centres on reproduction. It is this focus on reproduction and future generations that gives the heterosexual family its privileged status.

Section 28 was the first time in law that the family was explicitly assigned as only being heterosexual and the first legislation to describe gay and lesbian unions as pretended. Tamsin Wilton (1995) recognises the absurdity of this, stating that 'the implication that a lesbian mother may only pretend to a family relationship with her child exposes with appalling viciousness the extent to which a homophobic administration is simply able to write homosexuals out of the human race' (p.192).

Throughout the entire Section 28 era there was no legal or spiritual way of recognising same-sex relationships. Same-sex couples could not adopt children together until 2002, and were not entitled to IVF and embryology treatment on the same basis as heterosexual couples until 2009. In the 1980s, relationships between lesbians and gay men were largely seen as existing outside the family, if they were visible at all. Same-sex couples adopted creative and euphemistic ways of describing their relationships, usually with the aim of avoiding detection. For example, lesbians or gay men living together were commonly referred to as housemates or flatmates. Many would set up two bedrooms in their home to convince visitors that they did not share a bed.

However, evidence and opinion abound contending that, despite Section 28 attempting to wipe lesbian and gay couples from public consciousness, same-sex couples and families reacted by doing family differently. David Morgan (2011) argues in favour of 'family' as a verb. He refers to family as a set of practices that can create a social dynamic that troubles the traditional and heteronormative notion of the family as a social construct. Morgan observes that 'contemporary families are defined more by "doing" family things than by "being" a family' (p.178). Modern notions of family, especially in same-sex relationships, recognise the importance of personal networks that over time become the primary source of emotional, financial and social support (Takasaki, 2017). According to Kathleen Hull and Timothy Ortyl (2019), lesbian and gay families are confluent, drawing on expansive and innovative strategies that often exist outside biological family ties.

123

It was commonplace during the Section 28 era for some lesbian and gay people to be rejected by their families of origin. Small-c conservative parents would ask an adult child known to be lesbian or gay to leave the family home for fear of bringing shame on the family. In such circumstances, lesbian and gay people often looked to friends to replicate the support networks lost through their rejection by their families of origin. Since the repeal of Section 28 and other legislative and cultural advances for lesbian and gay people, it is far less common for families of origin to react negatively to a family member coming out as LGBTQ+. However, Hull and Ortyl (2019) observe that families of choice still exist for same-sex couples, but rather than being a replacement for families of origin, they often complement them with distinct shared connections and mutual support over an extended period of time.

The climate for lesbian and gay people in the 1980s was hostile enough that some individuals, despite knowing they were not heterosexual, entered into marriage and parenthood with a partner of the opposite sex. Inevitably, some of these relationships broke down, with lesbians and gay people coming out in later life and introducing children from heterosexual marriages to their same-sex partners when the courts permitted this. Sara Eldén (2016) explored the understanding of family by children, finding that children consider those who provide them with care as their families regardless of biological ties.

In the North of England, where I grew up, the titles of 'auntie' and 'uncle' were used as a mark of respect for the friends of my parents. It was common in the 1980s and 90s to refer to neighbours, family friends and people your parents saw regularly as 'auntie' and 'uncle'. As well as showing respect, it denoted a closeness established over the years as these people looked after you and spent time in your home. These aunties and uncles, though clearly without biological ties, were never referred to as 'pretend' or 'pretended'.

Stephen Russell (2019) observes that our heteronormative society sanctions those kinds of families that are permitted and those that are not, reasoning that when caregivers and supporters in the lives of others are not recognised by the communities in which they are based, this can have negative implications for the health and wellbeing of individuals.

Throughout the Section 28 era, the insistence that same-sex relationships were 'pretended' was compounded by the lack of appropriate language to describe caretaking relationships beyond the heterosexual family.

Like many same-sex couples, my partner, Jo, and I entered a civil partnership shortly after this was made legal in 2004, desperate to safeguard our financial security should one of us die unexpectedly. At the time, civil partnerships seemed like a major development towards lesbian and gay inclusion. Looking back, however, this legislation was deeply flawed. My first issue with civil partnerships is that, as a descriptor of one's status, it hardly trips off the tongue. Civil partnerships did not provide an equivalent adjective to 'married' and this caused the terms 'civil partnered' or, worse, 'civilly partnered' to enter common parlance. The former is austere, business-like and awkward in its phrasing; the latter suggests that courtesy and good manners form the basis of the union.

My second and more important issue with civil partnerships is that in declaring that one was in a civil partnership, one had to come out as lesbian or gay. The failure to name the union of a same-sex couple as marriage served to further secure the dominance of heteronormativity by positioning the civil partnership as a 'pretend' marriage. Celia Kitzinger and Sue Wilkinson (2004) state that 'the re-branding of marriage as "civil partnership" was useful to governments in enabling them to extend rights to, and control over, same-sex relationships while reserving the privileged status of "marriage" for heterosexuals only' (p.127).

Jacqueline Hudak and Shawn Giammattei (2010) call for a 'decentering' (p.55) of the family. Drawing on Judith Butler's theory of gender performativity (1990), they reject essentialist notions of the family and, like Morgan (2011), argue for family as a performative act in which fluid, ambiguous and diverse representations can prevail. Amaryll Perlesz et al. (2006) argue that conceiving of family as a performative act creates possibilities for relating and parenting outside the bounds of the heterosexual family. According to Hudak and Giammattei (2010), the performative act of family or 'doing family' (p.53) entails 'intentionally committing to add elements of responsibility and caretaking to the bonds of love, which usually embody roles traditionally assigned to kinship networks' (p.52). 'Doing family' transforms it from a static essentialist entity into a verb, encouraging new representations of caretaking and responsibility within loving relationships.]

Kathryn Rhodes (2020) posits that after the repeal of Section 28 in 2003, the family as a heterosexual-only construct started to unravel. However, same-sex couples would have to wait for 11 years after the repeal of Section 28 to have the 'pretend' descriptor finally lifted from their families, through the introduction of same-sex marriage in 2014.

As a lesbian and teacher for every year of Section 28, I contend that under this law, it was not just our families that were 'pretended'. Section 28 required us to pretend in almost every aspect of our professional lives as teachers, while the personal and professional lives of our heterosexual peers authentically overlapped and coexisted happily.

So how else did we, as lesbian and gay teachers, pretend in schools throughout Section 28? In my school workplaces, I pretended to live alone. It was custom and practice in staffrooms back then for colleagues to openly ask questions and make assumptions about one's private life. If one was unmarried by the age of 30, eyebrows began to be raised. If a housemate or flatmate appeared to have become a semi-permanent fixture, eyebrows were raised further. Although I lived with my partner in the house that we co-owned and shared, I coached myself to never refer to 'we' or 'us' at school, only to 'I' and 'me'. This, of course, led to some strange and strained conversations at break times. I would say *I* had been on holiday, or *I* had been out for a meal, or *I* had spent a weekend away in a hotel. How strange I must have seemed, doing all these things alone. However, at the time, it was better that my colleagues thought of me as strange than as a lesbian.]

Constantly reminding myself to use 'I', not 'we', and believing I was perceived as a loner, made me feel very self-conscious at school. I coped by pretending to be a private person who did not want to talk about my life outside school. Eventually, I revealed almost nothing about my life outside school and became adept at flipping the 'What did you do at the weekend?' question as soon as it was asked. Inevitably, pretending to be a private person became suffocating. I was hard work to sit with at break and lunch times because I was completely wooden, lacking in personality and devoid of fun. I was rarely invited on nights out as my colleagues believed, quite reasonably, that I was solitary and preferred it that way.

Early on in my teaching career, I tried making up boyfriends. The senior leadership team in my first school, a Catholic convent, were all nuns. Once they had given up hope that I might be saved and enter the convent, the nuns were determined that I should meet a nice young man. Some of the mostly female staff had met their husbands via a local walking group called the Catholic Ramblers. In common with many young people, I hated walking and, anyway, I wasn't even Catholic. So, I lied to the nuns (I'm crossing myself as I write this) and told them I had a boyfriend. My partner's name at the time was Julia, so when I was asked the name of my boyfriend, I simply called him Julian. Perfect! For a while, I felt liberated. I opened up a little in the staffroom about my life outside school. But I have a terrible memory and, as I let down my guard, I inevitably kept forgetting the 'n' on the end of Julia.

I also pretended throughout Section 28 not to hear homophobic language at school. Students often called each other 'dyke', 'faggot', 'homo', 'queer', and while I always intervened if I heard heteronormative name-calling such as 'slag' or 'dickhead', I made myself deaf to the homophobic slurs. To intervene when I heard homophobic name-calling was much too risky. The only teachers who could pull this off were the maternal, married, middle-aged ones who everyone knew were straight.

Finally, I pretended throughout Section 28 not to be ambitious or interested in school leadership. This was because becoming a headteacher involved a level of visibility that I did not believe would ever be open to me. The mostly male headteachers that I knew took their wives to the Christmas concert or summer fete and were pillars of the school community. Looking back, being a closeted lesbian was not conducive to being promoted at any level, as I tried at all times to remain as invisible as possible at school. To avoid staffroom conversations, I eventually would take myself off to Tesco at lunchtime or sit in my car and eat my packed lunch. Anything to avoid the stress of the staffroom and the pretence of trying to be someone I was not.

These recollections lead me into part II of this book. Having explored the historical and political landscape of Section 28 for lesbian and gay teachers, I now draw on the social and cultural climate of the time in a series of personal reflections. Beginning part II in 1979 with Margaret

Thatcher's election to prime minister, I go on to present diary extracts from each of the years that Section 28 was law. You will read of out-and-out homophobia and of other incidents that were only mildly uncomfortable. Each diary entry begins by describing some of the political and cultural events affecting the LGBTQ+ community in the UK and around the world.

If you were also a teacher during Section 28, my recollections may remind you of what school was like back then. If you attended school as a pupil between 1988 and 2003, you will get a sense of why you never had lesbian and gay teacher role models or learned about lesbian and gay people through the school curriculum. Whatever your personal history and interest in this book, I hope I can convey to you why, 20 years after the repeal of Section 28, we must not forget it. We should do everything in our power to ensure legislation of this nature is never passed again.

PART II

THE SECTION 28 DIARIES:
PERSONAL AND CULTURAL
PERSPECTIVES

INTRODUCTION

Part II represents a significant departure from the tone of this book so far. Here I reflect personally on my own experiences as a lesbian teacher throughout the Section 28 era.

As someone who has the dubious achievement of having taught in schools for every year of Section 28, I want to do what I could not do back then: tell my story. Covering in turn each of the years that Section 28 was law, I describe the cultural or political landscape for LGBTQ+ people and then share one of my own diary entries from that year that relates directly or indirectly to Section 28. I reflect on how the incident described affected me as a teacher and a person. To protect the identities of the people who appear in my diary entries, I have changed names, some dates and, where necessary, certain details of the events.

I hope that by sharing my personal recollections, I can help those who were not previously aware of Section 28 to understand how it affected me and countless other teachers. And I hope that the generation of people who attended school during Section 28 will learn why they had no lesbian or gay teacher role models, no pastoral support for their sexual identities, and never saw any lesbian or gay people in their school curriculum.

Lots of brave people protested against Section 28 in marches up and down the country. As a teacher, the legislation affected me more directly than many of those who stood up proudly in opposition to it; however, I did not march or protest. I hope that part II will explain why I could not march but how thankful I am to those who did.

I begin part II some nine years before the introduction of Section 28, in a significant year for the legislation. On 4 May 1979, the UK's first female prime minister, Margaret Thatcher, came to power in Britain. Thatcher was to become a prominent and recurring figure in my childhood and early teaching career. I attended a secondary school in Dinnington, South Yorkshire. Dinnington was a small mining town that emerged and prospered as a result of its colliery. Most of the students at Dinnington had fathers or brothers who were miners and so, in the mid-1980s, when Thatcher moved to close the collieries in northern England, Dinnington was hit especially hard. The steel mills further afield in Sheffield, where my grandmother had worked and lost her eye in an accident, were also in decline, leaving the employment landscape in South Yorkshire decimated.

As miners were starved from the picket lines by Thatcher, the once bustling high street of Dinnington soon declined, as did associated industries and local businesses. I saw some of my friends at school fall into poverty because of Thatcher. I am haunted especially by memories of Gary, a boy in my form group whose school shoes were so worn out that they flapped open at the toe like two hungry mouths, revealing equally worn-out socks. Schools did not take responsibility for the social and pastoral care of students, as they do today, and to my knowledge teachers did not do anything to support Gary and the many, many other students who were left hungry and vulnerable because of the miners' strikes.

I was unaware until I watched the film *Pride* (2014) of the way in which the lesbian and gay community had rallied to support the striking miners. Based on a true story, *Pride* depicts a group of lesbian and gay activists who raised money to help families affected by the miners' strike in 1984, at the outset of what would later become the Lesbians and Gays Support the Miners campaign. It was heartening to learn about the ways in which one of the communities to which I belong had helped another.

1979

In 1979, the first screen kiss between two men on British TV featured in the BBC drama *Coming Out*. In the film, Lewis, a closeted gay writer of romantic novels, pens an article on gay issues under the pseudonym of Zippy Grimes. The article is a remarkable success and leads to correspondence from other gay men who are leading a double life. Lewis opts to meet some of these letter-writers and ultimately is forced to come out.

For me, personally, 1979 was the year in which my best friend, Richard, and I went our separate ways as secondary school beckoned. In 1979, I was carefree and happy in my own skin. Richard and I were so similar and close that he felt like my twin. We shared an interest in activities, most of which were traditionally male but some of which were not. Richard is now heterosexual and married, yet I am a lesbian. I have tried many times to reflect on this period of my life. Did my tomboy behaviour cause me to be a lesbian or was it, rather, an early sign that I was already gay?

AUGUST 1979. THE END OF A FRIENDSHIP

Richard and I are in the back garden enjoying our summer holiday extension to bedtime. We are chatting casually as we play our made-up ball game, which entails kicking a tennis ball to each other, with one touch only, through the simple post-and-rail fence that separates the small gardens behind our adjoining semi-detached houses. We are lifelong friends. We ride our bikes together, build dens on the building site of the new houses up the road and make up complicated games that only we can understand and play.

Richard and I call for each other every morning and walk to school together. Sometimes we write notes for each other that we exchange in the morning without self-consciousness. We read the notes silently as we walk side by side to school. The notes contain drawings of us together and simple statements about our friendship and our plans to be best friends forever.

As we play our game on this warm August evening, Richard's dad is working on his Ford Capri in the garage behind us. He has no shirt on and his thick jet-black hair is slicked back with Brylcreem. I think he looks like Elvis. Richard is scared of him and so I am scared of him too. Richard's dad watches us play our football/tennis ball game as he stands just inside the garage, wiping his oily hands on a rag. I catch his eye and smile at him as we play, but unusually I get a blank stare in return. Suddenly, he shouts, 'Richard. Here. Now!'

Richard immediately leaves our game and runs towards his dad in the garage. Unsure of whether to wait for him, I remain in the garden, picking up our tennis ball. I pull nervously at its yellow fluff and listen while they talk.

'You know it's about time you stopped playing with a girl. You're not a baby any more, and Jonno and Pete will call you a poof. She shouldn't be playing football either, it's not ladylike.' Glancing in my direction, but stopping short of addressing me directly, Richard's dad adds: 'You two need to leave each other alone now. Do you hear me?'

Richard's pale, frightened face nods in agreement. He stands by the garage, unsure of what to do next.

'Right. In. Bath time,' his dad says. Richard turns as if to casually wave to me, but then appears to think better of it and runs off into the house. I never play with Richard again.

I stand in the garden with our tennis ball and a handful of yellow fluff. Richard is my best friend. I don't really have any other friends. I wonder what I am going to do now.

I burst through our kitchen door and blurt out my account of events in the garden to my mum. Surely she will have a word with Richard's dad and sort it out for us. Mum tells me to keep my voice down as the walls between our 1960s semi-detached houses are thin. She listens to what I have to say but doesn't seem in the least bit surprised or concerned.

'Well, I think it's for the best,' she says. 'You'll be going to high school in September and it's about time you made friends with some girls. You know, Gail down the road seems a nice girl. Perhaps you could pal up with her.'

My mum has lost her mind. I raise my voice again: 'Gail? Gail? Why would I want to be friends with her? She hasn't even got a bike.'

Gail has angelic white-blonde hair and is insipid and pale. She is always off school ill, and her idea of play involves walking up and down our road in make-up wearing her mum's tights and high heels. Gail and I are not going to be friends.

But Richard doesn't call for me again and so, after a conversation between Gail's mum and mine, my 'free' time is spent imprisoned in Gail's pink bedroom listening to *Parallel Lines* by Blondie. I sit on Gail's bed and stare through the Venetian blinds into the glaring sunshine, longing to be playing football or riding my bike or building a den.

At the time, it didn't cross my mind that my parents and Richard's might have colluded in pushing us in opposite, gender-appropriate directions. I thought my mum had simply been indifferent towards the stand taken by Richard's dad. In hindsight, perhaps it was planned between our two families, but I have never challenged my mum about this. I like to think she just wanted my transition to secondary school and young adulthood to go smoothly and felt the societal pressures of gender conformity on my behalf. I think she feared that if Richard and I continued to spend all our time together, we would be uncomfortable among the rest of our peers as we matured and entered adolescence. I can't speak for Richard, as I don't know how he felt, but for me this day set the blueprint for the rest of my life. I learned that life would never again be as simple as just being who you really are.

[handwritten: I wonder if that's a generational thing, the "why me?" narrative, like it's a cancer diagnosis]

Perhaps my parents look back and wonder whether they might have saved me from my lesbianism had they intervened in my tomboy friendship with Richard earlier. I'm not sure why I am a lesbian, but I believe very strongly that if this incident had any bearing at all on my sexuality, it was that forcing me into gender-appropriate expressions disorientated and disillusioned me, teaching me that living a lie was a normal part of social participation. *[handwritten: I've questioned if I'm gay but never why]*

My mum strongly encouraged me to present myself in a gender-appropriate manner before transferring to high school. She took me shopping for school skirts and bought me my first pair of slip-on shoes. I soon learned, when I arrived at secondary school, that I would be unable to present myself honestly there. I didn't recognise or like the self I had to be, and the people around me provided the roadmap for an identity that felt less and less like me the further I travelled down it. For example, there were expectations and enquiries about boyfriends, and so I had relationships with boys. Relationships with boys led to excruciating conversations with family and friends about my dream wedding plans, and so on. The heterosexual imperative ran away with me and by my mid-teens I had no idea who I was.

Although school was difficult, I opted to enter teaching. There is a saying that you can't be what you can't see, and this was the case in my career choice. The only person I suspected might be a lesbian and knew in real life was my PE teacher. I had no idea back then that lesbians worked in every sphere of employment. I visited Liverpool's IM Marsh College of Physical Education for the day and saw lesbians playing pool, drinking pints of lager in the college bar and mending their own cars. For the first time, I saw two women holding hands. I liked sport but was not particularly talented at it. However, by 16, determined to get to IM Marsh, I was fit, I was on school sports teams, and I worked part time at the local swimming baths to gain the experience I needed to apply to be a PE teacher. I was accepted to IM Marsh and while I gained my teaching degree, I had my first relationships with women. I graduated – and Section 28 and I entered teaching at the same time.

Now you know a little bit about my background before teaching, it is time to recall the first of the Section 28 years. As with each of the years, I start with the legislative and cultural events of note affecting the LGBTQ+ community, before sharing an extract from my diary for that year related directly or indirectly to Section 28.

1988

1988 was the year in which Section 28 of the Local Government Act was enacted as an amendment to the UK's Local Government Act 1986. The act was introduced by Margaret Thatcher in England and Wales, and almost identical legislation was enacted for Scotland. Also in that year, Princess Margaret opened the UK's first residential support centre for people living with HIV and AIDS, the London Lighthouse. The actor Sir Ian McKellen came out as gay on BBC Radio 3 in response to the proposal for Section 28 by Thatcher's government. It was rare at the time for celebrities to come out and McKellen stated that he was motivated in his decision by the counsel and support of his friends, including the author Armistead Maupin, who wrote the *Tales of the City* series of books about the gay community in San Francisco.

David Norris, an Irish scholar, independent senator and civil rights activist, took a case (*Norris v. Ireland*) to the European Court of Human Rights, where he claimed that Ireland's criminalisation of sex between consenting adult men was in breach of Article 8 of the European Convention on Human Rights (right to respect for private and family life). In 1988, the European Court ruled in favour of Norris, although homosexuality remained unlawful in Ireland for another five years.

Elsewhere in the world in 1988, Sweden became one of the first countries to introduce anti-discrimination laws that protected gay men and lesbians from prejudice when it came to access to social services, inheritance and taxes. In Canada, the age of consent for homosexual activity between two men was lowered to 18. Belize and Israel decriminalised homosexuality for men. In the US state of Minneapolis, Stacy Offner became the first openly lesbian rabbi employed by a mainstream Jewish congregation. The American dressage rider Robert Dover became the first Olympic athlete to come out as gay.

MAY 1988. *THE SIX O'CLOCK NEWS*

I remember where I was when Elvis died. It was 1977 and I was in the Dinnington chip shop getting chips and scraps (batter bits from the fryer) with my best friend, Richard. The news of Elvis's death was reported on a portable black and white TV perched on a ledge above the head of the server. I fainted and came to as I was being dragged out of the shop by my legs by a man. I did not faint because Elvis had died. I fainted because Richard and I had cycled into Dinnington, I hadn't eaten and it was really hot in the chip shop.

For the older lesbian and gay community in the UK, the question 'Where were you when lesbians interrupted *The Six O'Clock News*?' is a little bit like the question 'Where were you when Elvis died?'

I am home from school before *The Six O'Clock News*. I enter the shared terraced house in Liverpool after a day of teaching; I drop my kit bag in the hallway and plonk myself down on the floral two-seater sofa in the living room. The sofa's exposed cane arms and frame hint at its previous life, almost certainly in the conservatory of the landlord and landlady from whom we, as a bunch of new teachers, rent the house.

Gill, my housemate and fellow PE teacher, sits to my left, dressed in our old PE college sweatshirt and the royal blue trousers of the college-issue tracksuit. Sandy puts on the kettle in the kitchen and then joins us. She is off sick from her PE teacher post, having had her wisdom teeth removed.

As is common when we reconvene from our jobs as new teachers, we say very little in the early evening. After four fun years at PE college, we are exhausted and a bit shocked by the energy required to actually do our teaching jobs. We are also quite depressed that unlike our student teaching practice, where we counted down the days to the end of school placements, there is no end in sight and this is probably it for the next 40 years. Our heads of department are all formidable women with firm expectations of how we and our classes should behave, yet we are barely older than the oldest students. The sporty students want to be our friends and the naughty students exploit our inexperience and delight in the most public of confrontations.

Our TV is Gill's portable from her childhood bedroom. It sits on a teak sideboard at right angles to the cane conservatory sofa and matching chair. As the theme music to *The Six O'Clock News* begins, my mind wanders as I consider whether to eat something before starting tomorrow's lesson plans.

As the opening credits roll, a male voice announces as usual, '*The Six O'Clock News* from the BBC, with Sue Lawley and Nicholas Witchell.' Lawley and Witchell sit behind desks; Witchell is talking on a landline phone as if receiving the latest information. Lawley, in a cream suit, introduces the programme, saying, 'Good evening, the headlines at six o'clock.' The headlines feature the new poll tax laws, which are soon to be voted on in the House of Lords. Footage of a meeting between the US president, Ronald Reagan, and the leader of the Soviet Union, Mikhail Gorbachev, is shown next as tensions between the two countries grow. The threat of nuclear war has reached new heights and the BBC drama *Threads*, set in my home city of Sheffield, has convinced a generation of us that nuclear war could actually happen. There is then a brief item describing the poor state of the roads in the UK.

When the cameras return to the presenters, Lawley, always the embodiment of professionalism and experience, looks wide-eyed, as if startled. Muffled voices are heard off-screen and Gill asks, 'Did someone just say Section 28?'

Next, a still picture of the Houses of Parliament creeps into the foreground and obscures the right-hand side of Lawley's head, before lurching into its intended spot. Witchell is now missing from his seat and appears not to be in the news studio at all. The muffled voices get louder.

I then hear for myself a woman's voice shout, 'Stop Section 28!' I look at Gill as Lawley says, 'I do apologise if you're hearing quite a lot of noise in the studio at the moment. I'm afraid that we have rather been invaded by some people who we hope to be removing very shortly.' Scuffles in the news studio are audible as Lawley continues to read from the autocue.

I know what Section 28 is. My friend Helen works behind the bar at the gay club I head to each Saturday night. Helen and her mates, some of whom live in squat-like flats in once-regal villas around Liverpool's Sefton Park, attended a march against Section 28 in Manchester in February. Despite Helen doing what she could to persuade me, I didn't go. I am aware that everyone already thinks PE teachers are all lesbians and if I was seen by anyone from school, that would be that. Section 28 is a subject to be avoided at all costs and that it has been mentioned on the BBC, if only off-screen and in muffled tones, fills me with excitement and fear.

It was the following day before I learned more about the incident on the news. The tabloid newspapers covered the event on their front pages in language that is now unacceptably homophobic but was common parlance at the time. According to Paul Baker (2022), *The Daily Star* declared 'Loony lezzies attack TV Sue' and the article itself described the lesbians as a 'screeching gaggle'. The left-leaning *Daily Mirror* focused on what Witchell had been doing while Lawley kept the programme on the air; the headline stated, 'Here is the six o'clock news: Beeb man sits on lesbian'.

The articles explained how four lesbians had entered the news studio to protest against the introduction of Section 28. One had handcuffed herself to Lawley's desk, while Witchell and a member of the crew had restrained another by sitting on her and covering her mouth. Baker (2022) states that according to the *Pink Paper*, one of the BBC news crew had shouted to Witchell to 'Give her one', to which he replied, 'I'm trying to give her one, but she won't fucking sit still.'

Although the protesters had displayed courage and admirable nerve to achieve maximum exposure for their protest against Section 28, by the time I arrived at my school the next day, Section 28 had become law.

Although I do not remember Section 28 ever being mentioned at the Liverpool Catholic school where I took up my first teaching post, the silence around it was somehow deafening. It was commonplace to hear students refer to members of our female PE department (and female PE departments up and down the country, no doubt) as 'lezzers'. I had done it myself through my own schooling, secretly fascinated that one or other of the PE department at my school might actually be in a relationship with another woman. But now, under Section 28, being a teacher and a lesbian took on a new significance, and the gravity of this new law made me feel uneasy.

At school, heterosexuality loomed large and was given extra emphasis by our obligation to uphold the teachings of the Catholic faith. I did not fit in at the school but I tried my best. The mostly female teaching staff would often tell me that I needed a boyfriend; they accused me of being my own worst enemy by playing netball, a women-only sport.

As time passed under Section 28, I imagined that my colleagues – and in particular the nuns in the school leadership team – had found out my secret. I was permanently worried that I had been seen leaving the gay clubs in Liverpool and imagined that the teachers were gossiping behind my back. I was paranoid that it was obvious I was gay. Every time a senior colleague wanted to speak to me, I imagined that it was to dismiss me or move me on to another school.

I suspected that there were other closeted lesbian teachers at school and I felt their hostility acutely. I sensed that they thought I was too young, reckless and naive to hold on to this secret we all shared. I admired these older women but they distanced themselves from me. My attempts to get to know them were quickly shut down. They were older and discreet, and I sensed that they thought I could not be trusted.

1989

A year into Section 28, the campaign group Stonewall was founded in response to the new law. Stonewall is an LGBTQ+ rights charity and the largest organisation of its kind in Europe, named after the riots of the same name in New York City in 1969. After years of cruel treatment by the police, patrons at the Stonewall Inn, a gay club in Greenwich Village, fought back when police raided the venue, prompting several nights of violence in the city.

A number of high-profile gay actors, including Michael Cashman and Ian McKellen, founded Stonewall in the UK, along with some lesser-known lesbians including Lisa Power. A sexual health and LGBTQ+ rights campaigner who was secretary general of the International Lesbian and Gay Association, Power also co-founded the prominent LGBTQ+ newspaper *Pink Paper* and was the first openly LGBTQ+ person to speak at the United Nations. Other co-founders included the activist and counsellor Olivette Cole-Wilson, the filmmaker Fiona Cunningham Reid, and the activists Jennie Wilson and Deborah Ballard. The *EastEnders* actor Pam St Clement also contributed to setting up this new lobbying group.

Stonewall was initially established to lobby for an end to Section 28, but the group went on to campaign for an equal age of consent, an extension to adoption and IVF rights to include same-sex couples, and an end to the ban on LGBTQ+ people in the armed forces. Stonewall also lobbied for the introduction of civil partnerships and eventually equal marriage.

In 1989-90, a series of unsolved murders took place in West London. Christopher Schliach, a barrister who was gay, was murdered in his home, stabbed more than 40 times. Henry Bright, a gay hotelier, was similarly stabbed to death. William Dalziel, a hotel porter who was gay, was found unconscious on a roadside and died from severe head injuries. Michael Boothe, a gay actor, died after being savagely beaten by a gang of men in a park (Richardson, 2002). In protest against these murders, hundreds of lesbians and gay men marched to Ealing Town Hall and held a candlelit vigil. This demonstration led to the establishment of the group OutRage, which demanded that the police stop arresting gay men and instead start to protect them from homophobic attacks. Soon after, the Lesbian and Gay Police Association was established, no doubt an attempt to improve the image of the police and help to end the perceived hostility towards the lesbian and gay community.

On television in 1989, the Stonewall co-founder Michael Cashman became the first actor in a British soap opera to kiss another man on the mouth. Cashman played Colin Russell in *EastEnders*; when Colin kissed his partner, Guido Smith (Nicholas Donovan), the BBC received a record number of complaints from the public and the scene was criticised by the tabloid press. Piers Morgan, then a writer at *The Sun*, referred to the kiss as a 'homosexual love scene between yuppie poofs' that was 'screened in the early evening when millions of children were watching' (Duffy, 2020). The comment by Morgan was typical of the era. In common with many others at the time, he portrayed lesbian and gay people as a danger to children, suggesting that the kiss was a direct threat to their innocence.

In the rest of the world in 1989, Western Australia decriminalised homosexuality and Denmark became the first country to enact registered partnerships for same-sex couples. Though the law excluded the right to adopt children and the right to marry in a church, it offered same-sex couples in Denmark almost all the rights of a heterosexual married couple.

JULY 1989. COMING OUT TO MUM

In 1989, I did not see representations of other lesbians in the media. I remember the excitement, then, of staying up late one night in my parents' house to secretly watch the film *Lianna* (1983). The sound was down so low

I barely heard the dialogue, but I followed the story of the title character, a part-time student and wife of a university professor, as she fell in love with her female tutor and left her husband. Inevitable heartbreak followed, leaving Lianna alone after squandering the security of her marriage for this lesbian affair. In the 1980s, the rare stories about lesbianism always resulted in death or misfortune for the lesbian protagonist. This was a cautionary tale from the male-dominated arts industry that there were no happy endings for women who lived without men.

As I hunched over the television, I reflected that not only was I being deceitful and secretive at school, but I was also being duplicitous with the people who had known me the longest and ought to know me the best: my parents. At the time, however, creeping around and pretending was my entire existence, except for Saturday nights on the gay scene in Liverpool or within the walls of my own room in my shared house in the city.

As I watched Lianna end up alone and ostracised, a rare wave of self-pity overtook me. I was feeling hollow after the recent break-up of my first lesbian relationship and my mum had noticed. 'Cheer up, Cath, you're home now,' she would say if she caught me looking pensive. Unusually, Mum never asked me why I seemed unhappy. Rather than taking this as a clue that she perhaps suspected and did not want to know why I was down, I decided I owed it to my parents to be honest about my sexual identity. In truth, I was sad and lonely and needed someone to talk to. My diary recalls what happened next.

> My dad is out cycling, my sister has her headphones on upstairs, and Mum and I are together in the kitchen.
>
> 'Mum, look, you need to know that I'm gay. I hope this is OK with you. Carla and I were in a relationship, and she has split up with me, and I don't know what to do.' I burst into tears before I can complete the speech I have been rehearsing in my head for days.
>
> Mum slams down the pan she is holding in the kitchen and pushes past me to go upstairs to her bedroom. I follow her, aghast as she climbs into bed and pulls the covers over her head. What is wrong with this person who has loved me unconditionally, empathised with my every struggle and done all she can to make me happy? My

sister, Carrie, has recently been diagnosed with epilepsy and I wonder whether this has upset Mum more than I had realised. Confused but slightly indignant, I slump on the floor next to her bed and try to justify my coming out to her.

'Mum, I can't help the way I feel. I thought you knew. Mum, I wouldn't have chosen this and I didn't do it to hurt you. You're not going to kick me out, are you? Mum, talk to me, I'm frightened.'

She doesn't respond. Hearing her sobs from beneath the bedclothes, I ask her why she is crying. After a long pause, she finally speaks to me from beneath the blankets.

'We've got our Carrie with her condition and you with yours. Why can't you both just be normal?'

'Mum, it's me. I'm just the same. Please don't do this.'

Why can't I just be normal? Shaping me was the occupation of both my mother and father. I was born as their blank page. They sent me off to teacher training college in Liverpool as a feminine heterosexual young woman, having written the first part of the intended text for me. All I had to do was fill in the rest of the pages in the same vein.

In that moment, when I am asked why I can't just be normal, I realise there is no space in my family home for me to be myself. As I sit on the floor by my parents' bed, I recognise that no one, not even my family, wants to know who I really am. My mum repeatedly told me throughout my childhood, 'Don't worry what others think, just be yourself.' However, in adulthood, I now know this is just a cliché and not a code for life.

Mum remains still and silent under the covers. I try to pull back the sheets to see her face, but she grabs them and tries to hide from me. We catch each other's eyes in the tussle; narrowing hers, she says, 'Don't you ever dare tell your dad. You will break his heart!'

I hadn't dreamed that Mum would be so upset. There had been an abundance of clues throughout my childhood: I played football, rode my bike, refused to wear dresses. I knew I was different and I thought my mum knew it too.

Mum's reaction to my coming out devastated my whole sense of self and rocked the core values I thought she had instilled in me. I went out to meet a friend that evening and, by the time I returned, Dad was home, Mum was out of bed and it was as if the incident had never happened. My sexuality was never again discussed with either of my parents. They did not attend my civil partnership, nor my wedding, and my wife would be referred to as my friend throughout our years together.

1990

In 1990, a novel by the lesbian author Jeanette Winterson was dramatised for television. *Oranges Are Not the Only Fruit* introduced viewers to Jess, an adopted girl growing up in Accrington, Lancashire, in the 1970s within a Pentecostal evangelical family. The novel was based on Winterson's own childhood and, in common with the author, Jess eventually realises that she is a lesbian. As Jess embarks on relationships with girls, the leader of her church, the Elim Pentecostal, tries to exorcise Jess of her lesbian identity.

Despite omitting some of the lesbian content that appeared in Winterson's book, the BBC series remained controversial. Jess's fanatically religious mother, played by Geraldine McEwan, restricts her life to the extent that even smiling is banned. But despite the homophobic cruelty in the name of Christianity, it is the happiness Jess discovers in love and friendship and the gentleness of her self-acceptance that make this BBC series a classic. McEwan won a Bafta for her performance and the series won best drama. Two decades later, in 2010, *The Guardian* named *Oranges* as the eighth best TV drama series of all time. Since the repeal of Section 28, Winterson's novel has been recognised for its literary quality and now occasionally appears on GCSE and A level reading lists in schools across England and Wales

After years of television devoid of references to lesbian relationships, 1990 provided a second drama series featuring a lesbian or perhaps bisexual protagonist. *Portrait of a Marriage* told of the affair between Vita

Sackville-West, the writer and garden designer, and the socialite Violet Keppel. The series also depicts the strength of Vita's enduring marriage to the diplomat Harold Nicolson and his affairs with men. Sackville-West was part of the Bloomsbury Group in the first half of the 20th century. She wrote 12 novels and was the inspiration for *Orlando*, a novel by her famous friend and lover, Virginia Woolf.

In 1990, Justin Fashanu, a footballer with clubs including Norwich City and Nottingham Forest, became the first professional footballer to come out as gay. Tabloid stories followed, including salacious tales of affairs between Fashanu and unnamed celebrities, MPs and other football players. Although Fashanu was a talented player, no football club would offer him a full-time contract after the revelations. Fashanu moved to the US, where further controversy about his sexuality followed. Eight years later, in May 1998, Fashanu was found hanged in a garage in East London. To this day, no Premier League footballer has come out as gay, though many of England's women's football team have managed to come out without negative impact.

Also in 1990, the architect of Section 28, Margaret Thatcher, was ousted from power. Thatcher's government turned against her over her dismissive attitude to the European monetary union. One of her closest allies, Michael Heseltine, launched a leadership campaign and Thatcher was eventually persuaded by her cabinet to step down. After holding an audience with the Queen and making one last Commons speech, on 28 November 1990 the so-called Iron Lady left Downing Street in tears.

Elsewhere in the world, homosexuality was decriminalised in Queensland, Australia, and the World Health Organization removed homosexuality from its list of illnesses. In the US, Dale McCormick became the first out lesbian elected to a state Senate, albeit in the liberal state of Maine. Six years later, when McCormick was running for Congress in 1996, her heterosexual male opponent addressed the State Democratic Convention and invited his wife and children on to the stage at the end of his speech. In response, at the end of her speech, McCormick invited her partner, Betsy, and daughter, Paley, to join her on the podium. They stood together for several minutes while everyone cheered. McCormick has said that she wondered whether this might harm her political career, but the following day a picture of her and her family appeared on the front page of the local paper; McCormick describes this as a 'wonderful affirmation of gay and lesbian families' (McCormick, n.d.).

Also in the US, the national bisexual network BiNet was founded in 1990. BiNet held its first conference in San Francisco, attended by more than 450 people from 20 states and five countries. After the conference, the mayor of San Francisco commended the 'bisexual rights community for its leadership in the cause of social justice' and declared 23 June as Bisexual Pride Day.

MAY 1990. CONSCIOUSNESS-RAISING

It is 1990 and I am single. After mourning my breakup with Carla for the best part of a year, I decide that I need to get back out there and find a new girlfriend. An older woman in a black vest, leather jacket and faded jeans often stands alone at the bar at the New Court gay club in Liverpool. My best mate, Sandy, and I have in the past joked about her age as her hair is greying slightly at the temples. Laughing, Sandy says, 'Cath, promise me you will shoot me if I'm still on the prowl when I'm 35.'

I laugh at Sandy but something about the woman intrigues me. Sandy is playing pool and so I begin chatting to her at the bar. She is suspicious of me initially but tells me she is a social worker with Liverpool City Council. I don't tell her what I do.

On the woman's necklace hangs a silver axe pendant called a labrys. This double-sided axe was a sacred symbol in ancient Minoan civilization, often associated with female divinity and the mythological Amazons. The labrys was adopted in the 1970s by lesbian feminists as a symbol of strength and empowerment. This labrys sits against the woman's ribs and I realise how skinny she is. We chat in the noisy bar, leaning into each other's necks to be heard as the music is so loud. She smells of Paco Rabanne aftershave, a lesbian staple. She heads down a corridor and joins the queue for the toilet; as Sandy is still on the pool table, I follow her. In the relative quiet and bright lights of the toilet, I learn my new friend is called Val. She kisses me and I hold on to her waist. I am not that attracted to her, but I am in awe of her maturity and the confidence she has in her own physicality.

Val and I remain together for the rest of the evening and, before Sandy and I head off to get a taxi home, she asks me what I'm up to on Sunday afternoon. She invites Sandy and me to a flat on Princes Street for a consciousness-raising meeting organised through the News From Nowhere bookshop. I occasionally read *Spare Rib*, the feminist magazine that serves as the closest thing we have to a UK lesbian periodical. In *Spare Rib*, I sometimes see advertisements for consciousness-raising meetings, but I am not sure what they are about or who they are for. Though I am excited by the idea of a group of women meeting to talk politics (inevitably Section 28), as a teacher, my involvement in something like this could be very risky.

Consciousness-raising was a form of feminist activism initially made popular in the late 1960s and the 1970s in the US. The purpose of consciousness-raising activity was to raise awareness of a cause usually related to inequality. During the 1980s in Liverpool, feminists, most of whom were lesbians, met in squats that had once been grand villas just north of Liverpool's Lime Street Station. According to Anna Rogers (2010), consciousness-raising groups were pivotal to the informally organised movement that transformed the lives of many women during the 1970s. Jo Freeman (1975) described them as 'probably the most valuable contribution by the women's liberation movement to the tools for social change' (p.451). According to Rogers (2010), in consciousness-raising groups, women talked among themselves about female liberation as a form of political practice. At the time, it was seen as a subversive act for women to meet in this way and married women would often attend without their husbands' knowledge.

The Sunday after my night in the New Court bar with Val, I drag a reluctant Sandy to the consciousness-raising meeting Val invited us both to. I'm keen to see my older woman again and we head out with a Liverpool A to Z to find the address I was given. Sandy and I get a taxi there. We have no money and, despite receiving full maintenance grants at PE college, we have endless student debt. However, now we are wage-earners we have a misplaced sense of entitlement to taxis, as if by going to work every day we have somehow earned a chauffeur-driven lifestyle.

We find the building and walk up the grand stone steps to the front door. A series of buzzers reveal themselves on the right-hand side of the door frame and we look for the number we need. The name next to the buzzer we need is smudged and the sticker is peeling at the corners, so we don't know who to ask for.

We press the button and someone immediately buzzes us in. Laughing with nerves, we cautiously push open the large door and enter a wide, damp-smelling hallway with several bikes propped up against the wall. Two butch women in leather jackets descend the stairs; one of them fleetingly looks Sandy and me up and down as they pass. The look is enough to make us both hesitate. As the women leave through the front door, Sandy and I climb the stairs, pausing at the first landing to glance at one another, stifling giggles at how out of our depth we suddenly are. We stop again on the second floor as we hear laughter coming from a door that is slightly ajar. Our eyes widen as we recognise the sweet and sticky scent of cannabis in the air.

From the smell of the weed, we surmise that these are what Sandy and I commonly refer to as 'hardcore lesbians', just like the leather-jacketed pair we met on the stairs. I start to weigh up the options available to us. I am curious to see Val again but this suddenly feels a bit scary. Sandy and I are teachers and we are about to enter a room where we will discuss the topic of the moment: Section 28 and gay liberation. And these women are taking drugs. I begin to wonder what might happen if the police raid the meeting. What if Sandy and I get caught in there? In my head, I run through a whole scenario of shame in which I've let everyone down – my parents and my head of department at school, who already considers me a bit of a tearaway. If Sandy and I are discovered here and arrested, we will never work as teachers again. We catch each other's eyes as we approach the door of the weed-filled room, knowing that in a few steps we will be at the door and spotted by those sitting just inside. I can tell Sandy wants to turn and run. Three steps from the door, she whispers, 'Abort, abort!'

We turn and run back down the stairs before we are seen. We open the heavy door and bound down the steps two at a time, landing on the pavement and dashing down an alleyway to our left. Once there we fall about laughing. 'Don't! I need a wee!' Sandy says, as she disappears behind a commercial wheelie bin, pulling down her jeans and pants as she runs.

We walk back to our shared house through the park, laughing about what might have been had we entered the room. I never did see my older woman again and I never did get to experience consciousness-raising.

1991

By 1991, media attention was focused on the AIDS crisis. The tabloid press feasted on the closeted gay men in public life who were cruelly outed by contracting the virus. The death of the actor Rock Hudson from AIDS in 1985 had shocked the world. On 23 November 1991, the Queen singer, Freddie Mercury, announced to the press that he had AIDS. In a statement he said:

> *Following the enormous conjecture in the press over the last two weeks, I wish to confirm that I have been tested HIV positive and have AIDS. I felt it correct to keep this information private to date to protect the privacy of those around me. However, the time has come now for my friends and fans around the world to know the truth and I hope that everyone will join with me, my doctors and all those worldwide in the fight against this terrible disease. My privacy has always been very special to me and I am famous for my lack of interviews. Please understand this policy will continue.* (Associated Press, 1991)

Mercury died the following day. Earlier in 1991, the Stonewall co-founder Ian McKellen had an audience with the new Conservative prime minister, John Major, to discuss lowering the age of consent for sex between men to 16, the legal age for heterosexual couples. Government files from the National Archives reveal Major's thoughts on McKellen's argument. He writes, 'I have to say that, whilst fully recognising the sensitivities of the subject, I had considerable sympathy with some of Sir Ian's points on the grounds of simple, straightforward equity' (Malvern, 2018).

During the meeting, which took place at 10 Downing Street, McKellen raised issues that were affecting the gay community, like police harassment and abusive language in the press. He pointed out to Major, 'If two men merely showed affection for one another in public, they could be charged under the gross indecency laws or for a breach of the peace.' The archives show that Major believed this was an 'extreme reading of the law', but he did acknowledge that the police sometimes used this legal loophole as 'an excuse for harassment' against gay men.

McKellen is said to have written warmly to Major after the meeting, stating: 'It's been encouraging to note the overwhelmingly positive response throughout the media ... There seems to be a general acceptance that the concerns of lesbians and gay men should now be firmly on the political agenda.'

In response to McKellen, Major stated: 'I too was pleased to see the generally positive response in the media ... although I am afraid that my postbag has contained more critical than sympathetic letters.'

It would take three more years for the age of consent for gay men in Britain to be lowered from 21 to 18.

In a Foreign Office speech in 2017, the former prime minister, now Sir John Major, reflected on the backlash that followed his meeting with McKellen:

> *There were subterranean rumblings that I should never even have spoken to him – let alone invited him into No 10. Such an attitude was simply astonishing. Personally, I never regretted that meeting – and learned a great deal from it.* (Duffy, 2017)

Elsewhere in the world in 1991, homosexuality was decriminalised in the Bahamas, Hong Kong and Ukraine. The red ribbon was used for the first time as a symbol of the fight against AIDS. Sherry Harris became the first out African American lesbian to be elected to public office in the US. Chicago opened the world's first Gay and Lesbian Hall of Fame to honour people and organisations who had made significant contributions to the quality of life or wellbeing of the lesbian and gay community in the city. The first lesbian kiss on US television occurred on the slick courtroom drama series *LA Law*, prompting an unprecedented number of complaints.

FEBRUARY 1991. THE POEM

I'm in work especially early today. I don't have a washing machine as there isn't room in the terraced house I'm renting in Liverpool, so my head of department has agreed I can use the washing machine in the communal PE office as long as I'm discreet.

I've set a whites wash going and while I wait I plan my netball practice for the lunchtime club. The washing cycle finishes and I open the door of the machine to find that everything is pink. I search for the red sock that must have gone in accidentally, only to find that the culprit is a red paper napkin left in the cream jeans I have borrowed from my new girlfriend. A knock on the door interrupts me as I inspect the damage and wonder what I'm going to say to my girlfriend about her ruined jeans.

A sixth-form girl stands at the office door. I recognise her but I'm not sure of her name. She isn't one of the girls from any of the sports teams, but she does take part in sixth-form leisure centre time on Tuesday afternoons. There, sixth-formers get the chance to choose between aerobics, ten-pin bowling or table tennis.

Her dark wavy hair frames her face and, although she is tall, she stands slightly hunched, with her feet crossed at the ankles. She hands me a white envelope with 'Miss Lee' written on the front. I'm confused. Sixth-formers are not required to bring notes from home if they wish to be excused from these leisure sessions. As young adults, they are encouraged to be more autonomous in preparation for university, polytechnic or the world of work. And anyway, it's Wednesday.

The girl quickly turns to leave, muttering something to me as she walks away. I don't catch what she says, so I walk out after her and ask, 'Sorry, what did you say?'

'Seeing you makes my day,' she replies in a hushed tone, almost without emotion, her hair covering her face as she picks up speed. Embarrassed, I turn around and walk away from her, back to the PE office. I close the door, keen to put a barrier between me and the encounter that has just taken place. I sit on the bench, taking care not to lean back against the iron pegs that jut out at head height. I open the envelope carefully, neatly prising the triangular flap away from its gum seal without making a tear, so that I might reseal it, as if the envelope were never opened.

A colourful page with exquisite calligraphy is contained within. Hearts and swirls surround a three-verse poem that sits neatly at the centre of the page. I read the poem a couple of times and feel my face flush as the girl's secret attraction to me is laid bare through the verses. Then I panic. How does she know I'm gay? Will people think I have encouraged her? Who else knows about the poem?

The moment is broken by a key in the office door. Finding it already unlocked, my head of department enters and is surprised to see me sitting in the office. 'Oh, you're here early,' she says.

I look up and stuff the letter into the pocket of my tracksuit bottoms, quickly zipping it up.

Throughout the day, I'm constantly aware that the letter is in my pocket, and I take care not to use the pocket for any other purpose in case it should accidentally fall out. Once I arrive home that evening, I sit alone on the sofa and read the poem again. I know from my own crushes on PE teachers how painful and confusing this period of adolescence can be. I admire the girl's temerity in presenting me with the letter in person, even though acute embarrassment was etched across her face. I wonder whether I ought to let my head of department know, but I do not want to betray the girl. I wonder whether any of her friends in the sixth form know about the poem and become anxious that if I keep the correspondence to myself, I will somehow be seen as accepting her feelings or, worse still, be accused of being in a relationship with her. After taking myself through a number of irrational and implausible scenarios, all of which conclude with me losing my job, I take the letter and its envelope into the tiny backyard behind my house and light the corner of it with my cigarette lighter. As the flames chase diagonally down the page and nearer to my fingers, I drop the letter and watch as the last of the hearts and swirls succumb to the flames, becoming black powdery flakes that rise in the wind and disappear over the wall.

1992

In 1992, Katherine Dawn Lang, known as KD Lang, burst on to the UK music scene, having previously enjoyed a career as a country singer in her native Canada. *Ingénue* was Lang's most successful album, with hits including *Constant Craving* and *Miss Chatelaine*. Lang's short, floppy dark hair and strong masculine look delighted lesbians across the world. She came out in an interview with *The Advocate*, a lesbian and gay magazine, confirming what all lesbians had hoped to be true. Many country radio stations in the US stopped playing Lang's music and she was quickly ostracised by the country music industry.

At the same time, Madonna was famously being playful with her own sexuality via her new album, *Erotica*. She met Lang and reportedly said of her later, 'Elvis is alive…and she's beautiful.' Lang became a promoter of lesbian and gay rights and one of the only lesbian musicians well known in mainstream pop.

Also in 1992, the Isle of Man repealed its sodomy laws, although homosexuality remained illegal until 1994. Brighton held its first Pride in the Park event and the inaugural EuroPride took place in London, attended by more than 100,000 people.

Elsewhere in the world, the age of consent was lowered to that of heterosexual sex in Iceland, Luxembourg and Switzerland, and homosexuality was decriminalised in Estonia, Latvia and Australia. Canada ended its ban on lesbian and gay people serving in the military, while anti-discrimination legislation offered protection for lesbians and gay men in the provinces of New Brunswick and British Columbia.

In New York City, the Lesbian Avengers organisation was founded by Anne-christine d'Adesky, Marie Honan, Anne Maguire, Ana Simo, Sarah Schulman and Maxine Wolfe. A flyer distributed at their first meeting invited 'lesbian, dykes, gay women' to get involved. The flyer said: 'We're wasting our lives being careful. Imagine what your life could be. Aren't you ready to make it happen?' The Lesbian Avengers movement soon spread to the UK, with a London-based group emerging from OutRage, the political group focused on improving lesbian and gay rights. The Lesbian Avenger Ann Northrop shared views that were typical of the movement, stating: 'We're not going to be invisible anymore ... we are going to be prominent and have power and be part of all decision making' (Salholz, 1993).

In New York City, the Lesbian Avengers targeted right-wing attempts to stifle diversity in schools and promoted a multicultural 'Children of the Rainbow' curriculum for elementary schoolchildren. The group also named and shamed schools with a homophobic and racist agenda. The Lesbian Avengers were committed to challenging homophobic stereotypes, but some members were opposed to participating in the schools campaign as they feared being labelled as child molesters. It was for this very reason that other members believed their Rainbow curriculum work was essential.

AUGUST 1992. THE BARCELONA OLYMPICS

In 1992, my girlfriend, an England hockey player and fellow PE teacher, avidly followed the progress of her senior Great Britain hockey teammates at the Barcelona Olympics. And they did rather well. Despite being part-time athletes with full-time jobs, the women's hockey team won a bronze medal, one of only 20 medals gained by Team GB that year. There were at least two lesbian couples within the hockey team, although this was never mentioned publicly and the women involved were very discreet. The hockey medal-winners went on to enjoy a degree of celebrity. Some appeared on the BBC's *Question of Sport* programme and all were invited to the BBC Sports Personality of the Year award ceremony. I recalled the following incident in my diary shortly after the Olympic Games concluded.

It's Sunday morning and my girlfriend, Tessa, has popped to our local newsagent for the papers. We have the house to ourselves as my housemates are away. She returns five minutes later, bursting through the door and collapsing on to the sofa looking ashen. The papers are strewn across the living room floor and I can see that in addition to our usual paper, Tessa has purchased a Scottish *Daily Record*.

Tessa points to the front page of the *Daily Record*. Two Scottish members of Great Britain's bronze-medal-winning hockey team have been outed by the newspaper as being in a lesbian relationship. A salacious article describes how one, a solicitor, had left her husband and become a lesbian, and the other, already a lesbian, is a primary school teacher. Tessa is terrified. She worries out loud for the other lesbian couple on the team and all the lesbians in the hockey squad. Like Tessa, many of them are PE teachers, the only way in which these amateur sportswomen can earn any money for their abilities. Tessa begins calling her friends on the squad who are PE teachers. I listen as they worry for their primary school teacher friend, wondering what will happen to her now Section 28 is law.

Days later, the radio DJ Chris Evans launched a campaign on BBC Radio 1 to find out which other hockey players in the 1992 Olympic team were lesbians. Evans invited members of the public to phone the programme with names of players they knew or suspected were lesbian.

When Tessa found out, she began to contact her teammates again to talk about what they could do. The way in which the hockey team's bronze medal success had thrust very private lesbians into the limelight had shaken all those involved to their core. Four years into Section 28, it especially terrified those who were PE teachers.

Fast-forward to the 2016 Olympics in Rio de Janeiro and the climate is very different for GB's lesbian hockey players. Kate Richardson-Walsh, captain of the women's hockey team, and her teammate wife, Helen Richardson-Walsh, win gold and an array of positive media pieces about the couple follow. In an interview, Helen states, 'To win a gold medal is a dream come true – to win it standing next to my wife is really special' (BBC News, 2016).

Before the Games, Kate spoke to the BBC about the couple's relationship:

> *The best thing is the reaction we've had from the public in that we've helped people feel more confident in themselves. People feel it's OK to come out as bisexual or gay or lesbian – that's been the best thing for me.* (BBC News, 2016)

While those lesbian hockey players who feared exposure in 1992 by Evans no doubt celebrated the success of the Rio hockey team, it is important to stress that Kate and Helen Richardson-Walsh and other lesbians in the team stood on the shoulders of very quiet giants, who years before them had succeeded in a climate of homophobia that must have been unimaginable to the squad of 2016.

1993

In 1993, KD Lang appeared on the cover of the August issue of *Vanity Fair*. The photograph, shot by Herb Ritts, featured Lang dressed in a waistcoat and tie, sitting in a barber's chair while the supermodel Cindy Crawford, wearing a swimsuit, appeared to shave Lang's foam-covered neck with a razor. That same year, Lang won a Grammy for her hit single *Constant Craving*.

As AIDS continued to spread among gay men, more celebrities announced they were HIV-positive. The British radio DJ and comedian Kenny Everett and the Frankie Goes to Hollywood singer Holly Johnson were among those to do so in 1993.

Around the world, civil unions for same-sex couples were legalised in Norway and homosexuality was decriminalised in Belarus, Gibraltar, Ireland, Lithuania and Russia (with the exception of the Chechen Republic). Equalities legislation was passed in several US states and New Zealand ended its ban on lesbians and gay men serving in the military. The Lesbian Avengers continued their work in the US, with 20,000 people marching in support of them in New York City.

Also in 1993, in the US, Brandon Teena was raped and murdered at the age of 21. Teena was an transgender man from Nebraska who was killed along with his friends Phillip DeVine and Lisa Lambert. His life and death would become the subject of the films *The Brandon Teena Story* (1998) and *Boys Don't Cry* (1999). In 1993, Teena moved to the Falls City region of Richardson County, Nebraska, where he started to live as a man full-time. Teena began dating Lana Tisdel and associating with two ex-convicts, John Lotter and Marvin Thomas Nissen. On 19 December 1993, Teena was arrested for falsifying cheques and was held in the female section of the county jail until bailed.

Later in the same month, during a Christmas Eve party, Teena was assaulted by Lotter and Nissen and forced to remove his underwear. He was driven to a deserted location near a factory in Richardson County, where he was gang-raped. The police investigating this crime were, however, more interested in Teena's gender identity than in apprehending the rapists. A week later, Lotter and Nissen broke into the house where Teena was staying with his partner and friends, and shot and killed Teena, DeVine and Lambert. Lotter and Nissen were later charged with murder.

Teena is buried in Lincoln Memorial Cemetery in Nebraska. His headstone is engraved with his birth name and the epitaph 'daughter, sister and friend'. Teena's murder, and that of the 21-year-old student Matthew Shepard in Wyoming five years later, heightened awareness of LGBTQ+ hate crimes in the US and around the world.

Also in 1993, the singer Melissa Etheridge came out as a lesbian. She did so at the Triangle Ball, a lesbian and gay celebration event to mark US president Bill Clinton's first inauguration. Etheridge supported Clinton's presidential campaign and, since coming out, has been a prominent LGBTQ+ rights activist.

Until 1993, lesbian, gay and bisexual people were banned from serving in the US military. On becoming president, Clinton passed the 'don't ask, don't tell' bill. Lauded at the time as an act of tolerance, 'don't ask, don't tell' was not quite all it seemed. As the name suggests, the policy sought to turn a blind eye to lesbian, gay and bisexual people in the military provided they were discreet and did not announce their sexuality to anyone or speak about their same-sex relationships. 'Don't ask, don't tell' prohibited military personnel from discriminating against or harassing closeted lesbian, gay or bisexual service members or applicants. It had been routine until this point for military personnel to have their belongings ransacked by those in authority, searching for clues to same-sex relationships in items such as personal letters and photographs.

While presented as a concession of sorts, 'don't ask, don't tell' continued to prohibit people who demonstrated 'a propensity or intent to engage in homosexual acts' from serving in the armed forces of the US, because their presence 'would create an unacceptable risk to the high standards of morale, good order and discipline, and unit cohesion that are the essence of military capability'. The policy specified that service members who disclosed that they were in a same-sex relationship or identified openly as lesbian, gay or bisexual would be discharged. Those who were prepared to keep their personal lives hidden could, however, remain.

JANUARY 1993. UNDER THE BRIDGE

In 1993, I bought a terraced house in the notorious 'under the bridge' area of Garston in Liverpool. This was the first home I owned. Securing a 100% mortgage from the Teachers Building Society on the £19,000 two-bed property was just about manageable and, if I struggled, I planned to get a lodger or ask my girlfriend to move in full-time.

This was the first place I lived where I could lock the door for the night. My previous places were shared digs with other teachers, and their friends, other halves or one-night stands would regularly come and go. It was my first adult place of safety: a home where I could watch *Lianna* without keeping the volume low or quickly changing the channel if someone else walked in. I put my lesbian books on my pine shelves. The green and white spines of the Virago books and the black and white stripes of the Women's Press books appeared to shout in celebration that I could at last be myself. Despite being heavily in debt and having only a Baby Belling countertop oven to cook on, the first thing I did was buy a large framed print of two women in bonnets and dresses walking along the beach, holding hands. I doubted they were lesbians – probably sisters or friends – but nonetheless I placed the print above the three-bar gas fire in an attempt to create my very own lesbian hearth, the heart of the home.

As a new PE teacher, I earned £604 a month and so my decision to buy a house alone led to compromises about the property's location. I chose the ability to lock my own front door and control who crossed the threshold over a shared house in a more salubrious area. The house had been on the market for a while and latterly the agents had added the price to the board, seeking to entice buyers with the £19,000 knockdown sum. One Saturday afternoon, as I sat on the living room floor assembling flatpack drawers, a group of teenagers, including some girls I vaguely recognised from my school, walked past the house, each jumping to punch, head or slap the 'sold' sign as they passed.

'Nineteen grand? I wouldn't give you 19 quid for that skanky shit heap,' one of the boys declared, as he ran and jumped to punch the sign.

'It's Miss Lee's house. She's a lez,' said one of the girls in the group and they all laughed.

'Ugh, dirty dyke,' shouted another of the boys, before they all ran off down the street into a side alley.

Predictably, the boys came back to the house regularly, spurred on by the girls from my school, who lurked further away but almost certainly encouraged the boys to be ever more daring. In my diary, I recall one such visit.

It's Sunday evening and Tessa and I are watching TV in the living room, which is at the front of our terraced house. The lights are off but the room glows from the three bars of the gas fire. A loud thud at the living room window, and then another, jolts us both and we jump to our feet. Tessa, a PE teacher at a school some 20 miles away, instinctively heads for the door in her slippers. She gives chase to four boys, who have already started running away to join some girls I vaguely recognise but who are much further down the street. I remain on the step and watch as egg yolks, whites and shells run down the living room window.

Tessa returns minutes later, out of breath but jubilant. 'I got one of them,' she says. 'He was shitting himself.'

My heart sinks. 'What did you say?'

'I told them I would report them to their school if they ever pulled a stunt like that again.'

Knowing we have no idea which school the boys attend, Tessa's threat is an empty one. Although I admire the way in which she has bravely taken on the boys, I fear she has made the situation much worse.

Two evenings later, alone in the house, I hear the letterbox snap. On my porch mat is a lit firework, sizzling and spinning. I grab it, open the door and throw it as far as I can down the street, to whoops and howls of laughter from the boys.

Now enjoying my reactions to their pranks, and no doubt impressing the girls who hide out of sight, the boys begin to target my car. The pale blue Ford Fiesta, parked on the street outside my house, is a source of immense pride. Although it is rusting slightly at the wheel arches, I keep it in pristine condition and am proud that I have almost paid back the loan taken out to buy it.

Initially, the boys walk casually past the car and punch the door with the outer side of their fists before sprinting off. I take no action, reasoning that they might get bored if I don't react. Instead, they become ever bolder and start to give the car a quick kick as they pass, making substantial dents in both doors.

I decide to involve the police, but do not want them to visit my house for fear that the boys (and the girls from my school) will see them. Instead, I visit the police station after school the following day and explain the series of events to the desk sergeant.

'What's someone like you doing under the bridge?' he asks. 'It's full of scallies and druggies. My best advice is to sell your house – if you can. Houses go for a penny down there sometimes. But cut your losses and get yourself a nice place in Allerton or Aigburth instead.'

'But I've only just moved in,' I reply.

'Did you not know about under the bridge?' he asks, now a little amused by my plight. I say that I knew it wasn't the best place in Liverpool but assumed I would be OK.

The desk sergeant tells me there is next to no chance of ever catching the boys, let alone proving what they did, and he reiterates his advice that I should sell up and move on. As I leave the police station and return to my car, an idea comes to mind. I could park my car on the side street outside the police station each night and walk home instead. Surely no one would vandalise a car outside a police station.

From then on, every evening after school, I drove to the police station and walked the mile and half back home. Although the walk was terrifying, especially in the dark, I felt a sense of victory over the boys. Looking back, it is hard to believe that I would risk personal physical harm by walking home in the dark in order to keep my car from further vandalism. But, in retrospect, this was symptomatic of the complete absence of self-worth I had at the time. Five years into Section 28, living a lie at work and facing harassment outside my home, I believed this was the inevitable price of being gay.

It seems inconceivable now that I said nothing at school about what was going on most evenings. Today, I would find the girls at school and take them myself to the headteacher. I would also find out which school the boys were from and contact their headteacher. But this was the era of Section 28 and they were calling me 'lez' and 'dyke'. I was far too ashamed to let anyone at school know what was happening.

1994

In 1994, the Liverpool-based soap opera *Brookside* made history by broadcasting the first pre-watershed kiss between two women. The kiss was between the characters Beth Jordache (Anna Friel) and Margaret Clemence (Nicola Stephenson) in a storyline concerning Beth's revelation to Margaret that she had been sexually abused by her father.

In her portrayal of Beth, Friel was adamant that Beth's sexual attraction must not be framed as a reaction to her past abuse. In an interview with the *Radio Times*, Friel stated, 'I am proud we took on such controversial storylines and it was new and innovative. I am proud that we got it in the contract that Beth would always stay gay; it wasn't because of her sexual abuse' (Dowell, 2016).

When London hosted the Olympic Games in 2012, the kiss between Beth and Margaret was included in the opening ceremony as part of a celebration of all things British. The kiss was screened to a global TV audience of billions without censorship. Crucially, it was broadcast in 76 countries where same-sex relationships were still criminalised, the first same-sex kiss ever to be shown on television in these countries.

Also in 1994, the Conservative MP Edwina Currie proposed an amendment to lower the age of consent for homosexual acts from 21 to 16. The amendment was defeated and the gay male age of consent was lowered to 18 instead. There was still no mention of sexual activity between women and it continued to be ignored, as it had throughout legal history.

In 1994, the charity Save the Children dropped Sandi Toksvig as the compère of its 75th anniversary celebrations after she came out as gay. Once again, the issue of lesbian and gay people as somehow harmful to children reared its head in the media. After a protest by the UK Lesbian Avengers, Save the Children was pressurised into apologising to Toksvig. The charity did not reinstate her, however, although the reason for this is not known. In 2014, Toksvig joked that Save the Children ended her contract as it did not want Princess Anne to meet a lesbian (O'Carroll, 2014).

Anti-discrimination legislation was introduced in 1994 in South Africa, where a National Coalition for Gay and Lesbian Equality was founded. Homosexuality was decriminalised in Bermuda, the Isle of Man and Serbia, and Japan held its first ever gay parade.

The American Medical Association declared its opposition to treatments aimed at curing homosexuality. The US military continued to struggle with its position on the inclusion of lesbian, gay and bisexual personnel when the South Boston Allied War Veterans Council cancelled its St Patrick's Day parade rather than allow a contingent of lesbian, gay and bisexual soldiers to march. This was the first time in almost a century that Boston had not held such a parade.

Also in the US, Washington adopted a policy prohibiting discrimination based on sexual orientation in the state's public schools. The Gay Asian Pacific Alliance joined the Chinese New Year parade in San Francisco, the first time gay Asian American communities had participated in a public celebration of their identities.

DECEMBER 1994. WHEN THE PERSONAL AND PROFESSIONAL COLLIDE

In 1994, the lesbian and gay scene in Liverpool was thriving and Tessa and I would spend most Saturday nights out at a bar or club with our friends. Since the introduction of Section 28, those of us who were teachers worried that we might be spotted entering or leaving the venues. The ultimate fear was of seeing a student inside one of the bars or clubs.

Tessa and I have our friends Sam and Diane over for the weekend. Living in the West Country, they are keen to go out in Liverpool and explore the gay scene. It is a freezing cold Saturday evening and, despite feeling wiped out, we agree to take our guests to a lesbian bar, hoping that once we get there we might find some energy and actually enjoy ourselves.

We descend the stairs into the dark, damp, musty space. Lesbian clubs are only ever underground in dingy basements, and this adds to my already well-embedded shame in being a lesbian. The seedy subterranean bars say you must stay hidden from view. They say lesbian relationships do not deserve daylight or windows.

As we reach the bottom of the stairs, I hear the deafening throb of dance music and feel the familiar sensation of the beer-soaked, sticky carpet squelching beneath my Caterpillar boots. Diane hands me a bottle of beer and bends in towards my ear to make conversation with me. I grin and nod in response; I have no idea what she says. We stand around in a circle, cradling our beers, trying to make conversation above the sound of the music. I am aware of someone behind me, watching our group. I turn to see Julie, a sixth-form student from my school, standing with another girl I don't recognise.

Julie catches my eye and we both look away. My stomach lurches. I have been caught in a lesbian bar by a girl from school and I have no idea what to do. Trying and no doubt failing to look undaunted by Julie's presence, I dare myself to look at her again. This time, I acknowledge her by raising my bottle of beer in her direction and turn back to face my circle of friends. Wide-eyed and dry-mouthed, I catch Tessa's attention and try to tell her what has happened. She can't really hear me but I am afraid to lean in closer or touch her. I finally make Tessa understand that we have to leave, and our confused and slightly annoyed guests finish their beers and follow us up to street level and out of the club.

We hail a taxi and head home. The night is ruined. I vow that I will never go out in Liverpool again and spend all night awake, second-guessing what will await me on Monday morning at school.

Our guests leave on Sunday, straight after breakfast. Relaxing a little at last, I burst into tears. I sit with Tessa and we plan how I should approach school on Monday. We discuss whether I should just go in and tell the headmistress, a nun, what has happened. I worry that the head will make an example of me. If I tell her, I will lose my job.

Monday arrives and I get into school early. I want to be there before Julie, the headmistress and my head of department arrive. All weekend I have imagined them colluding and ambushing me as soon as I enter the school building. Despite my fears, all seems as it should. There is no sign of Julie, no comments from students, no summons to see the head. The bell rings; registration and the first two lessons all conclude without incident. I begin to think I have got away with it.

I am not approached at break time by the headmistress or my head of department, and I allow myself to relax a little. After break, I head out on to the field with my Year 7 cross-country class, but as I start the stopwatch and set them off on the course, the gate to the field opens and I glimpse Julie standing behind me. I am immediately conscious of my vulnerability as the slowest of the runners disappears over the brow of the hill, leaving Julie and I alone on the field. It is not unusual for the sporty sixth-formers to help with the little ones during their free periods, but I doubt Julie has come out to help me. I don't know how to be, so I am curt with Julie, hoping that if I make it clear I am not in the mood to talk, she will return to the school building. I don't make conversation with her and she doesn't speak to me either, but she loiters by the gate, waiting, no doubt, for me to be the adult. After an unbearable silence, Julie asks, 'Miss, can I have a word with you about Saturday night, please?'

'I'm teaching, Julie. This really isn't appropriate,' I retort defensively, dreading what she might say next. My mouth is so dry that my lips stick to my teeth, but Julie stays put and seems determined that we will talk about seeing each other in the lesbian bar.

After a long silence in which I am the sullen child and Julie is the patient adult, she speaks again. 'I just want to say that I am really sorry for spoiling your night on Saturday and I just want to ask you not to tell anyone where I was, because if this gets round the sixth form, I'll just die.'

'You shouldn't be in a place like that,' I tell her, angrily. 'You're not even 18.'

Julie starts to cry and I feel a mixture of compassion and relief. 'I have thought for ages that I might be gay,' she blurts out between sobs, 'and I just wanted to see what it was like at a club.'

I take a deep breath, mustering some kindness beneath the anxiety that is engulfing me. I remember being her age. I remember the terror of realising I didn't think like the other girls or feel the same way about boys. But I am so vulnerable now that Julie has seen me and this occupies me far more than Julie's concerns for her own reputation. After a further silence, I try to close down the discussion and get Julie to return inside.

'Look, you're still very young and I promise you, you're not gay. And even if you are, don't be. That club is no place for you to be on a Saturday night. There are some people in there who are not very nice, so stay away. If the police raid it, everyone will know you were there: your mum, your dad, everyone.'

As I project my own adolescent fears on to Julie and her current circumstances, to my relief, the fastest of the cross-country runners appear over the brow of the hill.

'Look, you need to go back into school, but just think about what I've said,' I say, with a weak attempt at a reassuring smile. I turn away from Julie and she retreats through the gate. In case she considers coming back, I focus intently on the runners, going overboard by shouting loud and excessive encouragements as they finish the course.

That evening, I relay the story to Tessa. She looks at me critically, with her nose scrunched and her mouth to one side. I suddenly feel dreadful that I was not a bigger person. Julie did not exploit me as I expected her to, but rather reached out for some help, some empathy and support. In response, I provided her with the opposite of what she was seeking and needed from me as her teacher.

If Julie had told me she was pregnant, had been abused, was unhappy at home or struggling with her coursework, I would have ensured she got access to all the help she needed. But because of my fear of being exposed as a lesbian, I was cruel to her, betraying myself and the entire lesbian community. I told her that the club was for people who were 'not very nice'. Did that include me? Did it include Tessa and our friends? Looking back, this was my own internalised homophobia at work and betrays my lack of self-worth at the time. However, in my discussion with Julie, I did what was required under Section 28. I told Julie not to be gay. I perpetuated the idea of lesbianism as a forbidden lifestyle, a sordid little secret kept by people who went to seedy subterranean bars and were not very nice.

I assume this was Julie's first experience of coming out to someone. Research shows that this first experience can be key to the way in which young people go on to formulate their sexual identity (Casey, 2002; Jennett, 2004; Taylor, 2007). To this day, I feel ashamed of the way I treated Julie. I feel guilty for leaving her isolated and without support at such a challenging time in her adolescence. I was selfish and showed a lack of courage and strength, but my actions reveal something of the climate created by Section 28 in schools.

The following Saturday was one of Liverpool's highlights of the lesbian calendar: the annual women-only disco. The discos took place just along the road from the venue where I had bumped into Julie, but drew a larger and slightly older crowd. In particular, these nights attracted professional lesbians, many of whom were PE teachers from schools in the city and surrounding area. These women were the ones I umpired opposite when my netball team had a match. As a new PE teacher, I aspired to be just like them, devouring their advice, praise and encouragement when it was given. They were more established in the teaching profession and so better paid; their tracksuits and trainers were more expensive than mine and I hoped one day to afford the gear they wore. Branded sports goods and label snobbery were just emerging in the 1990s, and I envied their velour tracksuits by Tacchini and Ellesse – the type of tracksuits worn by famous tennis players in impractical colours like cream, pale blue and white.

At the women's discos, I studied the older lesbian PE teachers closely, a rare chance to see them relaxed and themselves. They were almost always in couples and, although they were discreet, it was usually known among the Liverpool lesbian population who lived with whom. I used to watch how comfortable they were with each other at the discos. They never kissed in public, but small gestures like a hand brushing an eyelash from a cheek revealed the tenderness and care these women had for one another. And they would dance, often in a quite old-fashioned way ('in hold', as they say on *Strictly*), twirling each other around between fits of giggles.

Tessa and I would always try to get to the disco really early to avoid the ordeal of making an entrance. Professional lesbians, especially teachers, were well aware of the risks of being seen at the women's disco and so all watched the door with a mix of caution and apprehension. Once inside, I would be an avid door-watcher, hoping to see professional lesbian couples arrive, seeking some of the same thrill I used to get from seeing my own PE teacher out in the car or at the local supermarket.

I relied on alcohol for my confidence but, not having a great deal of money, Tessa and I would drink at home before going out to make the night cheaper. The use of alcohol was a balancing act. Too much and I might approach the older lesbians I respected and talk at them, believing (wrongly) that I was witty, charming and interesting. Too little alcohol, however, would leave me stuck to the wall all evening, too self-conscious to dance, go to the toilets or head to the bar.

After seeing Julie in the club the previous Saturday, I vowed that I would never go out in Liverpool again. Our encounter during the cross-country lesson on the following Monday, though a relief of sorts, had not gone well. And Julie could be moody and unpredictable. It was common for a netball bib to be thrown to the floor if it was not the position she wanted to play; she would occasionally storm out of the gym, upset that I had asked her to start a match on the subs' bench or had, in her words, 'looked at her funny'. In retrospect, Julie needed to be noticed by me in much the same way I needed to be noticed by the older, professional lesbian teachers who turned up once a year for the women's disco.

I had no idea whether, having been at the club the week before, Julie would turn up at the disco. I worried that after our encounter during my cross-country lesson, she might feel aggrieved and want to get her own back. Rather than worrying about how Julie was coping, I was completely absorbed in anxiety and self-pity.

I decided it was far too risky to go to the disco, even though Tessa and I had bought our tickets months ago. Tessa took the opportunity to visit her mum instead, so I was left alone for the weekend, finding myself at home alone watching the television on a Saturday night.

The acronym FOMO (fear of missing out) is now used frequently, but it wasn't really articulated 30 years ago. It was not a feeling people readily admitted to. There were no mobile phones, no Instagram, no Twitter or TikTok showing people 'living their best lives' in real time, so if you weren't there, you could only imagine what was happening.

I was surprised at the strength of my emotions as I sat at home, wondering what I was missing at Liverpool's lesbian event of the year. I couldn't focus on the television. I imagined our friends Sue and Michelle, fellow PE teachers who had gone along without us, sitting at a table with Helen and Sarah, Jackie and Jen, the two couples we most wanted to be like and be around. I worried what they might be doing and imagined that they were playing pool together, or that Sue and Michelle might get a lift home in Helen and Sarah's smart new Roland Garros edition Peugeot 205. I worried that Sue and Michelle might be invited over to their houses; that they would share in-jokes from this evening spent together when we next all saw each other at a school netball or hockey tournament. In time, Sue and Michelle would become the next professional lesbian PE teacher couple, and Tessa and I would be left out and left behind.

I imagined that Julie was there too. What if she became part of the group – part of my group? In my head, Julie was sitting with the professional lesbians; they found her funny and took her under their wing. I became more and more anxious and paced around the living room as images of the disco, Julie, the professional lesbians, and Sue and Michelle churned in my head, distorting all perspective. Should I go down to the club? Yes, I must. I would drive down there to see for myself what was going on. If Julie was there, I would tell her to leave. I dashed upstairs to get dressed, pulling on my jeans, grabbing my white shirt and stuffing my feet into my oxblood Doc Martens. I found my car keys and headed outside into the dark, slamming the door behind me.

As the fresh air hit me, I stopped in the street. What was I doing? I would never have the confidence to walk into that disco on my own, let alone wade in among the professional lesbians and tell Julie she couldn't be there. And my car was a mile and a half away, outside the police station. I put my hands to my head and turned around. I was surprised at the distress I felt and was ashamed, not for the first time, of the selfishness and immaturity of my thoughts. I went back through the front door, got undressed and went to bed instead, remaining awake and tormented by what I imagined was going on at the disco. Only well into the early hours, when I was sure the evening would have drawn to a close, did I finally fall asleep.

1995

As the AIDS crisis reached its peak in the UK, more than 1700 people lost their lives to the disease in 1995 (House of Lords, 2011). Meanwhile, Stonewall, along with the campaign group Rank Outsiders, launched a major campaign to end the ban on lesbian, gay and bisexual people openly serving in the British military, after the Clinton administration had passed the 'don't ask, don't tell' law in the US in December 1993.

In 1995, the charity Mermaids was founded by a group of parents brought together by their children's gender dysphoria. Mermaids offers resources to transgender, non-binary and gender-diverse young people, their families and carers, and professionals. Today, it is one of the UK's leading LGBTQ+ charities, empowering thousands of people with its secure online communities, local community groups, helpline services, web resources and events.

Elsewhere in the world, civil unions between same-sex couples were legalised in Sweden, and anti-discrimination laws that encompassed sexual orientation were passed in the Canadian province of Newfoundland and Labrador. In the US, the Human Rights Campaign broadened its pursuit of an America where LGBTQ+ people were ensured equality and 'embraced as full members of the American family at home, at work and in every community'.

Also in 1995, Rachel Maddow became the first openly lesbian winner of a Rhodes Scholarship, an international postgraduate award that affords talented young people the opportunity to study at Oxford University in

England. Maddow would go on to become a political commentator and news anchor, and a lesbian icon in the US.

MARCH 1995. WHAT AM I AFRAID OF?

In 1995, I was invited to discuss my lived experience as a lesbian PE teacher by the academic Gill Clarke, as part of her PhD research. Under the pseudonym Caroline, I relayed to Clarke some of my challenges. She asked me what I was most afraid of, as a lesbian teacher teaching under Section 28. I struggled to answer Clarke's question initially, but later reflected on the question in my diary.

> What is the fear that ultimately paralyses me as a PE teacher? I can't quite believe I am committing this thought to the page but I suppose, as a PE teacher, I am afraid of being perceived as a pervert or a paedophile. That's often the first thing people think of when they know you're a lesbian and you teach PE. I know that statistics show that the majority of paedophiles are heterosexual men, yet I still worry far too much of the time that this is what people might be thinking about me – that I am not suitable to be around children.

Clarke's research suggests that I was not alone in holding this fear; some of the other lesbian PE teachers she interviewed shared the same concern.

> *Their chief fear … was that if their sexuality was revealed they would be viewed as paedophiles, child molesters and perverts.* (Clarke, 1996, p.201)

As a PE teacher, I was especially sensitive to the paedophile or pervert label because part of my job entailed supervising girls as they changed and showered. In 1993, Clare Sullivan wrote an autobiographical account of her experiences as a lesbian teacher in an inner-city school. Not a PE teacher herself, Sullivan made the following comment:

> *How lesbians who teach girls' physical education cope, I don't know. I would be paranoid that my sexuality would be discovered and that the tabloid press would have a field day fabricating salacious headlines.* (Sullivan, 1993, p.99)

It is unthinkable today that the sexuality of a teacher would be newsworthy but during the Section 28 era this seemed completely probable. While overt prejudice against LGBTQ+ people may no longer be acceptable, those wishing to justify their homophobic views back in the early 1990s needed simply to make a link with paedophilia, however tenuous.

As a lesbian who was also a PE teacher, I always felt uncomfortable at school and this was a significant contributing factor to my decision to leave PE after only six years. I was so self-conscious and I worried permanently, especially after the incident with Julie, that as a PE teacher I was especially vulnerable to allegations of wrongdoing. I shared my fear of losing my job in the interview with Clarke and it appeared Section 28 had created a climate of fear for all Clarke's lesbian teacher participants. Writing about the impact of Section 28, Clarke states 'it has nevertheless contributed to the situation whereby all the lesbian [PE] teachers in my research feared for their continued employment should their sexuality be revealed' (Clarke, 1998b, p.66).

Another of my diary entries from 1995 describes the impact of holding on to fears such as these in the long term. On the edge of depression and alone at home, I wrote:

> The necessity of living a lie, of being invisible at school, a nobody, can at times feel like spiralling free-fall into a black pit of obscurity. I don't let others get to know me and I'm starting to feel as though I don't know who I am either. It takes so much energy to be someone else. What did I say to her last time we spoke? What did say when I spoke to him the other week? It's hard work trying to remember all my layers of deceit. School feels very hard at the moment and, in truth, I wish I had chosen another career instead. I will never be able to have children myself, so why should I dedicate my career to ensuring the children of my heterosexual peers get the best start in life? All I ever wanted to be was a teacher but I thought I would be able to be myself. I'm only ever myself within these four walls. As soon as I step outside my front door, I have to be who everyone else expects me to be.

1996

In 1996, I discovered the film *Desert Hearts* (1985), adapted ~~watch/read~~ from the 1964 lesbian novel *Desert of the Heart* by Jane Rule. Set in 1959, *Desert Hearts* tells the story of a university professor who travels to Reno, Nevada, to obtain a quick divorce. While in Reno, the professor discovers her lesbian identity through a relationship with another, more self-assured lesbian who works in a casino. The film, starring Helen Shaver and Patricia Charbonneau, is considered to be one of the first films on general release to present a positive portrayal of lesbian sexuality. Ten years later, in 2006, my partner and our friends would visit Reno during a holiday to Nevada and California. On hearing the trains passing through the casino town blowing their deep horns, I was transported back to the final scene between the women at Reno train station. At last, a lesbian film in which the protagonists did not meet a sorry end.

Also in 1996, Muffin Spencer-Devlin became the first professional female golfer to come out as a lesbian. In the same year, the sitcom *Friends* featured the wedding of Ross's ex-wife, Carol (played by Jane Sibbett), and her partner, Susan (Jessica Hecht).

In real life in the US, same-sex marriage was facing a judicial struggle. Opponents of same-sex marriage claimed that it validated alternative family formations, destabilised monogamy, and encouraged incestuous relationships and polygamous marriage.

The Defence of Marriage Act (DOMA) was passed by the US Congress and signed into law by President Clinton on 21 September 1996. It defined marriage only as the union of one man and one woman, thus permitting individual states to not recognise the same-sex unions granted elsewhere. DOMA was introduced in part as a response to speculation that the state of Hawaii was about to legalise same-sex marriage. There was a fear that same-sex couples would head off to Hawaii to get married and then expect their marriage to be recognised in the state where they lived. After DOMA was signed into law, 40 states enacted explicit bans on same-sex marriage. DOMA also adversely impacted non-biological parents in same-sex couples. Non-biological parents were unable to define or establish a legal relationship with the child or children of their partner, and same-sex partners were unable to take family medical leave to care for non-biological children or for their partners. They could not adopt children or petition the court for child support, visitation or custody if the relationship ended.

It would take until 2013 for DOMA to be struck down by the US Supreme Court (*United States v. Windsor*). The provision of the law that had permitted states to refuse to recognise same-sex marriages performed in other jurisdictions was later invalidated by the Supreme Court in *Obergefell v. Hodges* (2015), which granted to same-sex couples the constitutional right to marry and to have their marriage recognised in other states.

NOVEMBER 1996. LOOK AT YER CAR, LOVE

In 1996, I was living with my partner, Tessa, in my house under the bridge in Garston. Feeling more secure in my home, as I no longer lived alone, I had stopped parking my car outside the police station and now parked it in front of our living room window. In my diary, I recall the following incident.

> At 2am, Tessa and I are woken by banging on the window downstairs. I leap up and pull on tracksuit bottoms, then rush downstairs to find out what is happening. Two men, friendly but clearly the worse for wear, stand on the pavement. Pointing at my car, one of them mouths through the window, 'Look at yer car, love.'
>
> Every window has been smashed. The car stands in a pool of broken glass, which makes it twinkle like some sick kind of gameshow prize.

I go out in my slippers and wade through the glass as the two men depart down the road and into the alleyway. Tessa hangs back inside until the men have gone, then joins me outside. I try the door handle and notice that each of the locks has been filled with a cement-type mixture. I reach inside the car, carefully avoiding the broken glass protruding from the window's seal, and open the glove compartment to see what has been stolen. To my surprise, the fascia of my stereo and my emergency £10 remain in the glovebox, exactly where I have left them. As I peer into the dark interior of the car, I see what has motivated the vandalism. In the same cement-type mixture, someone has written 'LEZ' across my dashboard. Tessa beckons me to come and look at the front of the car. Across the bonnet, in large letters, someone has gouged 'DYKE' into the paintwork. I always hate to hear the word, but I especially hate to see it written. The letters are angular and harsh; even the shape of the word looks as if it is designed to cause harm.

Tessa and I go inside and I call the police. Tessa will drop me off at school in the morning. Even if the windows were not smashed, I couldn't arrive in the school car park with 'DYKE' written across my car bonnet. I'll get a crime number for the insurance, but the police won't do anything as there will be no witnesses. And, anyway, I feel too embarrassed and ashamed at the word on the bonnet to pursue it further.

No one was hurt and my car was eventually repaired, but the regular and targeted nature of this harassment took its toll on Tessa and me – and ultimately on our relationship. I put the house on the market but it didn't sell. As the house was mine, I remained there and returned to the nightly ritual of parking my car at the police station. Tessa met someone else and moved to the Lancashire suburbs. I missed her and envied her new relationship. I also envied her life in an affluent area where she no doubt felt much safer than she ever did with me under the bridge.

1997

In 1997, Angela Eagle, the Labour MP for nearby Wallasey on the Wirral, became the first MP to come out voluntarily as a lesbian. Stephen Twigg became the first out gay MP to be elected to the House of Commons. Also in this year, gay and lesbian partners were granted the same rights to immigration as heterosexual couples in the UK.

The comedian Ellen DeGeneres' semi-autobiographical sitcom, *Ellen*, was hugely popular here in the UK and in the US. When the character Ellen came out as gay in an episode broadcast on 30 April 1997, shockwaves rippled through the television industry. In addition to her character's coming out, DeGeneres publicly shared that she was also gay, appearing on the cover of *Time* magazine under the headline 'Yep, I'm gay'.

Almost a year of preparation went into the episode, beginning in May 1996, when DeGeneres discussed the potential storyline with the show's writers. She hoped that, in addressing the fictional Ellen's sexuality, she might provide a new direction for the show and explain why her character lacked chemistry with male romantic partners.

Despite threats from advertisers and religious groups, the coming out episode was an enormous ratings success. It won several awards, was celebrated by the lesbian and gay community in the US and the UK, and became a cultural phenomenon. Nevertheless, DeGeneres and her show quickly garnered mainstream criticism. Her onscreen relationship with Laura Dern made some viewers uncomfortable and, as a consequence, the series was cancelled the following season. Despite her popularity and obvious talent, DeGeneres faced a career backlash and was left without work. It would take until 2001 for DeGeneres to return to American network television.

Elsewhere in the world in 1997, homosexuality was decriminalised in Ecuador, Venezuela and the Australian state of Tasmania. Fiji also introduced limited rights for same-sex couples.

JANUARY 1997. LOUISE

Although no one was hurt and my car was eventually repaired, the damage to the car left me feeling vulnerable, especially as I was living alone again. However, I accepted this at the time as an inevitable part of being a lesbian. What shook me more was a homophobic attack on a student teacher friend. I recorded the details in my diary.

> As my friend Sue and I near the doors to the ward, my stomach lurches, as it always does in hospitals. I feel slightly giddy with the adrenaline and sense of anticipation as we look around for Louise. Suddenly we see Louise's partner, Lisa, a PE teacher, waving at us from her chair at the far end of the ward. I then glimpse Louise, propped slightly upright in the bed beside her.
>
> As we get nearer to the bed, the extent of Louise's injuries becomes apparent. The right side of her face is a maroon swollen expanse of skin. Her nose has been swallowed by her cheek. Her right eye is closed tight and black coarse stitches sit across her eyelid. Louise's right arm is in plaster. The loose neck of her hospital gown reveals bruising that runs down her skinny frame from her shoulders and chest before disappearing beneath the hospital covers.
>
> Sue, ashen and clearly shaken, is the first to speak. 'What happened? How did they do this?'
>
> Lisa takes a deep breath before recalling the event that has changed them both forever.
>
> 'We were walking home from the college disco on Friday night. As we rounded the corner into the lane by the park, there was no sign

of anyone, so I held Louise's hand as we walked. Suddenly, Reece and Darren [fellow students from Louise's PE teacher training course] appeared from the side entrance to the park and barged into us, knocking us both over.'

Lisa begins to cry as she continues. 'They were just shouting "Fucking dykes" over and over. They didn't seem that interested in me but, as Louise lay on the ground, they kicked her over and over. I didn't know what to do. I got up and I was just screaming at them, hitting them, running up and down the road to get help, anything to try to stop them.'

Sue puts her arm around Lisa. I look again at Louise. In the hospital gown she looks small, half the size she is in her tracksuits or leather jacket. I know of Reece and Darren and picture them towering above her as she lies on the ground by the gates to the park. I think about all the times, fuelled by alcohol and emboldened by the darkness, Tessa and I walked home through the Liverpool streets holding hands, always looking left, right and behind to check we were completely alone. There was something exhilarating about being out in public and getting away with a sign of affection, however brief or slight.

It was Louise this time, but it could have been any one of us. Louise will make a full physical recovery, but the legacy of this incident will affect all of us for years to come.

After the assault on Louise, both men were tried and Reece was given a custodial sentence. I like to think that neither man realised his goal of becoming a PE teacher, although this was well before the vetting and barring processes we have today and so I cannot be sure.

The attack on Louise happened 25 years ago and, thankfully, towns and cities across the UK are now more accepting places for LGBTQ+ people. It is commonplace to see same-sex couples holding hands and homophobic attacks nowadays sometimes cause moral outrage. At the time, however, there was a sense that if we were reckless and brazen enough to hold hands in the street then we were asking to get beaten.

The attack on Louise affected the entire community of lesbian PE teachers in Liverpool, deeply and quite profoundly. Although I am no longer in touch with Louise, I think about her in her hospital gown to this day. For years afterwards, as a teacher, when I heard the word 'gay' flung carelessly as an insult between students in the school corridor, or when I heard a homophobic joke in the staffroom, I could not help but wonder how many steps away this was from the sort of deep-seated hatred expressed by the would-be teachers who attacked Louise. She was assaulted not by a stranger but by two fellow student teachers; supposedly decent, educated human beings from her course. These were people Louise reasonably thought she was safe with. A few days after visiting Louise and under the shadow of Section 28, I wrote the following reflection in my diary. I had heard pupils at school call each other 'gay', 'queer', 'lez' and 'dyke' almost constantly that day and Louise was still very much at the front of my mind.

> What if I was braver, if I challenged the homophobic name-calling I hear in the school corridors? I could tell the kids that what they were saying was personally offensive to me. I could tell them about Louise, that would shut them up. However, my own fear of these names is visceral. I am paralysed when I hear what they call each other and panic that they will turn the names on me. As a teacher, it is my job to educate young people, but I can't educate them about the very thing I care about most.

1998

By 1998, Section 28 had been law for 10 years and there was no sign of it being repealed. However, popular culture was beginning to become a little more LGBTQ+ inclusive. The BBC launched a women's football primetime drama called *Playing the Field*, based on a book by Pete Davies entitled *I Lost My Heart to the Belles*, written about a real-life women's football club, the Doncaster Belles. *Playing the Field* ran for five series, from 1998 to 2002, with writers including Kay Mellor, Sally Wainwright and Gaynor Faye. The show also featured a lesbian couple, Angie (Tracy Whitwell) and Gabby (Saira Todd). The pair split at the end of the first series but by the end of the second were back together.

Julie Hesmondhalgh joined the British soap opera *Coronation Street* to play Hayley Patterson. Hayley was the first transgender character in a soap and the first permanent transgender character in a serialised drama. Hesmondhalgh, regretfully, was not herself trans, but she won an abundance of awards for her portrayal of Hayley and spent 16 years on *Coronation Street*.

Lord Alli, a Labour life peer and Muslim, became the first openly gay member of the House of Lords. The Labour party, elected to government in 1997, introduced an amendment to the Crime and Disorder Bill to set the age of consent at 16 for homosexual men. The amendment was later rejected by the House of Lords, preventing it from passing into law.

Beyond the UK, Rita Hester, an African American trans woman, was murdered in Boston, US, on 28 November 1998. After an outpouring of grief and rage among the Massachusetts LGBTQ+ community, Hester's death inspired a 'Remembering Our Dead' web project and the annual Transgender Day of Remembrance. Matthew Shepard was also murdered in 1998. A gay student at the University of Wyoming, Shepard was beaten, tortured and abandoned in a rural area outside Laramie. He died in hospital six days later, on 12 October 1998. The suspects, Aaron McKinney and Russell Henderson, were arrested and charged with first-degree murder. There was substantial media coverage of the attack and the role Shepard's sexuality played as a motive.

Also in 1998, South Africa and Romania ended the ban on lesbians and gay men serving in the military. Dana International became the first transgender singer to win the Eurovision Song Contest, representing Israel with the song *Diva*.

JUNE 1998. THEY DIDN'T MEAN IT PERSONALLY

By 1998, I had relocated to Suffolk to live with my new partner and was head of learning development in a large secondary school. I was closeted among school colleagues and felt anxious in my new school. I was particularly wary of the large groups of Year 10 and 11 boys who hung around in the corridor outside my office. They regularly hurled homophobic insults at one another and I dreaded that one day they would turn these insults in my direction. Though I no longer taught PE or wore a tracksuit, I was convinced that everyone could tell that I was gay and it was just a matter of time before someone pointed it out. When I was tired, I would envisage that once one person mentioned to another that I was gay, there would be, in this huge school, a moment of simultaneous realisation among the staff and students, like the moment in *The Emperor's New Clothes* when all agree that he is naked. Someone would call me gay and, just like that, my position would be untenable.

The boys in the corridor did turn their homophobia on me and, for a while, like the emperor in the children's story, I felt utterly exposed. My diary in 1998 recalls the incident.

It's lunchtime and I am in my office with the door closed. Since I started at my new school at Easter, I have found it difficult to fit in and, despite a few friendly faces telling me it's hard to start a new job in the summer term, I am finding the staffroom a very daunting place. I can't seem to catch the rhythm of the rest of the staff, who all seem so at ease with one another. There is a younger crowd of smokers, but they all seem achingly cool. Then there are the teachers and teaching assistants who gossip relentlessly – sometimes about me, I suspect.

I sit at my desk with my marking and long to be elsewhere. I especially long to be at home. I look at the picture of my cat I have brought into school in a half-hearted attempt to make my new office my own. This is the only kind of personal picture I can risk. My colleagues personalise their offices with photos of partners, husbands, wives and, of course, their children, but I know that to have any evidence of my partner at my workplace would be inviting trouble.

My musings are broken by thuds against my office door. As I get up from my desk and instinctively make my way towards the noise, my office door bursts open and a tangled ball of Year 10 boys falls into my office and falls into me.

'Lesbian!' they shout, before retreating at top speed down the corridor. I look around, desperate to check who else has heard this.

As I lean on my open office door, I feel a familiar tightness in my chest. It must be so obvious to everyone; I must be ridiculous. I begin to wonder if I should report this incident to the headteacher but talk myself out of it immediately. What would I say and what on earth would he think of me? Just as I begin to close the door, I become aware of Martin, the head of maths who has, I realise, witnessed the whole incident from the top of the stairs.

'Are you OK?' he asks.

'Yes, I'm fine,' I reply, forcing a weak smile and wishing to be anywhere but here. Fortunately, Martin moves on and leaves me to my thoughts. I retreat to my desk, closing the office door behind me.

Minutes later, I am startled as my office phone rings. Ian, the assistant head, asks to see me in his office. I set off down the corridor, following in the footsteps of the boys. I feel as though all the students congregated by radiators and in stairwells are laughing at me. I am sure I hear whispers from them as I pass – 'Lezzer', 'Dyke' – but I don't dare look up and can't tell whether the voices are real or in my head. I take a diversion across the playground to get some air and try to avoid further taunts, real or imagined.

I arrive at Ian's office. He is always jocular and larger than life. 'Come in, come in,' he beckons, shifting a pile of folders so that I can sit down. 'Martin's just been down to tell me what happened earlier. What they called you was a disgusting name, especially such a nice girl like you. It's unacceptable and I'm not standing for it. I'm going to have those boys and I've already sent Martin to fetch them all.'

I don't know how to respond. Does Ian know that I am actually a lesbian? He reaches across the desk and takes my hand in his. 'Don't worry,' he says. 'They didn't mean it personally. They just wanted to say something spiteful to provoke a reaction because you're new here. Listen, I know it's not true and you know it's not true, so try not to take it to heart.'

Ian is warm and fatherly. In this moment, he is the kindest person I have met at the school so far but also, unwittingly, the cruellest. I tell him I'm fine and thank him for sending for the boys, but I want to get out of his office before Martin brings them to the door. I stand up and return Ian's folders to the chair. I smile at him, thank him for being supportive and leave the room.

I will leave this shitty school and these shitty people as soon as I can find somewhere else to go.

1999

In the spring of 1999, a nail bomb exploded at the Admiral Duncan, a gay pub in Soho, London. The bomb was planted by the former British National Party member David Copeland and killed three people. It was the third bomb planted by Copeland in a campaign to target London's black, Bengali and gay communities.

Shortly after 6.30pm on Friday 30 April 1999, an unattended bag aroused the suspicions of people in the Admiral Duncan; the bomb inside the bag exploded just as the pub manager was examining it. In addition to the three deaths, 79 people were injured. Four of the survivors needed limb amputations.

Copeland was arrested at his home later the same evening. On the Sunday after the attack, a meeting was organised in Soho Square and was attended by thousands of people from London's gay community. Speakers included the Metropolitan Police's assistant commissioner, who then stationed a crime scene van outside the Admiral Duncan staffed entirely by gay and lesbian police officers. This was the start of a more positive relationship between Soho's gay community and the Metropolitan Police.

Also in 1999 in the UK, an amendment to Labour's Crime and Disorder Bill, including an equal age of consent clause, was rejected again by the House of Lords. Michael Cashman, the *EastEnders* actor involved in the first mouth-to-mouth kiss between men on a British soap opera in 1989, became the first openly gay UK member elected to the European Parliament.

Elsewhere in the world in 1999, civil unions between same-sex couples were legalised in the US state of California, but stopped short of including the joint adoption of children. In France, it became possible to register same-sex partnerships, and South Africa granted immigration benefits to same-sex couples for the first time.

JULY 1999. AN UNEVEN EXCHANGE

In 1999, I attended a three-day course for teachers that explored research in the classroom. This was part of a package of CPD provided by Suffolk local authority at its teachers' centre. On the first day we looked at interviewing in schools. I wrote the following in my diary.

I find myself nervously sitting around a long table with 20 or so fellow teachers. I am sitting next to Joyce, a teacher some 10 years older than me. After introductions, we are asked to pair off and get to know each other in a task that encourages us to reflect on our interviewing technique. Joyce and I decide to make the most of the July sunshine and head into the garden of the teachers' centre. My stomach twists as I think about what this task will require me to share about myself. After these three days I will probably never see Joyce again. There is no need to tell her my secret.

Before we even find a place to sit, Joyce asks me if I'm married. Although I have anticipated this question for the duration of our walk in the garden so far, I have not settled on a suitable answer. I reach, therefore, for the modus operandi that has seen me through so many networking events with other teachers in the past. I talk about my partner, Jo, without identifying her gender, describing the job she does or where we live, using the pronouns 'they' and 'them' throughout. Joyce seems to accept my narrative, though I note she uses the pronouns he and him for Jo. As we practise our questioning, I take every opportunity I can to flip the conversation back to Joyce and her life, and so we engage in a sort of polite ping-pong game.

Joyce presses on with questions and disarms me again by raising the issue of children. I explain that I don't have any and Joyce looks a little shocked. I don't have an excuse prepared. I'm not sure why my 'husband' Jo(e) and I wouldn't have children. While I freeze, Joyce fills the silence with ever more intimate details about herself and her family. She tells me all about her husband's depression, their increasing financial debt, her drug-addicted daughter and how unhappy she is in her marriage. Joyce presents herself with such extraordinary vulnerability that I start to feel guilty about the unevenness of our exchange, so with a deep breath I turn to Joyce and confess.

'I haven't been entirely honest with you. My partner, Jo, is actually a woman, It's Jo as in Joanne. We don't have children because, well, just because.'

I search Joyce's face, trying to decipher whether it is my lesbianism or my lying that has stunned her into silence. After what feels like an endless period of contemplation, she finally speaks.

'Catherine, hopefully you won't take this the wrong way, but it's such a waste – you're lovely.' Joyce and I sit in silence while she presumably ponders the deceit and my sexuality, neither of which, from the look on her face, has pleased her. Does she want me to go? To leave her sitting in the garden? I can't take back what I've said. What happens now?

We eventually continue our interview practice, talking about the safer subjects of our schools and our teaching experience. We steer well clear of anything else that is vaguely personal.

In this uneven exchange, Joyce has openly shared with me her own vulnerabilities, but I had not initially felt able to share similarly intimate information about my life. And when I do, it is too late – I have lied. But Joyce doesn't understand the burden of Section 28. I doubt she has even heard of it.

Joyce's revelations are a coming out of sorts for her, and I realise in that moment that lesbian and gay people do not have the monopoly on coming out. We all feel the need to come out for lots of different reasons. The difference between Joyce's coming out about her family problems and my coming out sits in the fact that Joyce's disclosures are squarely in the context of her heterosexuality. They could not jeopardise her career, as my revelation might.

This is the first morning of three days I have to spend alongside Joyce and as I return to the meeting room to feed back, I am not sure what to do. I contemplate feigning illness and going home. I wonder if I should swap seats but then worry we may have to feed back as a pair. All I know is that I no longer want to be here on this course that requires I share personal information with strangers.

2000

At the turn of the century, the New Labour government finally made a move to repeal Section 28 in England and Wales. The bill was defeated, however, by Conservative peers in the House of Lords. Scotland was more successful and abolished Clause 2a, as Section 28 was known there, in October 2000.

Also in 2000, the ban on lesbian, gay and bisexual people serving in the British armed forces ended, after the European Court of Human Rights ruled it unlawful. LGBTQ+ citizens can now serve openly in all the armed forces, and discrimination on the grounds of sexuality or gender is forbidden.

In the US, Hillary Clinton became the first spouse of a president to march in a Pride parade. The Transgender Pride flag was displayed for the first time at a Pride parade in Phoenix, Arizona, and same-sex partnerships were legally recognised in the state of Vermont.

In South Africa, the Promotion of Equality and Prevention of Unfair Discrimination Act was enacted as a comprehensive piece of anti-discrimination legislation. It prohibited unfair discrimination by the South African government and by organisations and individuals. It also made hate speech and harassment illegal. The act specifically listed race, gender, sex, pregnancy, family responsibility or status, marital status, ethnic or social origin, HIV/AIDS status, colour, sexual orientation, age, disability, religion, conscience, belief, culture, language and birth as 'prohibited grounds' for discrimination, but also contained criteria that courts could apply to determine grounds to prohibit discrimination based on other characteristics. This was a significant development for a country that had for decades operated under apartheid.

In Germany, the Bundestag federal parliament formally apologised to gays and lesbians persecuted under the Nazi regime. In Israel, the Supreme Court recognised a lesbian partner as the legal mother of her partner's biological son: Nicole Brener Kadish became the adoptive mother of the son of her partner, Ruthy Brener Kadish, setting an important precedent for other lesbian couples.

MARCH 2000. SHANNON'S HAT

In March 2000, I was teaching three hours of netball a week to help out the PE department in my new upper school. That's the problem with being new in September: the timetable is done and you're not there to have a say about what you will and will not teach in the following academic year. After moving to Suffolk, I tried to reinvent myself professionally, first as a special educational needs coordinator (SENCO) and then as a learning development lead, teaching English to those students in mainstream schools who struggled with literacy. But I trained as a PE specialist and my PE credentials hung around me stubbornly. Keen to secure the post, I had at my interviewed agreed I would teach a little PE if required, hoping that showing willing would get me the job but dreading that I might be required to actually teach any PE.

Since leaving PE for the classroom, it felt much easier to manage the intersection of the professional and personal. I missed the fun, the banter, the camaraderie of the netball clubs, the away fixtures on coaches with the school teams, everything I had revelled in during my first post as a PE teacher in Liverpool. But it was evident that despite the incident with the boys outside my office door at my last school, I was far less likely to hear the stinging jibes of 'lez' or 'dyke' when I wasn't walking the corridors in a tracksuit day after day. However, after a particularly challenging episode while helping out in PE, I wrote the following in my diary.

It is Year 10 netball today and I have changed into my tracksuit and trainers in the ladies' toilets next to the staffroom. I don't know the PE team well and am not comfortable enough to change in front of the others in the PE office. I am aware that the male and female heads of PE are married to each other and, although I have no evidence, I get the distinct feeling that this PE department isn't gay-friendly. Since Section 28, I perceive that some straight female PE teachers seem almost hostile to their unmarried, more masculine-presenting peers. I sense this is because the well-worn trope of the lesbian PE teacher has taken on a certain gravity in light of Section 28, and those of us that are a bit butch are seen as giving the profession a bad name. Or maybe this is just my paranoia.

The students at this upper school know me as the teacher who helps those with special needs. I work with a small percentage of the students, who rarely acknowledge me outside the safety of my classroom, as coming to me is usually something they feel ashamed of. None of the students in this school know I trained in PE or played sport at county level. To them, I am an ageing woman in an untrendy tracksuit and trainers who is helping out the proper PE staff.

Year 10 PE lessons are always an ordeal. The sporty girls hate it because the standard of sport is so low. The cool girls are self-conscious in their PE kits and, feeling insecure, deflect their vulnerabilities by being unkind to the sporty girls. This results in the sporty girls feigning disinterest in PE to ensure they don't get picked on. When they do get picked on, of course, the names they are called for being good at sport are 'lez' or 'dyke'.

It is a sunny morning and I'm aiming to take the girls over to the courts for netball. The fiercest of all the Year 10s is Shannon. She has a note (forged) excusing her from the lesson. She is wearing a baseball cap with the initials FCUK, from the fashion retailer French Connection UK. Being deliberately similar to the word 'fuck', the branding has caused widespread controversy and so, inevitably, teenagers love to wear it. Baseball caps are not allowed in school and nor is FCUK branding. I am wary of Shannon, however, so initially I turn a blind eye.

Shannon is in the changing room as the rest of the class get changed. I stay outside in the corridor. Twelve years into Section 28, I know better than to make myself vulnerable to accusations of staring at the Year 10 girls while they change.

From the changing room, I suddenly hear Shannon shout, 'Ooh, look at her knickers, the dirty bitch.' The class laugh and I hear scuffles break out. I quickly enter the room to find that Shannon has pinned one of the sporty girls to the floor. The girl is wearing her school shirt and her pants, which unfortunately are stained with blood from her period. 'Fat bitch,' the sporty girl shouts at Shannon. 'Fuckin' dyke,' Shannon retorts. The class, laughing with nerves and excitement, gather around the churning ball of limbs on the changing room floor.

I pull Shannon away and tell her to stand outside in the corridor. My heart goes out to the other girl, who rushes to put her school trousers back on, shaking from the humiliation of this ordeal.

One of the first things I learned as a newly qualified teacher was to never tell off a student when you are angry. It always goes wrong. That's why students are sent out of classrooms, to give the teacher and them time to calm down before a fair and proportionate sanction can be determined and restorative work can take place. Today, I break that golden rule.

I bound out of the changing room, boiling from Shannon's cruel behaviour. The fact that Shannon's taunts were homophobic adds to my fury. Shannon waits against the narrow corridor wall, hot and breathing heavily from the exertion of the fight. As I stand opposite her, she repeatedly steps forward into my personal space and soon it is me with my back to the corridor wall.

Shannon is almost my height and her FCUK baseball cap peak protrudes close to my face as she steps ever further into my personal space. Our eyes lock. Who does she think she is? I'm now angrier than ever and Shannon clearly has no intention of backing down. I grab the peak of the baseball cap and remove it from Shannon's head. 'Caps are not allowed in school,' I say, by way of justification, suddenly panicking that I have crossed a line.

'Give me my cap back, you fucking dyke,' Shannon yells, reaching to grab the cap from my left hand, which I now hide behind my back.

'No,' I say, standing my ground, albeit now almost pinned against the corridor wall. Shannon's head moves closer to mine and I can smell her breath, which is sweet with the scent of bubblegum. Shannon spits in my face. 'Give – me – my – cap – back – you – fucking – dyke,' she says again, this time more slowly, emphasising each of the words.

My pulse is racing. I peel away sideways, under Shannon's arm. Shaking, I drop the cap on the floor, head straight out of the gym door and into the school car park.

One of the other PE teachers follows me. Sensing her behind me, I call out, 'I'm fine, I just need a minute.'

'I'll take your group with mine,' she says. 'Go and get a cup of tea.'

Still in my tracksuit, I retreat to my classroom base and watch as the male head of PE marches Shannon across the car park and the playground to the headteacher's office.

I change back into my clothes and wait for the headteacher to contact me to tell me that Shannon has been suspended. I am sure the incident is the talk of the staffroom but, given the 'fucking dyke' part, I can't face going in there today. Lunchtime ends and the headteacher hasn't been in touch. But Shannon is notorious for outbursts and I have no doubt she has been sent home for at least the rest of the week.

Later that afternoon, as I move between classrooms to teach, I see Shannon in her baseball cap in the art room with the rest of her class. I am furious. I turn in the opposite direction to my next class and run down the corridor to the head's office. 'Can I see him, please,' I say to his PA, not dignifying the headteacher with a name.

'Yes, he's not with anyone,' she says, cheerily. 'Knock on the door.'

'Come in,' he shouts, and I open the door and walk in. 'Ah, Catherine. I've spoken to Shannon, but she says you took her hat off her head.'

'I know, I shouldn't have done that. I'm sorry, but Shannon spat at me.'

'Shannon says she didn't mean to do that. It was an accident when she was speaking to you.'

'Well, she swore at me,' I offer in reply, stopping short of referencing the 'dyke' part.

'Yes, she admits that, but is sorry. Look, we all know Shannon's got issues, but I think we should give her the benefit of the doubt. It's best she stays in school; we all know that home is far from ideal.'

In my head I seethe, stifling the urge to say, 'Either she goes home or I do.' I feel hot tears of frustration brimming in my eyes and am determined to get out of the head's office before they run down my cheeks. I turn, thank the head for seeing me and run back to my class, drying my eyes on my sleeves as I go.

2001

In 2001, the European Court of Human Rights found that its convention was being violated in the UK. It judged that the UK government was being discriminatory by having a higher age of consent for sex between men (18) than for heterosexual sex (16). In response, New Labour, four years into government, proposed a bill to reduce the age of consent between gay men and, under pressure from the rest of Europe, the bill was passed. On 8 January 2001, the Sexual Offences (Amendment) Act came into force, lowering the age of consent for gay men to 16 in England, Wales and Scotland, and 17 in Northern Ireland. Under the act, consensual group sex for gay men was also decriminalised.

Elsewhere in the world, the Netherlands approved same-sex marriage, also permitting same-sex couples to adopt children jointly; Helene Faasen and Anne-Marie Thus became the world's first lesbian couple to legally marry. Same-sex civil partnerships or unions were permitted in Finland, Germany and Portugal; however, the laws initially stopped short of permitting the joint adoption of children. The age of consent was equalised in Albania, Estonia and Liechtenstein, and homosexuality was declassified as an illness in China.

In the US, a memorial honouring LGBTQ veterans was dedicated in Desert Memorial Park, California. Also in California, Pink Triangle Park was opened in San Francisco as a memorial to the thousands of LGBT people persecuted and killed by the Nazi regime.

SEPTEMBER 2001. THE WRONG BADGE

In the research I have conducted with lesbian, gay and bisexual teachers, I frequently hear that coming out in the school workplace feels like oversharing. Somehow, saying that one is lesbian, gay or bisexual directs the person receiving this information to the sexual activity associated with that identity. In contrast, the dominant presumption of heterosexuality directs the person to one's familial status, not to what one does in bed.

Thirteen years into Section 28, I continued to self-censor in the school workplace, but it became ever more stifling and draining. My continued need to manage my personal identity, I realise retrospectively, was exacerbated by the fact that I moved teaching jobs frequently. I was too quick to decide I was unhappy, did not fit in at a school and would be better off elsewhere. Every two years or so, I would start again, in a new staffroom with a new set of strangers. As a teacher with a secret, I was permanently withdrawn and never gave myself sufficient chance to build relationships in staffrooms. This diary entry records my first day at what would be the final school in my teaching career.

> It is my first day in my new teaching position. Despite this being my fifth teaching post in 10 years, first days at new schools remain as terrifying as my first day at primary school back in the early 1970s. I am handed a temporary name badge to wear until mine arrives. In large black letters it says 'MRS LEE'. As I pin it to my jacket, I feel unsettled by this inaccuracy. Nobody knows me and they will assume from my badge that I am married. I don't want to be found out as gay but, equally, I don't want to paint a false picture of my circumstances. In fact, I don't want to paint any picture at all. With each new introduction to a colleague, I feel the need to point to my badge and say, 'I'm not married, they got my name wrong.' I unnecessarily bring attention to the fact that as a woman in my mid-thirties, I am single and have never been married. This is not the way to blend in on the first day at a new school.

2002

In the UK in 2002, same-sex couples were granted rights to adopt children together. The new law was fiercely resisted by members of the House of Lords. For example, Baroness O'Cathain said:

> By extending the category of would-be adopters to include homosexual couples of both genders and cohabiting heterosexuals, I contend that the Bill is now being used as an instrument of social engineering ... Is it political correctness? Is it social engineering? Or – perish the thought – is it the permanent downgrading of marriage and the family? (Stonewall Cymru, n.d.)

Also in 2002, Alan Duncan became the first Conservative MP to come out as gay without being first outed via the tabloid press. The former *Big Brother* contestant Brian Dowling became the first openly gay children's television presenter in the UK, on SMTV Live. Phillip Schofield had, of course, been on children's TV since 1985, but he would not come out as gay until 2020. Dowling's appointment was one of the few times in the Section 28 era that a gay man in the public eye was associated with children without the tabloid press reminding the country that gay men and lesbians were unsuitable to be in contact with young people.

Elsewhere in the world, civil union laws were passed in Quebec, Canada, and Buenos Aires, Argentina. Same-sex couples in South Africa and Sweden were granted the right to adopt children together. The age of consent was equalised in Austria, Bulgaria, Cyprus, Hungary, Moldova, Romania and Western Australia.

In the Netherlands, the openly gay Dutch politician Pim Fortuyn was assassinated by Volkert van der Graaf outside a radio studio in Hilversum. The assassination was not motivated by homophobia: van der Graaf said at his trial that he killed Fortuyn to stop him exploiting Muslims as 'scapegoats' and targeting 'the vulnerable sections of society' in seeking political power.

DECEMBER 2002. THE SCHOOL CHRISTMAS PARTY

In December 2002, I took the step of coming out to a few close colleagues. It was almost Christmas; I was tired and had little of the required energy left to manage my personal narrative in the school workplace. I certainly had no energy left to manage the annual school Christmas party problem. Each year I pondered the same questions: do I avoid the celebrations altogether? Do I go alone and present myself as a heterosexual single woman? Or do confess all and take my partner, Jo, with me?

Over 14 years and in five separate schools, I had never attended the school Christmas party. Recently, however, I had begun to relax a little with two female colleagues who had classrooms close to my own. Chatting on the corridor between lessons, they asked whether I would like to join them and their husbands at the local pub for unofficial Christmas drinks. I recorded the exchange in my diary.

> I have suspected for a while that Becky and Mel know I'm gay. They ask me to the pub with them and their husbands, for unofficial Christmas drinks. 'More fun than the official school do,' they say, trying to persuade me. They are younger than me, so I imagine that my being gay is not a huge concern to them, but at that moment, on the corridor in the middle of the school day, as my buttoned-up self, I am caught off-guard by their invitation. The question lingers and I feel my neck and cheeks flush. Stuck for a response, I pull a face and say, 'You're all taking your other halves. I'd be on my own.'
>
> 'Don't you have a partner?' asks Becky. I'm now sure they both know that I have.

I freeze. I like Becky and Mel and think a night at the pub would be fun. And I don't want to lie to these two women who have gone out of their way to be friendly at school.

Mel leaps to my rescue. 'You should bring her. It's all right, we know you're gay. So you're gay, what's the big deal?'

And that was that. I was out to two teachers and the world had carried on pretty much as before. For the first time in 14 years, I felt as though I had friends at school – people who knew I was gay and still wanted to be around me.

For any LGBTQ+ teacher in 2023, out at school, perhaps running a Pride club and enjoying a full social life with their colleagues, I recognise that this account and perhaps this whole book portrays me as overly cautious, unnecessarily guarded and almost obsessively wary of others. However, we are all a product of the experiences we have had and the times through which we have lived. Over time, Section 28 manifested in me as shame, deceit and, frankly, a good deal of loneliness. My self-esteem and self-regard were low. I had internalised the homophobia surrounding me. Internalised homophobia manifests itself as isolation, fear of discovery, deception and passing as heterosexual (Szymanski & Chung, 2002). It produces self-hatred and shame, and often involves adopting negative attitudes about other gay and lesbian people, meaning that alliances between lesbian and gay people in heteronormative spaces are rare. Emery Hetrick and Damien Martin (1987) describe internalised homophobia as 'a form of stress that is internal and insidious' (p.34) and suggest it develops as a consequence of continued exposure to anti-gay attitudes.

The experiences I have drawn on throughout part II of this book made it really hard for me to keep up with the growing acceptance and tolerance of LGBTQ+ people. I ought to have been prepared to trust people as attitudes changed, but I was firmly rooted in the past and previous incidents had destroyed my confidence and faith in people.

The week after coming out to Becky and Mel, I was to learn, however, that careful management of my personal identity was still vital in the school setting, even during downtime with my two new friends in the staffroom.

The usual crowd are grabbing their after-school wind-down cup of tea in the staffroom. Around a large rectangular table, several conversations are taking place and Becky, Mel and I are covering the usual ground. We are moaning about difficult classes and competing to be the person with the biggest marking workload that evening. The conversation eventually moves away from school, turning to television and comedy shows specifically. I ask whether Becky or Mel saw *Absolutely Fabulous* with Jennifer Saunders last night. They both did. As the discussion goes on, it becomes clear that they didn't find it quite as funny as I did. I begin to wish I hadn't mentioned anything and backtrack a little bit. I feel silly and embarrassed, like I've told a joke that has fallen flat. Rather than moving the conversation on, I search for something to say to justify why I liked it.

'I like Jennifer Saunders. I think she's really attractive,' I offer.

My two friends look down into their mugs, clearly uncomfortable, as other conversations around the table seem to stop at the precise time I make my utterance. No one speaks for what feels like forever. What was I thinking? They don't know how to respond to my comment. I feel flushed and heat creeps up from my neck into my cheeks, making my shame clear for all in the staffroom to see. I don't speak again and listen to the others as the conversation slowly resumes. I have completely misjudged what it means to come out at school.

In the car on the way home that evening, I am really angry with myself. I had begun to think that I fitted in; that my new friends had given me permission to be myself. But the silence and awkwardness I caused made me feel ashamed and isolated again.

I know I have done the wrong thing but I can't articulate why at first. Why had my comment about Jennifer Saunders jarred with Becky and Mel so much? After all, most of the women in our staffroom spend hours debating the attractiveness of everyone from George Clooney to the visiting firemen, or the new male PE teacher. So why has my comment made us all feel so awkward, when it was supposedly 'no big deal' that I was gay?

I ruined things with Becky and Mel today. I crossed a line from their new gay friend to someone actually attracted to women. Becky and

Mel accept my gayness as a quirky label, but they are not at all prepared to think of me as someone who might be attracted to women. I relaxed too much and far too quickly. I thought I had permission to be myself with them, but I don't. When they said it didn't bother them that I was gay, what they actually meant was: if you're discreet, we will turn a blind eye. I wasn't discreet today though. I let them down.

2003

In 2003, Section 28 was finally repealed in England and Wales. New employment equality regulations made it illegal to discriminate against lesbian, gay or bisexual people in any workplace, including schools. Also in 2003, the British academics Celia Kitzinger and Sue Wilkinson were legally married in British Columbia, Canada, where Wilkinson worked at the time. On returning to Britain, the couple found their relationship had no legal status. In 2004, when the Civil Partnership Act was enacted, their relationship was automatically converted to a civil partnership. But Kitzinger and Wilkinson brought a case to the High Court, supported by the human rights organisation Liberty and the grassroots LGBTQ+ campaigning organisation OutRage, seeking to have their marriage recognised as such.

Kitzinger and Wilkinson lost their case. The judge, Sir Mark Potter, president of the Family Division of the High Court, acknowledged that the women were subject to discrimination (when compared with a heterosexual couple married abroad). However, he ruled that the discrimination was justified to protect the tradition of marriage and the heterosexual nuclear family.

Outside the court, Kitzinger and Wilkinson read out a statement in which they said: 'This judgment will not stand the test of time. We look forward to the day when there is full equality in marriage – not just for us, but for all same-sex couples.'

Elsewhere in the world in 2003, Belgium passed a same-sex marriage law and civil unions were permitted in Argentina, Tasmania, Austria and

Croatia. In Australia, Alex MacFarlane, an intersex person born with XXY sex chromosomes, was the first person to acquire a birth certificate and passport showing an indeterminate gender.

Russia ended its ban on lesbians and gay men serving in the military, and homosexuality was finally decriminalised in every one of the United States of America.

In popular culture, Jennifer Finney Boylan's autobiography, *She's Not There: a life in two genders*, became the first book by an openly transgender American to become a bestseller and the fantasy TV series *Buffy the Vampire Slayer* showed the first lesbian sex scene on US network television.

SEPTEMBER 2003. WE DON'T TEND TO TOUCH HOMOSEXUALITY

In 2003, Section 28 was finally taken off the statute books in England and Wales. As the new academic year commenced, the word 'gay' had become endemic as an insult between students in my own school and in schools up and down the country. I had been placed on the personal, social and health education (PSHE) teaching team to fill in for a colleague on long-term sick leave and so was exposed to what was done, via the curriculum, to teach our students about equality and diversity. There was very little at all and I found no mention of sexuality anywhere in the PSHE schemes of work. By now, a few more teachers knew I was gay and, as Section 28 had been repealed, I felt buoyed by a new sense of freedom. I was also doing the head of PSHE, Shirley, an enormous favour in teaching for a term, so I thought I could legitimately ask her where the teaching about sexuality took place in PSHE. The following extract from my diary details our conversation.

> After the PSHE team meeting tonight, I hang around in Shirley's classroom as the other staff leave. I ask her if she can talk me through what the students learn about sexuality in their PSHE lessons. She is one of a handful of colleagues I have come out to and I feel relatively safe with her. She seems a little vague but offers a reply.
>
> 'We do, you know, sex education and then discuss race and disability as part of our diversity unit. But, to be honest, we don't tend to

touch homosexuality at all. Perhaps we should, but I tend to steer clear from opening that can of worms. You know how it is, Section 28 and all that.'

'Section 28 has been repealed,' I tell her. Shirley raises her eyebrows in casual acknowledgement, making it clear that this is news to her. I press her further: 'Do you think we should cover sexuality in diversity?'

'Well, the boys in Year 8 cover sexuality all by themselves: they say everything and everyone is gay,' she laughs.

'What do you say to them when they're calling each other and everything gay?' I ask.

'Oh, I tend to let it go because I don't think "gay" means gay any more. I think that these days "gay" just means rubbish or no good. The kids don't mean any harm by it,' Shirley replies, making light of my challenge.

Shirley is right. For many children (and adults) the word 'gay' became in the early noughties a byword for anything that was rubbish, boring or stupid: 'Your trainers are gay', 'This worksheet is gay', 'This lesson is gay'. But as David Watkins (2008) asks: 'Would students' language remain as unchallenged if their vocabulary changed to include use of the phrases "don't be so Jewish" or "this work is so paki"?' (p.108).

I take a deep breath and challenge Shirley. 'But I'm gay, Shirley, and when the word is associated with anything rubbish and no good, it means that I'm rubbish and no good.'

I say the very words that I dream of saying to the students every time I walk down the corridor and hear the word 'gay' being hurled around as a joke or an insult.

Aware of my irritation, Shirley attempts to refocus. 'Perhaps we ought to be more PC, but the kids are only young. Even at 14, they're not sexual yet, so I'm not sure they need to know about homosexuality.'

I become braver, surprising myself. 'Is heterosexuality about sex?' I reply. 'I don't think it is. I think it's about identity and family, and same-sex relationships are no different. I'm not advocating we teach the kids about gay sex, but I do think they should know that there are people who are gay, who aren't rubbish or no good, who might live on their street or even, God forbid, be their teacher.'

'Oh, I agree completely,' Shirley replies, sensing my growing frustration. 'But you know what it's like here – what would the parents say? There would be letters and phone calls. You know how they can be.'

Shirley has touched on the crux of the whole issue. As teachers, we are the moral guardians of the children of our peer group. We are entrusted to perpetuate the conservative values of the community in which our school is set. There is evidence of a stubborn and misplaced belief among some parents that if schools expose their child to homosexuality, this will make them gay. This principle does not seem to extend to other curriculum content. For example, it would be ridiculous to assume that if a child learns about Norway in geography then they will want to live there, but still parental concerns about exposure to homosexuality prevail. And unhappy parents can create unwelcome publicity for schools such as ours.

I am aware that Shirley is the parent of a child at our school, so I ask her whether, as a parent, she would be concerned about sexuality being included in the PSHE curriculum.

'You know, Catherine, I'm about as gay-friendly as you can get but, if I'm honest, I wouldn't want my Emma being taught about sexuality. You've said yourself, it's hard work being gay. I don't want my Emma to have that struggle if she doesn't have to. I think it's best that parents keep control of this. It's not our place at school.'

Shirley has entirely missed the point. Being gay is hard work for me precisely because of views such as hers. With that, our discussion is concluded and our self-described gay-friendly PSHE lead leaves the room, clearly irked by my challenge. Despite my anger and blinding sense of frustration, I cringe as she departs, imagining the conversation she is about to have with our colleagues back in the staffroom.

CONCLUDING THOUGHTS
A PRODUCT OF MY PAST

While compiling these stories and assembling this book in 2022, I have wondered throughout why, as a teacher, I wasn't braver and more prepared to be my authentic self. I know now that no teacher was prosecuted as a consequence of Section 28 and the legislation, given its awkward and vague phrasing, was pretty much unenforceable. I didn't know that at the time, though. I hope that, through my diary entries, I have demonstrated how challenging the climate was for lesbian and gay teachers under Section 28. I have tried to strike some sort of a balance with the diary extracts chosen: I wanted to represent the everyday alongside more memorable incidents. Yet, seeing the stories together, I recognise that at times they make for quite depressing reading.

Since leaving teaching and entering a career in higher education, I have through my research and work with trainee teachers had ample opportunity to reflect on the Section 28 era. Finding, in my university workplace, an environment in which it is easy to be out, I have thrived. I have been appointed MBE for services to equality in education and have achieved professorship and National Teaching Fellow status for my work on LGBTQ+ inclusion. And I have never been happier.

The experiences outlined in part II are not unique to me. Lesbian and gay teachers in the 1980s and 90s all have similar stories to tell; what happened to me was in no way unusual or especially unfortunate. It was just what happened to some of us, especially those of us who lived well away from the capital, in provincial cities and towns or in rural school communities.

In the final part of this book, I examine current perspectives related to LGBTQ+ inclusion in schools. I reflect on my own leadership development work with LGBTQ+ teachers through a programme called Courageous Leaders, and argue that some of the adversity we may experience as LGBTQ+ teachers can equip us with skills that are effective for school leadership. I also explore recent advances in equalities policies and guidance that have helped to improve the school climate for LGBTQ+ staff and students. I conclude the book by describing how my diary entries from the Section 28 era led to my involvement in the most unimaginable and joyous opportunity – one that almost made the adversity of Section 28 seem worthwhile.

PART III

PROGRESS SINCE THE REPEAL OF SECTION 28: CURRENT PERSPECTIVES

INTRODUCTION

I am determined that current and future generations of LGBTQ+ teachers will have a more positive experience in schools than I did. When a Julie turns up in their lesson, needing a chat about how they are feeling, I want LGBTQ+ teachers to be the role models to young people that I could never be.

To that end, in 2016, funded by the Department for Education, I worked in partnership with schools to introduce the UK's first leadership development programme specifically for LGBTQ+ teachers, called Courageous Leaders (www.courageousleaders.org.uk). Through my work on this programme, I have learned that the skills and coping mechanisms developed by LGBTQ+ teachers to navigate their hetero- and cis-normative school workplaces equip them with a distinct set of attributes. These attributes make them ideally placed to be excellent school leaders.

CHAPTER 9
COURAGEOUS LEADERS

Despite advances in equalities legislation – for example, the Equality Act 2010 and the Marriage (Same Sex Couples) Act 2013 – many LGBTQ+ teachers do not yet feel safe or adequately secure in their school workplaces (Lee, 2020). The mere mention or presentation of identities that transgress the heterosexual and cisgender norms compromise the discourses of power in the school, and still have the potential to create moral panic (Piper & Sikes, 2010). Section 28 was the first state-sanctioned example of such moral panic, but more recently, in 2019, moral panic reared its head yet again when parental and faith group protests took place at school gates against the introduction of compulsory relationships, sex and health education (RSHE) that is inclusive of LGBTQ+ relationships.

For LGBTQ+ teachers, substantial energy and caution is required to navigate the hetero- and cis-normative school community. They still describe remaining as invisible as possible in their schools so as to not draw attention to themselves, a strategy hardly conducive to job promotion (Rudoe, 2010). LGBTQ+ teachers all too often avoid opportunities for promotion to leadership roles, as promotion would increase their visibility within the school community. Yet some of the strategies used by LGBTQ+ teachers to navigate the hetero- and cis-normative school workplace, if practised over time, provide them with distinctive traits that are advantageous for effective school leadership.

There are five key leadership attributes that LGBTQ+ teachers may have in abundance:

1. Emotional intelligence.
2. Sensitivity to the inclusion of others.
3. Connecting with others and building teams.
4. Managing uncertainty and stressful situations.
5. Courage and risk-taking.

EMOTIONAL INTELLIGENCE

LGBTQ+ people often have outstanding emotional intelligence. This is because they have highly developed instincts from years of proceeding warily with people new to them, as a means of protecting themselves from those with homophobic or transphobic views. Through extensive practice, LGBTQ+ people are perceptive and adept at reading situations and people, in order to gauge whether or not it is safe to be out. Every time an LGBTQ+ teacher enters a new environment or meets someone new, they must quickly get a sense of the nuanced behaviours of others, before deciding whether or not it is safe to be their authentic selves – or whether it is better to assume a pseudo-heterosexual and cis-gendered professional self. LGBTQ+ teachers learn, then, to be very insightful, making them perfectly positioned to make good judgements when recruiting employees, assigning responsibilities and being sensitive to the requirements of others.

SENSITIVITY TO INCLUSION

LGBTQ+ teachers typically have considerable experience of feeling othered or marginalised, either in the workplace, within their families of origin or during their own educational experience. They know all too well what it feels like to be on the fringes and to be the odd one out. Having suffered exclusion and marginalisation, LGBTQ+ teachers are likely to be highly sensitive to inclusive behaviours, in their classrooms and among their colleagues. They often have an enhanced appreciation of those on the margins of their school communities and instinctively look for ways to make sure these people feel included. LGBTQ+ teachers may have personal experience of oppression, providing them with a keen sense of social justice. This is likely to equip them with a wealth of empathy for pupils, parents and colleagues who may be marginalised based on other protected characteristics such as race, faith, disability or social class.

CONNECTING WITH OTHERS

LGBTQ+ people spend the majority of their time in hetero- and cis-normative spaces. They become proficient in recognising where it is possible to connect with others with whom they do not have a natural affinity. They may embark on delicate transactional discourses, perhaps by coming out themselves; in doing so, they encourage others to share similar intimate information. Making connections with others is crucial for school leadership, especially when working with a diverse array of stakeholders across the school community. Finding common ground helps LGBTQ+ teachers to build teams. When they can come out to colleagues, they report closer working relationships and greater levels of trust from their colleagues.

MANAGING UNCERTAINTY

LGBTQ+ teachers are used to enduring a good deal of uncertainty. They often do not know which school stakeholders suspect them to be LGBTQ+, yet they suppress ambiguity and adopt a business-as-usual approach, while inwardly controlling a degree of individual turmoil. School leaders must sometimes shield their school communities from uncertainty, adversity or bad news, and LGBTQ+ teachers learn to function under great personal stress while giving away nothing in their professional demeanour.

COURAGE AND RISK-TAKING

Finally, LGBTQ+ teachers regularly hone their skills of courage and risk-taking. When they apply for a new job in a new school, they must determine whether this workplace will afford them a secure and welcoming space to be their authentic selves, or whether they will be silenced through an unspoken 'don't ask, don't tell' arrangement with their colleagues and school leaders. It takes significant courage for an LGBTQ+ teacher to present themselves authentically in a new school. Those teaching during the Section 28 era know all too well the risks of personal and professional identities colliding; they have, then, extensive experience of navigating hazardous and uncertain school workplaces.

The five leadership attributes identified here form the basis of the Courageous Leaders programme, the UK's first leadership programme exclusively for LGBTQ+ teachers. Courageous Leaders has worked with almost 100 teachers across the UK since it was established in 2016, supporting them to gain leadership roles as their authentic selves. Throughout the year-long programme, LGBTQ+ teachers, within a safe and inclusive space, are given the tools to reflect on the nexus of their personal and professional identities, confront hetero- and cis-normative school practices, and appreciate their own leadership potential. The quotations below, from three participants, capture the benefits of the programme and are typical of a number of similar stories.

> Today I was offered and accepted a role as deputy head here at XXX. This was completely unexpected and represents me moving not one but two steps upward from my teaching role into senior management. I would like to personally thank the Courageous Leaders team for how the course changed my perspective about how I can use my diversity to my advantage. (Jack)

> I have, thanks to my amazing mentor, at last got a headship. And I got that headship as me. I start in January and I'm already out to everybody. (Jess)

> The network of people I met through the programme made me feel braver and more able to be myself. As a direct result of this programme, I had the confidence to pursue and achieve my dream of becoming a headteacher. (Jamil)

Most people would agree that in order to prosper in school, young people need diverse role models, committed teachers and authentic school leaders. When LGBTQ+ leaders become visible within our schools, they embody a distinctive type of leadership through the acquisition and application of the five attributes identified. When LGBTQ+ teachers become school leaders, they disrupt hetero- and cis-normative practices in their schools and, through their visibility, allow students, parents and colleagues to also be themselves.

Courageous Leaders has been able to work with 0.01% of the LGBTQ+ teacher population and the Department for Education withdrew its funding for the programme in 2020. At a time when a quarter of primary headteachers and a third of secondary headteachers leave the profession within five years (Batchelor, 2022), it is vital that government investment is returned for distinct school leadership, so that schools can attract, recruit and retain talented school leaders who reflect the diversity of our society.

CHAPTER 10
LGBTQ+ INCLUSION IN SCHOOLS: A NEW ERA

My work on the Courageous Leaders programme, and with trainee teachers, persuades me that there have been significant positive changes in schools since I left the teaching profession 13 years ago. Thankfully, society has also changed for the better, creating a climate for LGBTQ+ people that I never could have envisaged during Section 28.

EQUALITY ACT 2020

Since I left teaching in 2010, important milestones in the UK and around the world have positively impacted the lived experience of LGBTQ+ people in schools. The first is the Equality Act 2010. The act brought together a number of protections in education, the workplace and wider society to provide a single, consolidated source of UK discrimination law. It replaced existing equality legislation – such as the Race Relations Act 1965, the Disability Discrimination Act 1995 and the Sex Discrimination Act 1986 – with a single duty.

The government distilled aspects of the Equality Act that were relevant to schools into a single guidance paper (Department for Education, 2014). The paper specifies that stakeholders must not be discriminated against on the grounds of their sex, race, disability, religion or belief, or sexual orientation. It also emphasises that, for the first time, protections are extended to students who are pregnant or have recently given birth, or who are undergoing gender reassignment.

The guidance stresses that the Equality Act calls for flexibility. For example, the act does not extend to gender and school uniforms, but schools are cautioned that blanket uniform policies must not discriminate on grounds of race, religion or belief, gender, disability, gender reassignment or sexual orientation. It calls for particular flexibility in relation to uniform rules when meeting the needs of students undergoing gender reassignment.

The guidance also covers bullying. The paper notes that bullying motivated by prejudice is a particularly sensitive issue, but stresses that the relationship between one pupil and another is not within the scope of the Equality Act. Rather, schools must ensure all forms of prejudice-motivated bullying are taken seriously and dealt with equally and firmly, including homophobic and transphobic bullying.

Protection from discrimination on the grounds of gender reassignment is defined in the Equality Act as applying to anyone who is undergoing, has undergone or is proposing to undergo a process (or part of a process) of reassigning their sex by changing physiological or other attributes. This definition means that, in order to be protected under the act, a student does not necessarily have to be undertaking a medical procedure to change their gender, but should be taking steps to live in the opposite gender. Gender reassignment guidance from the government for teachers and other adults in schools is covered via the Gender Recognition Act 2004.

Schools are instructed under the Equality Act to make sure that all 'gender variant' students, or the children of transgender parents, are not singled out for different and less favourable treatment (Department for Education, 2014). They should check that there are no practices that could result in unfair or less favourable treatment. On sexual orientation and in particular the teaching of marriage and civil partnerships, the guidance notes that schools must make sure pupils who identify as LGBTQ+ or are the children of LGBTQ+ parents are not singled out for different and less favourable treatment.

On the teaching of marriage, still open only to heterosexual couples at the time of the Equality Act 2010, secondary schools are reminded of their legal requirement to teach about the 'nature of marriage' in a sensitive, reasonable, respectful and balanced way. When they are delivering sex education, schools must do so in a way that is appropriate to the age and level of understanding and awareness of the pupils. The guidance paper states that no school, or individual teacher, is under a duty to support, promote or endorse marriage of same-sex couples.

The paper provides instruction to schools on how to navigate the relationship between the protected characteristics of religious freedom and sexual orientation. It states:

> *Many people's views on sexual orientation/sexual activity are themselves grounded in religious belief. Some schools with a religious character have concerns that they may be prevented from teaching in line with their religious ethos. Teachers have expressed concerns that they may be subject to legal action if they do not voice positive views on same sex relationships, whether or not this view accords with their faith. There are also concerns that schools with a religious character may teach and act in ways unacceptable to lesbian, gay and bisexual pupils and parents when same sex relationships are discussed because there are no express provisions to prevent this occurring.*

> *Schools with a religious character, like all schools, have a responsibility for the welfare of the children in their care and to adhere to curriculum guidance. It is not the intention of the Equality Act to undermine their position as long as they continue to uphold their responsibilities in these areas. If their beliefs are explained in an appropriate way in an educational context that takes into account existing guidance on the delivery of Sex and Relationships Education (SRE) and Religious Education (RE), then schools should not be acting unlawfully.*

> *However, if a school conveyed its belief in a way that involved haranguing, harassing or berating a particular pupil or group of pupils then this would be unacceptable in any circumstances and is likely to constitute unlawful discrimination.*

> *Where individual teachers are concerned, having a view about something does not amount to discrimination. So it should not be unlawful for a teacher in any school to express personal views on sexual orientation provided that it is done in an appropriate manner and context ... However, it should be remembered that school teachers*

are in a very influential position and their actions and responsibilities are bound by much wider duties than this legislation. A teacher's ability to express his or her views should not extend to allowing them to discriminate against others. (Department for Education, 2014)

MARRIAGE (SAME-SEX COUPLES) ACT 2013

Though not directly linked to schools, the Marriage (Same-Sex Couples) Act 2013 was an important milestone towards LGBTQ+ inclusion in the UK. A government document entitled *Marriage (Same Sex Couples) Act: a factsheet* states that marriage is a hugely important institution in the UK, adding that the principles of long-term commitment and responsibility bind society together. Then, in the first declaration of its kind by any Conservative government (albeit a coalition government with the Liberal Democrats at the time), the following statement is made:

> *The Government believes that we should not prevent couples from marrying unless there are very good reasons – and loving someone of the same sex is not one of them.* (Government Equalities Office, 2014)

The factsheet argues that opening up marriage to same-sex couples demonstrates respect for all individuals, regardless of their sexuality, making society fairer and more inclusive. It adds that this move strengthens the institution of marriage and 'ensures that it remains an essential building block of modern society'.

The Marriage (Same-Sex Couples) Act was passed on 17 July 2013, and the first marriages of same-sex couples took place on Saturday 29 March 2014. Same-sex couples who were married abroad under foreign law and subsequently treated as civil partners in England and Wales were recognised as being married under the new act.

The act still discriminates against same-sex couples, as no religious organisation or representative is forced to conduct or participate in same-sex marriage ceremonies. Religious organisations and their representatives can continue to act in accordance with their doctrines and beliefs on this issue. Today, there is some indication that the Church of England may be considering permitting same-sex marriages in churches in the near future (Sherwood, 2020), but at the time of writing religious institutions are not compelled to extend marriage ceremonies to same-sex couples.

The government factsheet provides guidance for teachers on how same-sex marriage should be taught in schools (Government Equalities Office, 2014). It states that teachers have the right to express their own beliefs, or those of their faith, about the marriage of same-sex couples as long as this is done in an appropriate and balanced way. In a distinct departure from the Section 28 era, the government indicates that it trusts teachers to deal sensitively and professionally with many issues in the classroom, such as divorce and contraception, and says it has no reason to think they will do otherwise when teaching about same-sex marriage.

The factsheet also stresses that teachers are not expected to promote or endorse views that go against their beliefs. Teachers in faith schools are entitled to express their own beliefs in a balanced way, and are expected to act according to the tenets of the religion of the school.

INCLUSIVE RELATIONSHIPS, SEX AND HEALTH EDUCATION

The final recent development I want to explore is inclusive relationships, sex and health education (RSHE). Since September 2020, schools in England have been required to teach RSHE that includes reference to LGBTQ+ relationships. Provision in primary and secondary schools differs, with primary-age children receiving relationships education, secondary-age students receiving relationships and sex education, and children in all phases receiving health education. The Department for Education (DfE) recommends that primary schools deliver sex education as well, although this is not mandatory.

It is of note that, in contrast to previous sex and relationships education guidance, the new guidance puts the word 'relationships' before the word 'sex' in the title. The DfE has been at pains to stress that teachers are not expected to teach children about sex between LGBTQ+ people but simply that 'teaching should reflect the law … as it applies to relationships' (Department for Education, 2019a). In 2019, schools in England were instructed to draw up a policy for teaching relationships education/ relationships and sex education to be made readily available for parents and carers before the teaching started.

The new guidance states that schools should teach about different families, which 'can include for example, single parent families, LGBT parents, families headed by grandparents' and so on (Department for Education, 2019a). For secondary schools, the guidance states that 'sexual orientation and gender identity should be explored at a timely point' and that 'there should be an equal opportunity to explore the features of stable and healthy same-sex relationships', which 'should be integrated appropriately into the RSE programme, rather than addressed separately or in only one lesson'.

With its emphasis on healthy relationships rather than prevention and risk, the guidance is designed to educate young people in preparation for relationships and life in a diverse society. Inclusive RSHE aims to teach children and young people how, when and where to ask for help, and seeks to create schools that are supportive and safe environments for all children, young people and adults regardless of their sexual or gender identity.

Demonstrations by parents and faith groups against plans for the new compulsory RSHE took place outside schools across England and were widely reported in the mainstream media. The most vociferous of the protests continued for a number of months outside a primary school in Birmingham, Parkfield Community School. The protests began as a specific demonstration against efforts by an out gay male senior teacher to teach a series of storybooks about equality and diversity, featuring different sorts of families and in some cases LGBTQ+ characters. The aim of the No Outsiders project by Parkfield's assistant headteacher, Andrew Moffat, was to help all children and young people to grow up with respectful and positive attitudes towards people who are different to them. No Outsiders also aims to proactively tackle prejudice-related bullying towards those with protected characteristics and those who are just different to their classmates.

The angry response outside the school gates to plans for the new RSHE and the No Outsiders programme created a moral panic that left some pupils upset and teachers needing counselling. A second Birmingham primary school, Anderton Park, applied for and won the right to form an exclusion zone around the school, prohibiting parents and faith group representatives from continuing to gather at the gates to protest against inclusive RSHE.

In October 2019, fearing an escalation in the protests, the DfE issued guidance for local authorities and headteachers entitled 'Primary school disruption over LGBT teaching/relationships education'. In it, the DfE anticipated considerable further disruption by parents and faith groups, warning that protesters may eventually prevent children and staff in some parts of the country from getting to and from school. The DfE also warned against the 'public victimisation of teachers, parents or children in relation to this topic' (Department for Education, 2019b).

The DfE anticipated that wellbeing support would be required for staff, stating that disruptive activity, particularly where sustained over a period of time, could have an adverse impact on wellbeing and mental health. However, the DfE stopped short of naming what was at the root of the objections by parents and faith groups, namely the inclusion of LGBTQ+ identities in relationships education. Nor did it say whether it expected LGBTQ+ teachers, parents and other school stakeholders to be more at risk during this period. This guidance was unprecedented and unlike any other communication from the DfE before or since. Not since Section 28 had there been such moral panic about LGBTQ+ identities and schools.

September 2020 was the date set for the introduction of inclusive RSHE in English schools. However, in March 2020, the prime minister at the time, Boris Johnson, instructed every person in the UK to remain at home as Covid-19 spread around the world. He closed schools and, for the next 12 months, staff and pupils learned to pivot quickly between online learning and face-to-face teaching in the wake of late and contradictory instructions from Johnson's government. In light of the pandemic, inclusive RSHE became the least of any school's concern and became policy without further protests from parents or faith groups.

CHAPTER 11
CULTURAL DEVELOPMENTS
TOWARDS LGBTQ+ INCLUSION

Beyond the UK, there have been, over the past decade, similar positive developments to encourage greater inclusion for LGBTQ+ people. In June 2011, the United Nations Human Rights Council passed the UN's first-ever resolution on human rights violations based on sexual orientation and gender identity. In 2012, Barack Obama became the first US president to express support for gay marriage. Obama was also responsible for repealing the 'don't ask, don't tell' policy introduced by the previous Democratic president, Bill Clinton. In 2015, same-sex marriage was legalised in all states of the US, as the Supreme Court ruled that refusing to grant marriage licenses to gay and lesbian couples violated the 14th Amendment to the United States Constitution.

Also in 2015, the Republic of Ireland became the first country in the world to approve same-sex marriage by a public referendum. Two years later, in 2017, Leo Varadkar became Ireland's first openly gay Taoiseach, joining other current and former LGBTQ+ heads of state including Per-Kristian Foss of Norway, Jóhanna Sigurðardóttir of Iceland, Elio Di Rupo of Belgium and Xavier Bettel of Luxembourg.

There was less progress elsewhere, however. In Russia and China, laws were introduced curbing the expression of homosexuality, with those protesting against this ban facing cruel treatment at the hands of law enforcers. On the election of Donald Trump as US president in 2016, the country began to see an erosion of some of the freedoms previously granted to the LGBTQ+ community. The Trump administration reinstated the ban on transgender people serving in the military and repealed protections in schools for transgender students.

Most recently, the US has seen the introduction of Section 28-style legislation in Florida schools. In 2022, lawmakers in Florida passed an act banning teachers from discussing sexual orientation or gender identity in their classrooms. The Parental Rights in Education Act, nicknamed the 'don't say gay' law by its critics, prevents teachers and other school staff from providing support to LGBTQ+ students without first gaining permission from their parents. Florida follows other states with similar statutes that restrict teachers from discussing same-sex relationships with their students. Parents can sue school districts for damages if they believe a teacher has broken the law and talked about sexual or gender identity with their child without first obtaining their permission. The act also mandates that sex education is restricted to teaching that promotes 'honor and respect for monogamous heterosexual marriage' (Lee, 2022).

The 'don't say gay' law is Section 28 by another name: the act is similarly suspicious of teachers and advocates parental vigilance. Just like Section 28, the Parental Rights in Education Act positions every teacher and student in the binary position of potential abuser and potential abused. However, the champion of the act – Ron DeSantis, Florida's governor and a 2024 Republican presidential hopeful – has stated: 'Parents must have a seat at the table when it comes to what's going on in their schools' (BBC News, 2022). One cannot help but remember a similar quote made in 2000 by the Conservative MP Theresa May: 'Most parents want the comfort of knowing Section 28 is there' (Becket, 2017).

As Florida school districts implement the Parental Rights in Education Act for the academic year 2022-23, the state of Pennsylvania looks set to follow suit. We can only hope that 'don't say gay' does not endure for anything near the 15 years that the UK lived with Section 28.

On a personal note, a good deal has changed for me since I left teaching in 2010. My partner and I upgraded our civil partnership to a marriage in 2016. I continue to do everything I can, through my research and university role, to ensure education is as LGBTQ+ inclusive as it can be for staff and students.

There is much that I regret about my years as a teacher during Section 28, and revisiting my diaries for this book has been painful and frustrating at times. I have wondered, time and again, why I wasn't braver. There is, however, a silver lining to my Section 28 story: in the final chapter of this book, I describe how my Section 28 diaries provided me with the most unexpected and welcome of opportunities.

CHAPTER 12
BLUE JEAN

On BBC Radio 4's Today programme, Nick Robinson's voice is especially grave. Russia's Vladimir Putin has done the unthinkable and invaded Ukraine. Sleet falls gently on the windscreen as I drive from the North East of England down the A1 towards my home in Suffolk. Ordinarily I would be avidly following the news, especially on such a momentous day, but today I am distracted. For the past few days I have been on the set of a film, *Blue Jean*, which takes inspiration in part from the diary entries that recalled my experiences during Section 28.

In 2018, I was contacted by a film director, Georgia Oakley, and producer, Hélène Sifre, who had seen one of my academic journal articles about the legacy of Section 28 for LGBTQ+ teachers. They were hoping to secure funding for a film about the experiences of a lesbian PE teacher in the North of England during the Section 28 legislation.

Letting them know that I was a PE teacher during Section 28, I chatted at length to both women about the Section 28 era and told them all about my experiences. I also sent them some of the diary entries that feature in part II of this book, including the time I encountered Julie, a student on my netball team, in a lesbian bar in Liverpool.

Then the Covid-19 pandemic hit and I thought no more about the film, assuming the plans would have evaporated as a result of the multiple lockdowns that decimated the arts and associated industries. But, in 2021,

Hélène got back in touch to say the film had received funding from the BBC and the British Film Institute, and that my stories had helped to inspire the film's screenplay.

Blue Jean tells the story of a closeted lesbian PE teacher in the North East of England during Section 28. The film's promotional material reads:

> *It's 1988. Thatcher's government have just passed a law that stereotypes lesbians and gays as paedophiles, recruiting children for their 'deviant' lifestyles. Female PE teachers are prime targets for homophobic accusations, and as a result, Jean is forced to lead a double life. During the week she's a respected member of staff; on the weekend she slips surreptitiously into Newcastle's gay scene with her girlfriend Viv. But when she's confronted by one of her students in a lesbian bar, Jean is pushed to extreme lengths to save her job and her sanity.*

In the following months, I met with the actor cast in the role of Jean, Rosy McEwen. I also met with the costume department and shared photographs that showed what I wore during the late 1980s, both out on the gay scene in Liverpool and in my first teaching post. I reviewed the script and provided feedback to Georgia and Hélène.

I was employed as an adviser when the filming of *Blue Jean* commenced in February 2022. I would initially spend three days with the cast and crew, setting up and leading the netball scenes. Not at all sure what to expect, and worrying about how old and uncool I was, I headed off to the North East, arriving as instructed at a school that had been empty and unused since the 1980s. As I waited nervously outside the location manager's office, I watched the crew come and go with equipment and costumes. Nowadays, I am usually confident when I encounter new people in my professional life, but I felt on edge in an environment that was entirely new to me and one that seemed glamorous and exciting when compared with education.

After a warm welcome from everyone, I visited the set in the gym where the netballers, a mixture of established young actors and netball players from local clubs, sat on the old gym benches waiting for the crew to set up the scene. I hadn't expected entering the gym to affect me so profoundly. The heavy hydraulic-hinged oak door, with its panel of grid-patterned glass, closed slowly behind me and I was back in the 1980s. After being unused for years, the magnolia satinwood walls of the gym were almost peach; they told of hundreds of PE lessons and netball practices in that space. The lower parts of the walls were scuffed with plimsoll and trainer footprints; sticky tape remained where posters had long since fallen from the walls; small, smeared diagrams of drills hinted at match preparation from decades ago.

The wall bars partially covered the windows and frosted glass obscured any view outside. The heavy metal window frames had an uneven texture, where layer upon layer of magnolia gloss paint had been added by contractors without first sanding down the frames.

Weaving in and out of the wall bars were four ropes suspended from the top bar. They were as thick and leaden as I remembered, with pale blue waxy ends preventing them from fraying. I never mastered how to climb a rope and rarely saw a student able to do it well. Like me in my school days (and at PE college), girls in my lessons would jump, grab the rope and try to push themselves up with their feet, letting go when their hands began to smart from rope burn. Eventually, most students would wrap the rope beneath the backs of their legs and, holding it taut, use it as a swing, until the whistle blew to signal their move to the next apparatus. I'm still not sure why ropes were such an enduring feature of school gyms.

Lighting rigs and white sheets framed the gym, and coloured gaffer tape marked the actors' places on the worn oak floor. The sound team were in the gym equipment cupboard. Monitors, thick cables and metallic cases dominated, but gym mats, coloured cones, bags of basketballs and rugby balls resisted the takeover. Students would queue at large cupboards just like this one while I handed out bibs and balls for my netball practices. After a midweek night out, I had even been known to sneak an occasional nap on the mats if I had a free lesson.

Rehearsing the next scene, the netballers entered the gym through the heavy door, laughing and chatting as they took their places in front of Jean, their teacher. Self-conscious in grey velour shorts, some of the girls pulled their oversized sweatshirts down towards their knees. Most of the girls had their arms folded, betraying how defensive, awkward and embarrassed they felt. I was, at that moment, reminded of the way in which girls of that age held themselves in PE lessons, perpetually uncomfortable in their changing bodies.

I looked at the rows of training shoes as the netballers positioned themselves where they had been directed, toes up to their gaffer tape cue. I remember most of the shoes and had several of the styles myself: the white leather Diadoras with the gold forked stripe, the Nike nylon wally waffles with the pale blue swoosh, and the Reebok aerobic shoes with the perforated toes.

Jean, their PE teacher, stepped forward to address the girls. Her grey fleece jogging bottoms were tucked into white socks, just as we did back in 1988. Her grey sweatshirt had short wide sleeves rolled back almost to the shoulder – I once had a sweatshirt just like it. Jean cradled a netball as she spoke quietly to her team. The ball performed the dual function of providing comfort for Jean and placing a barrier between her and the girls.

I had spoken at some length with Rosy, who played Jean, about the 'noise' in my head as a PE teacher during Section 28. I was always a sentence or two ahead of myself in school, checking what I was about to say before it left my mouth, in case it might betray me in some way. A voice on repeat in my head, day after day, reminded me to be careful: 'Say nothing personal, don't give anything away.' My netball girls were only a few years older than me; they were funny and made me laugh a lot. I enjoyed our time together on buses travelling to and from games, waiting on the sidelines of netball courts between matches and, of course, practising in a gym just like this one. But I was never in the moment, never entirely present at school, and I never relaxed.

Jean was present in the gym, but she wasn't *there*. Rosy had perfectly captured a hollowness in her eyes and an anguished expression that barely disguised her fear that she may be outed or accidentally betray herself. As I watched the scene being rehearsed, I recalled my own paralysis every time a teacher or student mentioned anything about life beyond school.

The costumes for the school scenes featured pale blues, creams, greys and whites. I huddled around a video monitor in the PE changing rooms with the costume, hair and makeup people, who were waiting for the appropriate moment to go out on to set, readjust appearances and ensure continuity. On the monitor, the film looked fantastic, with the muted pale colours managing simultaneously to look both bleak and warm. The claustrophobia of the gym and Jean's double life was cloying in the images. I was immediately transported back to chilly winter mornings before the heating had kicked in, when the gym was only just preferable to being on the netball courts outside on the playground.

In a later scene, Jean teaches Lois, the netballer from the gay bar, how to defend. PE teaching is about physicality. It is about showing students how to move their bodies in certain ways to be most effective at their sport or activity. Demonstration was and still is an important part of the PE teacher's role – physicality takes over when language has gone as far as it can. I watched for years as my heterosexual PE teacher and netball coach peers physically handled their students, moving them from one space to another, adjusting the position of their arms and their legs, shaping their bodies for them by moving one limb and then another into the desired position. They would also put an arm around a student after they lost a match or were disappointed when subbed off during practice. For me, however, Section 28 created a level of self-consciousness and anxiety that took the physical from my role as a physical education teacher. I couldn't bear to make physical contact with any of my students – I constantly worried that I may unwittingly embody the trope of the lecherous lesbian teacher.

In the film, Jean is bolder than I ever was. She shows a netballer, Siobhan, how to defend. Jean places Siobhan in position by standing behind her and moving her; first her shoulders and then her hips. Jean then realises that, to complete the demonstration, she has to do the same with Lois, the girl she encountered at the gay bar. Jean is hesitant and senses she is placing herself in a vulnerable position. Her frame shrinks. I see myself in Jean with utter clarity. As I stand well behind the camera, crew and lighting, a wave of pity for Jean engulfs me. 'It's all in your head,' I want to shout. 'No one is thinking what you think they are thinking.'

Over lunch, I sit with Rosy and Lucy, the actor who plays Lois, the young netballer who is finding her own lesbian identity. I show them a photo of my netball team that I had found when sorting out photos for the costume department. I point out Julie to Lois. The photo had been taken not long after I had seen Julie in the gay bar in Liverpool; she is looking away from the camera as if she could not bear to look in my direction while I took the photograph. Lucy asks what Julie was like and I tell her about the times Julie would flounce in and out of the gym, throwing off her netball bib because she wasn't in the A team or didn't get her favoured position in the practice session. I describe how wretched it felt when I couldn't talk to Julie when she came on to the cross-country field seeking my support.

After lunch, I watch as a scene between Jean and Lois is rehearsed. It is the day after they have encountered each other in the gay bar and Lois peers through the grid-patterned panel of the gym door. Seeing Jean alone inside the gym, laying out cones, Lois opens the door and the two women silently stare at each other. Jean breaks the silence first, saying, 'Changed your mind, then?', referring to an invitation for Lois to join the netball practice issued before they had seen each other in the bar. Lois nods and walks in, bringing the scene to an end. I see the raw fear etched in the eyes of both young women and, although I haven't experienced that fear myself for many years, it is achingly familiar.

In the next scene, Lois and her nemesis, Siobhan, the red-haired, confident ringleader, both vie for Jean's attention and approval during the netball practice. I have known lots of Siobhans as both a pupil and a teacher, and have witnessed the way in which they control, manipulate and dominate. The action is over by the changing-room doors. Siobhan blocks Lois's way, asking what type of man she fancies and whether she is still a virgin. The other girls laugh and encourage Siobhan. Buoyed by their laughter, Siobhan asks Lois whether she prefers women to men and what women do in bed. Provoked and longing to leave the gym, Lois pushes Siobhan and tries to get past.

'Get off me, you fucking dyke,' Siobhan shouts and a fight between the two girls ensues. I haven't heard 'dyke' uttered aggressively for years, yet it was such a familiar word in the Section 28 era. Men would shout it as I walked in Liverpool with friends or girlfriends. During my own schooling, my own Siobhan, a girl named Denise, suggested it should be printed on the back of my school coat. As a teacher, I ignored the word if I heard it while passing down a corridor, pretending not to hear it in case it was meant for me, or in case it might be turned on me if I intervened in a spat between girls. I ignored it in full knowledge that those girls in receipt of this homophobic slur were really struggling. And now, as I saw Lois struggle as Siobhan spat out the word, I was overwhelmed with guilt for failing to support or protect Julie and countless other girls from homophobic assaults like the one I was witnessing.

As the stunt coordinator led multiple takes of the scene, the line 'fucking dyke' was repeated over and over, echoing around the cold school gym. My chest felt tighter and tighter with every take and I felt hot tears start to burn my eyes. How many Julies did I let down? 'You fucking slag' would have me rushing across the gym or the playground to break up a fight, but not 'You fucking dyke'.

I'm aware I'm getting melancholy now, but *Blue Jean* is very much a happy ending to my Section 28 story, so let's get back to the positive parts of being on set.

Throughout my days as an adviser, I hoped the team might invite me to be a supporting artist (or extra) in the film. Although I can't stand to have my photo taken, much less see myself on video, when the invitation finally arrived to be in *Blue Jean*, I jumped at it. The cream and black Puma nylon tracksuit selected for me by the costume team was one I recognised from the 1980s, and although the filming of my scene didn't begin until almost 5.30pm, I was dressed in it and ready to go by 11am.

I was to be the away team netball teacher, umpiring the match opposite Jean. I tossed a coin to begin the game, then walked to the sideline of the netball court. It wasn't a stretch to do the role and I slipped easily back into being both PE teacher and umpire. After a minute or two of filming, the final whistle was blown, signalling the end of the match. My team, the away team, had lost. As I walked back to our bench with the young actors playing the defeated netballers, I remembered all the school fixtures that had ended this way. I also remembered the palpable disappointment felt by the girls who had tried their very hardest. I always stopped short of putting a comforting arm around them, just in case.

At that moment, transported back to my old life, but with the hindsight and freedom I have now, I decided I wanted to make up for all the times I stopped myself from comforting my disappointed netball teams. I stretched out my left arm and placed it around the shoulder of the girl playing goal attack with a quick consolatory pat.

My final task was to shake hands with Jean and congratulate her on the win. As filming stopped, I turned around to see the director, Georgia, cupping her hands in a heart shape in my direction. She was smiling broadly and, relieved I hadn't let her down, I felt a wave of euphoria engulf me. For 20 years as I teacher, I had never offered a consoling arm to a student, but my involvement in this film afforded me the chance to literally go back in time and change the narrative.

As we filmed the scene again and again, I looked over at Jean, umpiring across the court from me. She was small and pale in her cream tracksuit and blonde hair. I felt sorry for Jean and was really angry with her. I wanted to hug her and then shake her and tell her not to be so small, so timid, so diffident. In years to come, no one would have the right to tell Jean who she was allowed to love and what she could and couldn't talk about at school.

The conclusion of the netball match scene signalled the end of my stint on set for a few weeks and, knowing I would not see the netball girls again, the cast assembled for team photos. Then I hugged Rosy. I am usually self-conscious when hugging straight women; a legacy of Section 28 is my own fear that straight women might worry the hug means more to me than it does to them. But I hugged Rosy without self-consciousness.

I returned to my hotel room for the final night, filled with joy and excitement. The gym had been flooded with simulated daylight all evening, and this had distorted my body clock and stopped me getting off to sleep. But my moment in the film, and my goodbyes with the cast and crew, had left me floating on a high rarely experienced at any time in my life.

The costume team commented on several occasions that, as I had a 'proper' job in education, being on set must have felt like a frivolous way to spend my working hours. I do admit that that was my expectation before arriving on the set of *Blue Jean*, but it turned out to be one of the most authentic and profound experiences of my life. It seems a cliché to liken my experience to that of Ebenezer Scrooge in Dickens' *A Christmas Carol*, but in some ways that was exactly what it was like. I visited my younger self, in what should have been my dream job, and saw how miserable and frightened and alone I was because of Section 28.

But it would be all right. Eventually, I would leave teaching and work in higher education, where I would take my authentic gay self to work every single day. I would research LGBTQ+ inclusion in education and run the UK's first ever LGBTQ+ leadership development programme for teachers. And one day, I would be an adviser to a film about Section 28, helping in some small way to show those who never knew about this law the damage it did to people who just wanted to do a good job and live a quiet life with the person they loved.

In the car on the way back home, tears fell down my face. I was tired from the hours spent on set and the artificial daylight, and I was sad to be leaving people who had made me feel so welcome. I was sad for Ukraine. And although I had no right to be, in comparison with the poor Ukrainians, I was also sad for me. Chatting with the young actors playing the netballers reminded me of the fun I had, and often stopped myself from having, with my own netball teams. No teacher ever lost their job to Section 28, but my involvement in *Blue Jean* made me realise it was the cruellest of laws.

What I wouldn't give to be like Scrooge and wake up in 1988 as a young lesbian PE teacher with my whole career ahead of me. I would do things very differently. I would take my whole self to school and talk openly about my partner and our home life, what we did at the weekends and our holidays together. I would have children with my partner and we would be proud lesbian mums. There would be no self-censorship, no thinking two sentences ahead, no stopping halfway through a sentence in case I outed myself. I would place my arm around the shoulders of a disappointed netballer and move their arms into place if their netball technique wasn't quite right. I would be the lesbian role model that Section 28 denied a generation of young people.

But, driving back from the set of *Blue Jean*, I also felt extremely happy. Thanks to Georgia Oakley and her inspirational cast and crew, the story of Section 28 was at last being told. The thousands of us who were lesbian teachers during Section 28 would finally be seen, after years of state-sanctioned invisibility.

At the time of writing, *Blue Jean* will have its world premiere at the 2022 Venice Film Festival, and I have been invited to attend alongside Georgia, Hélène, Rosy and others. I am excited to see *Blue Jean* in full and will be forever grateful to these inspirational women for giving a voice to all the teachers silenced by Section 28.

There is a saying: when life gives you lemons, make lemonade. While the 15 years of Section 28 was the 'lemons' part of my life, being lucky enough to make a small contribution to *Blue Jean* has most definitely been my 'lemonade' moment.

CONCLUDING REMARKS
A CALL FOR FURTHER INCLUSION

I feel fortunate to have had the opportunity to share some of my Section 28 experiences through the publication of *Pretended* and via *Blue Jean*. However, I am conscious that there are many lesbian and gay teachers who have never had the opportunity to share their stories; some are still silenced by the long shadow of Section 28. My experiences were not unusual or extreme. My lesbian and gay teacher friends at the time suffered too, and in some cases experienced far worse.

This book, then, is for all the lesbian and gay teachers between 1988 and 2003 who never got to tell their story. It is also for all the LGBTQ+ young people at school during that era who never had a role model, never saw themselves reflected in the curriculum and never had an adult to talk to at school.

As part III has shown, legislation and policy directly and indirectly affecting schools has done a good deal over the past two decades to improve the climate for LGBTQ+ teachers, adults and young people. The Equality Act 2010 prevents teachers from being dismissed or discriminated against on the grounds of their sexual or gender identities. The Marriage (Same-Sex Couples) Act 2013 has pushed schools into celebrating the weddings of teachers in same-sex relationships in much the same way as they always have the nuptials of heterosexual teachers. And, while some schools are still on something of a journey with it, inclusive RSHE means young LGBTQ+ people now learn they are not alone. The growth in children's literature about different families, alongside projects like Andrew Moffat's

No Outsiders, shows children with same-sex parents that their families are just like any other. Pride Month in June and LGBT History Month in February serve as annual touchpoints for even the most conservative of schools to celebrate LGBTQ+ identities within their communities.

But we rest on our laurels at our peril. If we think we have achieved LGBTQ+ inclusion in UK schools, we are mistaken. For many of our trans and non-binary students and teachers, this era is their Section 28. We have, in the current Conservative government, leaders with a concerning track record on LGBTQ+ inclusion and, in particular, trans inclusion. In April 2021, when Liz Truss was minister for women and equalities, the government's LGBT Advisory Panel was disbanded after a series of resignations over her inaction on a ban on conversion therapy. Panellists reported finding Truss completely disengaged; the LGBT action plan was put to one side, and members described feeling as though they were hitting their heads against a brick wall (Attitude, 2022). An article in *The Guardian* stated that a 'damning report' from the Women and Equalities Committee had 'accused the government of sidelining the push for equality', adding that this 'risked regression on equal rights after decades of progress' (Topping, 2021). One of Truss's first acts when she briefly became prime minister in September 2022 was to remove the word 'women' from the equalities minister job title.

Where the US leads, the UK often follows, and so it is important to conclude this book by reflecting on the current state of affairs in Florida. As discussed in chapter 11, the Parental Rights in Education Act 2022, nicknamed the 'don't say gay' law by critics, is Section 28 by another name. There are reports that some schools across Florida have removed LGBTQ+ inclusive books from their libraries and withdrawn textbooks containing references to LGBTQ+ people (Brangham & Hastings, 2022). Teachers with same-sex partners have been compelled to remove photographs of their loved ones from their desks, fearing that being out at school could make their roles untenable under the new law. This is all remarkably familiar.

I hope that through this book, and in particular my Section 28 diaries, I have been able to convey the toxic and damaging climate in schools for those of us who identified as lesbian and gay under Section 28. We have, though, come a long way since the repeal of Section 28 and there is much to celebrate in UK schools at present. I am always thrilled to visit schools and see the way in which they celebrate LGBT History Month and Pride and are now largely safe and welcoming environments for LGBTQ+ staff and students. Trans and non-binary school stakeholders are still struggling, however, as the media delight in pitching the LGB and the T against each other. While we in the LGBTQ+ community are disagreeing between ourselves, we are wasting time and squandering energy that could be more usefully spent supporting one another and working together to demand equality.

Section 28 is a cautionary tale of division, othering and exclusion. We must now, as educators, come together and do everything we possibly can to create truly inclusive school communities. No one in school should have to pretend.

REFERENCES

Abbott, J. (1991) 'Accomplishing "a man's task": rural women teachers, male culture, and the school inspectorate in turn-of-the-century Ontario', *Gender and Education in Ontario*, pp.51-72

Allen, J.B. (1982) *The Ethical Poetic of the Later Middle Ages*, University of Toronto Press

Anderson, E. (2002) 'Openly gay athletes: contesting hegemonic masculinity in a homophobic environment', *Gender & Society*, 16(6), pp.860-877

Anderson, J. (2016) 'The Tory party at prayer? The Church of England and British politics in the 1950s', *Journal of Church and State*, 58(3), pp.417-439

Apple, M.W. (1985) 'Teaching and "women's work": a comparative historical and ideological analysis', *Teachers College Record*, 86(3), pp.455-473

Ashley, M. (2003) 'Primary school boys' identity formation and the male role model: an exploration of sexual identity and gender identity in the UK through attachment theory', *Sex Education*, 3(3), pp.257-270

Associated Press. (1991) 'Freddie Mercury, 45, lead singer of the rock band Queen, is dead', *The New York Times*. Retrieved 23 November 2022 from: www.nytimes.com/1991/11/25/arts/freddie-mercury-45-lead-singer-of-the-rock-band-queen-is-dead.html

Attitude. (2022) 'Liz Truss: the LGBTQ rights record of the UK's new prime minister'. Retrieved 2 December from: https://attitude-uk-production. nextgear.nl/article/liz-truss-the-lgbtq-rights-record-of-the-uks-new-prime-minister/27392

Averill, L.A. (1939) *Mental Hygiene for the Classroom Teacher*, Pitman

Bailey, D.S. (1956) *Sexual Offenders and Social Punishment: being the evidence submitted on behalf of the Church of England Moral Welfare Council to the Departmental Committee on Homosexual Offences and Prostitution, with other material relating thereto*, Church of England Moral Welfare Council

Baker, P. (2022) *Outrageous! The story of Section 28 and Britain's battle for LGBT education*, Reaktion Books

Batchelor, T. (2022) 'Number of headteachers quitting within five years of starting on the rise, data shows', *The Independent*. Retrieved 16 December 2022 from: www.independent.co.uk/news/education/teachers-quitting-school-education-naht-b2065513.html

Bates, A. (2018) 'How do you support your LGBT+ staff?', *Secondary Education*, 8(13)

BBC News. (2016) 'Rio 2016 hockey: Kate and Helen Richardson-Walsh celebrate "special" win'. Retrieved 23 November 2022 from: www.bbc. co.uk/news/uk-england-berkshire-37141969

BBC News. (2022) '"Don't Say Gay": Biden denounces "hateful" new Florida bill'. Retrieved 29 November 2022 from: www.bbc.co.uk/news/world-us-canada-60326418

Becket, A. (2017) 'How Theresa May defended the law banning schools from educating children about homosexuality', *Insider*. Retrieved 18 November 2022 from: www.businessinsider.com/how-theresa-may-defended-the-law-banning-promotion-of-homosexuality-2017-7

Bengry, J. (2014) 'Profit (f)or the public good? Sensationalism, homosexuality, and the postwar popular press', *Media History*, 20(2), pp.146-166

Berlant, L. & Warner, M. (1998) 'Sex in public', *Critical Inquiry*, 24(2), pp.547-566

Bérubé, A. & D'Emilio, J. (1984) 'The military and lesbians during the McCarthy years', *Signs: Journal of Women in Culture and Society*, 9(4), pp.759-775

Blount, J.M. (1996) 'Manly men and womanly women: deviance, gender role polarization, and the shift in women's school employment, 1900-1976', *Harvard Educational Review*, 66(2), p.318-339

Blount, J.M. (2000) 'Spinsters, bachelors, and other gender transgressors in school employment, 1850-1990', *Review of Educational Research*, 70(1), pp.83-101

Blount, J.M. (2003) 'The history of teaching and talking about sex in schools', *History of Education Quarterly*, 43(4), pp.610-615

Borg, S. (2017) 'Teachers' beliefs and classroom practices' in P. Garrett and J.M. Cots (eds.) *The Routledge Handbook of Language Awareness* (pp.75-91), Routledge

Borjas, G.J. (2007) *Labor Economics*, McGraw Hill

Braidwood, E. (2018) 'Theresa May says she "shouldn't have" voted against the repeal of Section 28', *PinkNews*. Retrieved 22 November 2022 from: www.pinknews.co.uk/2018/07/03/theresa-may-says-she-shouldnt-have-voted-against-the-repeal-of-section-28

Brangham, W. & Hastings, D. (2022) 'Critics say new school policies in Florida ostracize LGBTQ students', PBS. Retrieved 30 November 2022 from: www.pbs.org/newshour/show/critics-say-new-school-policies-in-florida-ostracize-lgbtq-students

Brown, S. (2018) 'Theresa May admitted she has made bad decisions and wants to be seen as an LGBT ally', *Attitude*. Retrieved 22 November 2022 from: www.attitude.co.uk/news/world/theresa-may-admitted-she-has-made-bad-decisions-and-wants-to-be-seen-as-an-lgbt-ally-296367

Bullough, V.L. (1976) 'Homosexuality and the medical model', *Journal of Homosexuality*, 1(1), pp.99-110

Bullough, V.L. (1988) 'Katharine Bement Davis, sex research, and the Rockefeller Foundation', *Bulletin of the History of Medicine*, 62(1), pp.74-89

Butler, J. (1990) *Gender Trouble: feminism and the subversion of identity*, Routledge

Card, T. (1994) *Eton Renewed: a history from 1860 to the present day*, John Murray

Casey, M.E. (2002) 'Young gay males' experiences of coming out in the context of school', *Youth and Policy*, 75, pp.62-75

Cavanagh, S.L. (2005) 'Female-teacher gender and sexuality in twentieth-century Ontario, Canada', *History of Education Quarterly*, 45(2), pp.247-273

Cavanagh, S.L. (2008) 'Sex in the lesbian teacher's closet: the hybrid proliferation of queers in school', *Discourse: Studies in the Cultural Politics of Education*, 29(3), pp.387-399

Clarke, G. (1996) 'Conforming and contesting with (a) difference: how lesbian students and teachers manage their identities', *International Studies in Sociology of Education*, 6(2), pp.191-209

Clarke, G. (1997) 'Playing a part: the lives of lesbian physical education teachers' in G. Clarke & B. Humberstone (eds.) *Researching Women and Sport* (pp.36-49), Palgrave Macmillan

Clarke, G. (1998a) 'Working out: lesbian teachers and the politics of (dis) location', *Journal of Lesbian Studies*, 2(4), pp.85-99

Clarke, G. (1998b) 'Voices from the margins: regulation and resistance in the lives of lesbian teachers' in M. Erben (ed.) *Biography and Education: a reader* (pp.64-78), Falmer Press

Clifford, G.J. (1989) 'Man/woman/teacher: gender, family, and career in American educational history' in D. Warren (ed.) *American Teachers: histories of a profession at work* (pp.293-343), Macmillan

Colgan, F. & Wright, T. (2011) 'Lesbian, gay and bisexual equality in a modernizing public sector 1997-2010: opportunities and threats', *Gender, Work & Organization*, 18(5), pp.548-570

Cooper, D. (1997) 'Governing troubles: authority, sexuality and space', *British Journal of Sociology of Education*, 18(4), pp.501-517

Coulter, R.P. & Greig, C.J. (2008) 'The man question in teaching: an historical overview', *Alberta Journal of Educational Research*, 54(4)

Dane, C. (1917) *Regiment of Women*, Macmillan

Dane, C. (1926) 'A problem in education', *The Women's Side*, H. Jenkins

Davis, K.B. (1929) *Factors in the Sex Life of Twenty-Two Hundred Women*, Harper & Brothers

DePalma, R. & Atkinson, E. (2009) '*No Outsiders*: moving beyond a discourse of tolerance to challenge heteronormativity in primary schools', *British Educational Research Journal*, 35(6), pp.837-855

Department for Education. (2014) *The Equality Act 2010 and Schools: departmental advice for school leaders, school staff, governing bodies and local authorities*. Retrieved 29 November 2022 from: https://dera.ioe. ac.uk/20312/1/Equality_Act_Advice_Final.pdf

Department for Education. (2019a) *Relationships Education, Relationships and Sex Education (RSE) and Health Education: statutory guidance for governing bodies, proprietors, head teachers, principals, senior leadership teams, teachers*. Retrieved 29 November 2022 from: https://assets.publishing.service.gov.uk/government/uploads/system/ uploads/attachment_data/file/1090195/Relationships_Education_RSE_ and_Health_Education.pdf

Department for Education. (2019b) 'Primary school disruption over LGBT teaching/relationships education'. Retrieved 29 November 2022 from: www.gov.uk/government/publications/managing-issues-with-lgbt-teaching-advice-for-local-authorities/primary-school-disruption-over-lgbt-teachingrelationships-education

Department for Education. (2021) *Staffing and Employment Advice for Schools*. Retrieved 15 November 2022 from: https://assets.publishing. service.gov.uk/government/uploads/system/uploads/attachment_data/ file/1026591/Staff_Advice_Handbook_Update_-_October_2021.pdf

Dowell, B. (2016) '*Marcella* star Anna Friel: I love playing "more womanly" roles', *Radio Times*. Retrieved 25 November 2022 from: www.radiotimes. com/tv/drama/marcella-star-anna-friel-i-love-playing-more-womanly-roles

Drescher, J. (2015) 'Out of DSM: depathologizing homosexuality', *Behavioral Sciences*, 5(4), pp.565-575

Duffy, N. (2017) 'Sir John Major: "I learned a great deal" about gay people from Ian McKellen', *PinkNews*. Retrieved 22 November 2022 from: www. pinknews.co.uk/2017/07/12/sir-john-major-i-learned-a-great-deal-about-gay-people-from-ian-mckellen

Duffy, N. (2020) 'Piers Morgan apologises for anti-gay article attacking *EastEnders* over "yuppie poofs"', *PinkNews*. Retrieved 22 November 2022 from: www.pinknews.co.uk/2020/01/29/piers-morgan-the-sun-eastenders-yuppie-anti-gay-michael-cashman-g2

Education Support Partnership. (2018) *Teacher Wellbeing Index 2018*. Retrieved 22 November 2022 from: www.educationsupport.org.uk/media/drdlozbf/teacher_wellbeing_index_2018.pdf

Edwards, L.L., Brown, D.H.K. & Smith, L. (2016) '"We are getting there slowly": lesbian teacher experiences in the post-Section 28 environment', *Sport, Education and Society*, 21(3), pp.299-318

Eisenmann, L. (2001) 'Creating a framework for interpreting US women's educational history: lessons from historical lexicography', *History of Education*, 30(5), pp.453-470

Eldén, S. (2016) 'Book review: *Couple Relationships in the 21st Century*', *Acta Sociologica*, 59(1), pp.86-88

Ellis, D.M. (1971) *Seven Thousand Men*, Ontario Institute for Studies in Education/Ontario Public School Men Teachers' Federation

Epstein, D. (1996) 'Corrective cultures: *Romeo and Juliet*, Jane Brown and the media', *Curriculum Studies*, 4(2), pp.251-271

Epstein, D. & Johnson, R. (1998) *Schooling Sexualities*, OUP

Faderman, L. (2013) *Scotch Verdict: the real-life story that inspired The Children's Hour*, Columbia University Press

Ferfolja, T. (2009) 'State of the field review: stories so far: an overview of the research on lesbian teachers', *Sexualities*, 12(3), pp.378-396

Ferfolja, T. (2010) 'Lesbian teachers, harassment and the workplace', *Teaching and Teacher Education*, 26(3), pp.408-414

Foster, T. & Newman, E. (2005) 'Just a knock back? Identity bruising on the route to becoming a male primary school teacher', *Teachers and Teaching*, 11(4), pp.341-358

Freeman, J. (1975) *The Politics of Women's Liberation*, David McKay

Gillard, J.W. (2018) 'An initial analysis and reflection of the metrics used in the Teaching Excellence Framework in the UK', *Perspectives: Policy and Practice in Higher Education*, 22(2), pp.49-57

Gilmore, L. (1994) 'Obscenity, modernity, identity: legalizing *The Well of Loneliness* and *Nightwood*', *Journal of the History of Sexuality*, 4(4), pp.603-624

Godfrey, C. (2018) 'Section 28 protesters 30 years on: "We were arrested and put in a cell up by Big Ben"', *The Guardian*. Retrieved 11 November 2022 from: www.theguardian.com/world/2018/mar/27/section-28-protesters-30-years-on-we-were-arrested-and-put-in-a-cell-up-by-big-ben

Government Equalities Office. (2014) *Marriage (Same Sex Couples) Act: a factsheet*. Retrieved 29 November 2022 from: https://assets.publishing.service.gov.uk/government/uploads/system/uploads/attachment_data/file/306000/140423_M_SSC_Act_factsheet__web_version_.pdf

Gray, E.M. (2010) '"Miss, are you bisexual?" The (re)production of heteronormativity within schools and the negotiation of lesbian, gay and bisexual teachers' private and professional worlds', doctoral thesis, Lancaster University

Gray, E.M. (2013) 'Coming out as a lesbian, gay or bisexual teacher: negotiating private and professional worlds', *Sex Education*, 13(6), pp.702-714

Gray, M. (2022) 'Section 28: impact and legacy' (blog post), HFL Education. Retrieved 15 November 2022 from: www.hertsforlearning.co.uk/blog/section-28-impact-and-legacy

Griffin, P. (1992) 'From hiding out to coming out: empowering lesbian and gay educators', *Journal of Homosexuality*, 22(3-4), pp.167-196

Griffin, P. (1998) *Strong Women, Deep Closets: lesbians and homophobia in sport*, Human Kinetics Publishers

Griggs, G. & Biscomb, K. (2010) 'Theresa Bennett is 42…but what's new?', *Soccer & Society*, 11(5), pp.668-676

Grimley, M. (2009) 'Law, morality and secularisation: the Church of England and the Wolfenden Report, 1954-1967', *The Journal of Ecclesiastical History*, 60(4), pp.725-741

Grindley, L. (2016) 'UK's new prime minister, Theresa May, evolved on LGBT rights', *Advocate*. Retrieved 18 November 2022 from: www.advocate.com/world/2016/7/11/englands-new-prime-minister-theresa-may-evolved-lgbt-rights

Hall, G.S. (1905) 'Certain degenerate tendencies among teachers', *The Pedagogical Seminary*, 12(4), pp.454-463

Hamer, E. (2016) *Britannia's Glory: a history of twentieth-century lesbians*, Bloomsbury

Hammond, P. (1996) *Love Between Men in English Literature*, St. Martin's Press

Hantover, J.P. (1998) 'The Boy Scouts and the validation of masculinity' in M. Kimmel & M. Messner (eds.) *Men's Lives* (fourth edition), Allyn & Bacon

Hardie, A. (2012) 'Lesbian teachers and students: issues and dilemmas of being "out" in primary school', *Sex Education*, 12(3), pp.273-282

Hetrick, E.S. & Martin, A.D. (1987) 'Developmental issues and their resolution for gay and lesbian adolescents', *Journal of Homosexuality*, 14 (1-2), pp.25-43

House of Lords. (2011) *No Vaccine, No Cure: HIV and AIDS in the United Kingdom*, Select Committee on HIV and AIDS in the UK, https://publications.parliament.uk/pa/ld201012/ldselect/ldaids/188/188.pdf

Hudak, J. & Giammattei, S.V. (2010) 'Doing family: decentering heteronormativity in "marriage" and "family" therapy' in J. Ariel, P. Hernández-Wolfe & S.M. Stearns (eds.) *AFTA Monograph Series: Expanding our Social Justice Practices: advances in theory and training* (pp.49-58), American Family Therapy Academy

Hufton, O. (1984) 'Women without men: widows and spinsters in Britain and France in the eighteenth century', *Journal of Family History*, 9(4), pp.355-376

Hull, K.E. & Ortyl, T.A. (2019) 'Conventional and cutting-edge: definitions of family in LGBT communities', *Sexuality Research and Social Policy*, 16(1), pp.31-43

i. (2022) '"I would vote differently now": six prime ministers on LGBT progress on Pride 50th anniversary'. Retrieved 18 November 2022 from: https://inews.co.uk/news/six-prime-ministers-lgbt-progress-pride-50th-anniversary-1716636

Jeffreys, S. (1997) *The Spinster and her Enemies: feminism and sexuality, 1880-1930*, Spinifex Press

Jennett, M. (2004) *Stand Up For Us: challenging homophobia in schools*, Crown

Jennings, R. (2006) 'The Gateways club and the emergence of a post-Second World War lesbian subculture', *Social History*, 31(2), pp.206-225

Jennings, R. (2007) *A Lesbian History of Britain: love and sex between women since 1500*, Greenwood World Publishing

Kelleher, P. (2022) 'All the ways Liz Truss or Rishi Sunak as prime minister would be bleak for LGBTQ+ rights', *PinkNews*. Retrieved 18 November 2022 from: www.pinknews.co.uk/2022/07/22/liz-truss-rishi-sunak-lgbtq-rights-tory-leadership-candidates

Khayatt, M.D. (1992) *Lesbian Teachers: an invisible presence*, State University of New York Press

Khayatt, D. (1997) 'Sex and the teacher: should we come out in class?', *Harvard Educational Review*, 67(1), pp.126-144

King, J.R. (2004) 'The (im)possibility of gay teachers for young children', *Theory into Practice*, 43(2), pp.122-127

Kissen, R.M. (1993) 'Voices from the glass closet: lesbian and gay teachers talk about their lives', paper presented at the annual meeting of the American Educational Research Association

Kissen, R.M. (1996) *The Last Closet: the real lives of lesbian and gay teachers*, Heinemann

Kitzinger, C. (1994) 'Should psychologists study sex differences?', *Feminism & Psychology*, 4(4), pp.501-506

Kitzinger, C. & Wilkinson, S. (2004) 'The re-branding of marriage: why we got married instead of registering a civil partnership', *Feminism & Psychology*, 14(1), pp.127-150

Kushnier, J.S. (2002) 'Educating boys to be queer: Braddon's *Lady Audley's Secret*', *Victorian Literature and Culture*, 30(1), pp.61-75

Lee, C. (2019) '15 years on: the legacy of Section 28 for LGBT+ teachers in English schools', *Sex Education*, 19(6), pp.675-690

Lee, C. (2020) 'Courageous leaders: promoting and supporting diversity in school leadership development', *Management in Education*, 34(1), pp.5-15

Lee, C. (2022) '"Don't say gay" bill: Florida should learn from the harmful legacy of Britain's section 28', *The Conversation*. Retrieved 2 December 2022 from: https://theconversation.com/dont-say-gay-bill-florida-should-learn-from-the-harmful-legacy-of-britains-section-28-176955

Lenskyj, H.J. (1997) 'No fear? Lesbians in sport and physical education', *Women in Sport and Physical Activity Journal*, 6(2), pp.7-22

Lewis, B. (2016) 'Homosexuals' (pp.202-232), *Wolfenden's Witnesses: homosexuality in postwar Britain*, Palgrave Macmillan

Litton, E.F. (1999) 'Stories of courage and hope: gay and lesbian Catholic elementary school teachers', paper presented at the annual meeting of the American Educational Research Association

Lugg, C.A. (2003) 'Sissies, faggots, lezzies, and dykes: gender, sexual orientation, and a new politics of education?', *Educational Administration Quarterly*, 39(1), pp.95-134

Lugg, C.A. & Tooms, A.K. (2010) 'A shadow of ourselves: identity erasure and the politics of queer leadership', *School Leadership & Management*, 30(1), pp.77-91

Malvern, J. (2018) 'National archives: Sir Ian McKellen key to lowering age of consent for gay men', *The Times*. Retrieved 23 November 2022 from: www.thetimes.co.uk/article/national-archives-sir-ian-mckellen-key-to-lowering-age-of-consent-for-gay-men-6r72cblll

Marshik, C. (2003) 'History's "abrupt revenges": censoring war's perversions in *The Well of Loneliness* and *Sleeveless Errand*', *Journal of Modern Literature*, 26(2), pp.145-159

Martino, W. (2009) 'Beyond male role models: interrogating the role of male teachers in boys' education' in W. Martino, M. Kehler & M. Weaver-Hightower (eds.) *The Problem with Boys' Education: beyond the backlash* (pp.284-302), Routledge

Mason, G. & Tomsen, S. (eds.) (1997) *Homophobic Violence*, Hawkins Press

Mayock, P., Bryan, A., Carr, N. & Kitching, K. (2009) *Supporting LGBT Lives: a study of the mental health and well-being of lesbian, gay, bisexual and transgender people*, Gay and Lesbian Equality Network

McCormick, D. (n.d.) 'Essay by Dale McCormick for *Out and Elected in the USA*'. Retrieved 23 November 2022 from: https://outhistory.org/exhibits/show/out-and-elected/1990/dale-mccormick

McGhee, K.A.C. (n.d.) 'The destruction caused by Clause 28', Glasgow Women's Library. Retrieved 11 November 2022 from: https://womenslibrary.org.uk/explore-the-library-and-archive/lgbtq-collections-online-resource/the-destruction-caused-by-clause-28

McKay, G. (2004) 'Subcultural innovations in the Campaign for Nuclear Disarmament', *Peace Review*, 16(4), pp.429-438

Meyer, I.H. (2003) 'Prejudice, social stress, and mental health in lesbian, gay, and bisexual populations: conceptual issues and research evidence', *Psychological Bulletin*, 129(5), pp.674-697

Morgan, D.H.G. (2011) 'Locating "family practices"', *Sociological Research Online*, 16(4), pp.174-182

Morris, M. & Griggs, C. (eds.) (1988) *Education: the wasted years? 1973-1986*, Routledge

Mullin, K. (2018) 'Unmasking *The Confessional Unmasked*: the 1868 Hicklin test and the toleration of obscenity', *ELH*, 85(2), pp.471-499

Munro, P. (1998) *Subject to Fiction: women teachers' life history narratives and the cultural politics of resistance*, McGraw Hill Education

National Archives: ADM 1/25754, Committee on Homosexual Offences and Prostitution: Memorandum by the War Office

Neary, A. (2013) 'Lesbian and gay teachers' experiences of "coming out" in Irish schools', *British Journal of Sociology of Education*, 34(4), pp.583-602

Nixon, D. & Givens, N. (2007) 'An epitaph to Section 28? Telling tales out of school about changes and challenges to discourses of sexuality', *International Journal of Qualitative Studies in Education*, 20(4), pp.449-471

O'Carroll, L. (2014) 'Sandi Toksvig: Save the Children fired me for being a lesbian', *The Guardian*. Retrieved 25 November 2022 from: www.theguardian.com/world/2014/nov/29/sandi-toksvig-lesbian-fired-save-the-children-princess-anne

Ofsted. (2021) 'Inspecting teaching of the protected characteristics in schools'. Retrieved 15 November 2022 from: www.gov.uk/government/publications/inspecting-teaching-of-the-protected-characteristics-in-schools/inspecting-teaching-of-the-protected-characteristics-in-schools

Olson, M.R. (1987) 'A study of gay and lesbian teachers', *Journal of Homosexuality*, 13(4), pp.73-81

Parkes, A. (1994) 'Lesbianism, history, and censorship: *The Well of Loneliness* and the suppressed randiness of Virginia Woolf's *Orlando*', *Twentieth Century Literature*, 40(4), pp.434-460

Perlesz, A., Brown, R., Lindsay, J., McNair, R., De Vaus, D. & Pitts, M. (2006) 'Family in transition: parents, children and grandparents in lesbian families give meaning to "doing family"', *Journal of Family Therapy*, 28(2), pp.175-199

Peters, D.W. (1934) *The Status of the Married Woman Teacher* (No. 603), Teachers College, Columbia University

Piper, H. & Sikes, P. (2010) 'All teachers are vulnerable but especially gay teachers: using composite fictions to protect research participants in pupil-teacher sex-related research', *Qualitative Inquiry*, 16(7), pp.566-574

Press Association. (2006) 'Most gay teachers suffer abuse, poll finds', *The Guardian*. Retrieved 23 November 2022 from: www.theguardian.com/education/2006/may/17/schools.uk3

Preston, M. (2018) 'Book review: *Queer Teachers, Identity, and Performativity*', *Journal of LGBT Youth*, 15(2), pp.145-147

Rasmussen, M.L. (2004) 'The problem of coming out', *Theory into Practice*, 43(2), pp.144-150

Renold, E. (2002) 'Presumed innocence: (hetero)sexual, heterosexist and homophobic harassment among primary school girls and boys', *Childhood*, 9(4), pp.415-434

Rhodes, K.N. (2020) 'Visibility and lesbian women working in UK schools at the end of the 20th century and into the 21st century', doctoral thesis, Cardiff University

Richardson, C. (2002) 'The worst of times', *The Guardian*. Retrieved 22 November 2022 from: www.theguardian.com/world/2002/aug/14/gayrights.comment

Ringrose, J. (2016) 'Postfeminist media panics over girls' "sexualisation": implications for UK sex and relationship guidance and curriculum' in V. Sundaram & V. Sauntson (eds.) *Global Perspectives and Key Debates in Sex and Relationships Education* (pp.30-47), Palgrave Pivot

Robinson, L. (2006) 'Three Revolutionary Years: the impact of the counter culture on the development of the gay liberation movement in Britain', *Cultural and Social History*, 3(4), pp.445-471

Rogers, A.E. (2010) 'Feminist consciousness-raising in the 1970s and 1980s: West Yorkshire women's groups and their impact on women's lives', doctoral thesis, University of Leeds

Roseneil, S. & Budgeon, S. (2004) 'Cultures of intimacy and care beyond "the family": personal life and social change in the early 21st century', *Current Sociology*, 52(2), pp.135-159

Roughead, W. (1931) 'Closed doors; or, the great Drumsheugh case', *Bad Companions*, Duffield & Green

Rudoe, N. (2010) 'Lesbian teachers' identity, power and the public/private boundary', *Sex Education*, 10(1), pp.23-36

Russell, S.T. (2019) 'Social justice and the future of healthy families: sociocultural changes and challenges', *Family Relations*, 68(3), pp.358-370

Salholz, E. (1993) 'The power and the pride', *Newsweek*. Retrieved 2 December 2022 from: www.newsweek.com/power-and-pride-193662

Sanders, S. & Spraggs, G. (1989) 'Section 28 and education' in C. Jones & P. Mahony (eds.) *Learning Our Lines: sexuality and social control in education*, The Women's Press

Sanderson, E. (2021) *London Police Stations*, Amberley Publishing

Sargent, P. (2005) 'The gendering of men in early childhood education', *Sex Roles*, 52(3), pp.251-259

Schofield, M. (1965) *Sociological Aspects of Homosexuality: a comparative study of three types of homosexuals*, Longmans

Sedgwick, E.K. (1990) *Epistemology of the Closet*, University of California Press

Sexton, P.C. (1969) *The Feminized Male: classrooms, white collars and the decline of manliness*, Random House

Sherwood, H. (2020) 'Church of England could rethink stance on LGBTQ+ issues by 2022', *The Guardian*. Retrieved 29 November 2022 from: www.theguardian.com/world/2020/nov/09/church-of-england-could-rethink-stance-on-lgbtq-issues-by-2022

Sigel, L.Z. (2011) 'Censorship in inter-war Britain: obscenity, spectacle, and the workings of the liberal state', *Journal of Social History*, 45(1), pp.61-83

Sinfield, A. (1994) *The Wilde Century: effeminacy, Oscar Wilde and the queer moment*, Columbia University Press

Singer, S.E. (1997) 'Voices from the margins: lesbian teachers in Nova Scotia's schools', unpublished master's thesis, Mount Saint Vincent University

Singh, F.B. (2020) *Scandal and Survival in Nineteenth-Century Scotland: the life of Jane Cumming*, University of Rochester Press

Smith, R. (2021) 'A comprehensive guide to Boris Johnson's infamous use of "tank-topped bum boys"', *PinkNews*. Retrieved 18 November 2022 from: www.pinknews.co.uk/2021/09/27/boris-johnson-tank-top-bum-boys-homophobic-peter-mandleson-history

Sparkes, A.G. (1994) 'Self, silence and invisibility as a beginning teacher: a life history of lesbian experience', *British Journal of Sociology of Education*, 15(1), pp.93-118

Squirrell, G. (1989) 'Teachers and issues of sexual orientation', *Gender and Education*, 1(1), pp.17-34

Steinberg, D.L. (1999) 'Pedagogic panic or deconstructive dilemma? Gay genes in the popular press' in D. Epstein and J.T. Sears (eds.) *A Dangerous Knowing: sexuality, pedagogy and popular culture* (pp.59-83), Continuum

Stonewall Cymru. (n.d.) '2002: Same-sex couples free to adopt with the Adoption and Children Act'. Retrieved 28 November 2022 from: www.stonewallcymru.org.uk/our-work/campaigns/2002-same-sex-couples-free-adopt-adoption-and-children-act

Sullivan, C. (1993) 'Oppression: the experiences of a lesbian teacher in an inner city comprehensive school in the United Kingdom', *Gender and Education*, 5(1), pp.93-101

Szymanski, D.M. & Chung, Y.B. (2002) 'Internalized homophobia in lesbians', *Journal of Lesbian Studies*, 7(1), pp.115-125

Takasaki, K. (2017) 'Friends and family in relationship communities: the importance of friendship during the transition to adulthood', *Michigan Family Review*, 21(1)

Taylor, Y. (2007) '"If your face doesn't fit...": the misrecognition of working-class lesbians in scene space', *Leisure Studies*, 26(2), pp.161-178

Thompson-Lee, C. (2017) *Heteronormativity in a Rural School Community: an autoethnography*, Sense Publishers

Thorp, A. & Allen, G. (2000) *The Local Government Bill [HL]: the 'Section 28' debate*, House of Commons Library

Topping, A. (2021) 'Liz Truss accused of treating equalities role as "side hustle"', *The Guardian*. Retrieved 30 November 2022 from: www.theguardian.com/politics/2021/sep/24/liz-truss-accused-of-treating-equalities-role-as-side-hustle

Toulouse, C. (1991) 'Thatcherism, class politics, and urban development in London', *Critical Sociology*, 18(1), pp.55-76

Underwood, J.L. (1995) *Shades of Pink: an exploratory study of lesbian teachers*, California State University

Waites, M. (2002) 'Inventing a "lesbian age of consent"? The history of the minimum age for sex between women in the UK', *Social & Legal Studies*, 11(3), pp.323-342

Waites, M. (2005) 'The fixity of sexual identities in the public sphere: biomedical knowledge, liberalism and the heterosexual/homosexual binary in late modernity', *Sexualities*, 8(5), pp.539-569

Wallis, A. & VanEvery, J. (2000) 'Sexuality in the primary school', *Sexualities*, 3(4), pp.409-423

Watkins, D. (2008) 'Heads in the sand, backs against the wall: problems and priorities when tackling homophobia in schools' in R. DePalma & E. Atkinson (eds.) *Invisible Boundaries: addressing sexualities equality in children's worlds* (pp.107-120), Trentham

Watt, N. (2009) 'Cameron apologises to gay people for section 28', *The Guardian*. Retrieved 18 November 2022 from: www.theguardian.com/politics/2009/jul/02/david-cameron-gay-pride-apology

Westwood, G. (1953) *Society and the Homosexual*, E.P. Dutton

Williams, Z. (2008) 'Boris Johnson for Mayor? Be afraid. Be very afraid', *The Guardian*. Retrieved 18 November 2022 from: www.theguardian. com/politics/2008/may/01/boris.livingstone

Wilson, A.R. (ed.) (1995) *A Simple Matter of Justice? Theorizing lesbian and gay politics*, Cassell

Wilton, T. (1995) 'Subject to control', *Lesbian Studies: setting an agenda* (pp.181-204), Routledge

Woods, S.E. & Harbeck, K.M. (1992) 'Living in two worlds: the identity management strategies used by lesbian physical educators', *Journal of Homosexuality*, 22(3-4), pp.141-166

Young, A. (2019) *From Spinster to Career Woman: middle-class women and work in Victorian England*, McGill-Queen's University Press